How to Make It BIG as a Consultant

FOURTH EDITION

WILLIAM A. COHEN, PH.D.

⊿AMACOM

American Management Association

New York • Atlanta • Brussels • Chicago • Mexico City • San Francisco
Shanghai • Tokyo • Toronto • Washington, D. C.

Special discounts on bulk quantities of AMACOM books are available to corporations, professional associations, and other organizations. For details, contact Special Sales Department, AMACOM, a division of American Management Association, 1601 Broadway, New York, NY 10019.
Tel.: 800-250-5308. Fax: 518-891-2372.
E-Mail: specialsls@amanet.org
Website: www.amacombooks.org/go/specialsales
To view all AMACOM titles, go to: www.amacombooks.org

This publication is designed to provide accurate and authoritative information in regard to the subject matter covered. It is sold with the understanding that the publisher is not engaged in rendering legal, accounting, or other professional service. If legal advice or other expert assistance is required, the services of a competent professional person should be sought.

Library of Congress Cataloging-in-Publication Data

Cohen, William A.
  How to make it big as a consultant / William A. Cohen. — 4th ed.
      p. cm.
  Includes bibliographical references and index.
  ISBN-13: 978-0-8144-1032-5
  ISBN-10: 0-8144-1032-4
  1. Business consultants. I. Title.

HD69.C6C57 2009
001—dc22

2008048569

Printing number

10 9 8 7 6 5 4 3 2

This edition is dedicated to
Peter F. Drucker
1909–2005
The Father of Modern Management
and
The World's Foremost Management Consultant

CONTENTS

Research—Voice-Activated Word Processing Is Here!—Scanning Documents and Photographs into Your Presentations—Instant Communication—Some Reading Suggestions—Summing Up

What Is the Internet?—What Do You Need To Get Online?—Preloaded Connection, Browser, and Portal Services—Internet Connections—Researching on the Internet—How to Use Search Engines—Evaluating and Using Your Results—Marketing on the Internet—The World Wide Web—Once You Have Your Site Developed, Then What?—Selecting an ISP—Selecting a Name—Why Not a Cybermall?—How Should You Market on the World Wide Web?—Publicity: The Number One Secret for Marketing on the Web—Using Banners—Cyberlinks—Giving Information Away—Why Not an E-mail Newsletter?—Books on Internet Marketing—Summing Up

Selecting the Legal Structure for Your Consulting Firm—The Sole Proprietorship—The Partnership—The Corporation—Other Legal Necessities—Obtaining a Business License—The Resale Permit—Fictitious Name Registration—Clients' Use of Credit Cards—Stationery and Business Cards—Insurance and Personal Liability—Keeping Overhead Low—The Telephone—Fax Machines—Anticipating Expenses—Necessary Records and Their Maintenance—Tax Obligations—Income Taxes—Excise Taxes—Unemployment Taxes—State and Local Taxes—Minimizing Tax Paperwork—Sources of Additional Information—Summing Up

Why My Recommended Approach to Strategy is Different—Principles, Resources, and Situational Variables—Example: Attacking a Market Leader's Top Product—How Lever Bros. Did It—Integrating the Principles—Looking at Resources—Lever Bros.' Secret Weapon—Enter the Great Depression—The Launch—Apply the Principles Scientifically—Summing Up

THE WORLD'S FOREMOST CONSULTANT AND HIS IMPACT ON THIS BOOK

IT HAS BEEN ONLY LAST YEAR that my book *A Class with Drucker: The Lost Lessons of the World's Greatest Management Teacher* (AMACOM, 2008) was published. I had the very great honor of being Peter Drucker's first executive PhD student and of maintaining a relationship with him over a 30-year period. This is significant because Peter Drucker was not only the greatest management teacher, but was also known as The Father of Modern Management. Moreover, he was also the most celebrated management consultant worldwide. Drucker Societies have sprung up all over the world to continue his ideas and his legacy. And no wonder: His ideas were not just fluff. Consider just one of his clients and one engagement.

DRUCKER'S CONSULTING

Jack Welch, the legendary former General Electric CEO, sat down with management consultant Drucker shortly after becoming CEO of GE. Drucker posed only two questions, but they changed the course of GE's future. Those two questions were worth billions of dollars over the course of Welch's tenure as CEO. The first question was, "If GE weren't already in a business, would you enter it today?" Then he followed up with, "If the answer is no, what are you going to do about it?" Welch decided that if GE could not be number one or number two in a market, the business would have to be fixed, sold, or closed. According to Welch, that strategy, which was based on his consultation with Drucker and the questions Drucker asked, was at the core of GE's success.[1]

Yet Drucker did not consult for just large corporations. He consulted for small businesses, nonprofits, governments all over the world, the military, and churches. Yet he had no giant consulting firm to back him up. He was a sole practitioner who even answered his own phone. He did not even have a secretary.

Many of the techniques and concepts in this book originated with Peter Drucker. I just did not realize their origins until I sat down with my notes from my time as his student and reflected on what he taught. So I am doubly enthusiastic about updating this book. Its errors, if any, are mine. But the debt I owe Peter—and that's what he asked all of his students to call him—for pushing me in the right direction and showering me with his wisdom, ideas, and friendship is significant. The incubation of many of the concepts and techniques contained in this book are surely his, and I am happy not only to acknowledge this, but to dedicate this edition, the fourth since 1985, to him.

HOW CONSULTANTS GET STARTED

Before we get into the nitty-gritty of consulting, you need to understand one thing. Like many others, I did not start out in life with a burning desire to become a consultant. I know that I am not alone in this regard, for I have talked to hundreds of other consultants, both full and part time, and very few started out with that intention. Most of them must have had an early experience like mine. Because my entrance into the consulting field was unplanned, the first time I performed consulting services I had no one to ask for advice.

This is true even of Peter Drucker. Drucker did not plan on becoming a consultant. I know this because Peter said that his first experience in consulting started not long after arriving in this country. Previously, he had been a newspaper correspondent and journalist as well as an economic analyst for a bank and an insurance company. However, because he had a doctorate (in international law, not in management), Peter's services were mobilized for World War II. Peter was told that he was to serve as a management consultant. Drucker said that he had no idea what a management consultant was. He checked a dictionary but could not find the term. He said he went to the library and the bookstore. "Today," he told us, "you will find shelves of titles. In those days, there was almost nothing." The few books on management did not include the term, much less explain it. He asked several colleagues and had no better luck. They did not know either.

On the appointed time and date, Drucker proceeded to the colonel's office, wondering all the way exactly what he was getting into. A receptionist asked him to wait, and an unsmiling sergeant came to escort him to the colonel. This must have been a little intimidating for a young immigrant who not too many years earlier had fled from the military dictatorship of Nazi Germany, most of whose party members wore one sort of uniform or another.

Peter was led into the office by yet another stern-faced assistant. The colonel glanced at Peter's orders and invited him to be seated. He asked Peter to tell him about himself. He questioned Drucker at some length about his background and education. But though they seemed to talk on and on, Drucker did not learn what the colonel's office was responsible for, nor was he given any understanding of what he would be doing for the colonel as a management consultant. It seemed as if they were talking round and round to no purpose.

Drucker was more than a little uncomfortable in dealing with the colonel. He hoped that the officer would soon get to the point and tell him exactly what kind of work he would be doing. He was growing increasingly frustrated. Finally, Drucker could take it no longer. "Please sir, can you tell me what a management consultant does?" he asked respectfully.

The colonel glared at him for what seemed like a long time and then responded: "Young man, don't be impertinent." "By which," Drucker told us, "I knew that he didn't know what a management consultant did either."

Drucker knew that someone who did know what was expected of a management consultant had made this assignment. Having lived in England and having read Arthur Conan Doyle's *Sherlock Holmes*, Drucker knew what a consulting detective did. With that knowledge and the insight that the colonel did not know anything about management consulting, Drucker asked direct questions about the colonel's responsibilities and problems. Peter then laid out some options about what should be done and the work that he, Drucker, should do. The colonel was interested and clearly relieved. He accepted Peter's proposals in their entirety. This proved to be Drucker's first successful consulting engagement. So Peter Drucker was not only the father of modern management; he may have been the father of modern management consulting as well.

MY INITIAL IGNORANCE ABOUT CONSULTING

Experience in other fields had taught me that whenever I lacked knowledge about something, my first step should be to find a book on the subject. Like Peter, I did just that. I visited several bookstores, and I checked with the libraries. But I found no books with the information I needed in 1973 when I became a consultant for the first time. The few books on consulting were all about consulting by the large consulting firms. They contained none of the specifics on what to do. It was only slightly better than when Drucker became a consultant. At least I knew what a consultant did.

But there was much I did not know. How much should I charge? Was a contract absolutely necessary? Did I need a business license or some other kind of license? What could I do as a part-time consultant without running into a conflict of interest with my full-time employer? How much could I make if I decided to devote myself full time to consulting? Also, if I consulted full time, how much time would I need to spend marketing my services versus actually consulting, and how should I go about marketing my services anyway? These and numerous other questions plagued me, but I had no single volume to turn to for answers.

Eventually I learned, but mainly it was the hard way: through experience. I made numerous mistakes, which in some cases cost me a lot of money and in all cases wasted time and brought frustration. However, I did finally learn what to do and how to do it, and I began to make money. I consulted for Fortune 500 companies, for small businesses, for start-up companies, and for the government.

Then in 1979, I received my doctorate and became a full-time university professor. (By the way, becoming a successful business consultant in most specialties does not require a PhD, an MBA, or in fact any business degree at all. More about that later.) In any case, becoming a business professor did not curtail my consulting activities. If anything, it intensified them.

AN ACADEMIC COURSE IN CONSULTING

At my university, I noticed that many students had a tremendous interest in business consulting—and not just business students. I was persuaded to develop an interdisciplinary course at California State University at Los Angeles on the subject of consulting for business. As the course developed, we did not stop at theory; every quarter I invited practicing consultants from many fields to share their experiences. The speakers ranged from those in small, one-person operations to staff consultants employed by multimillion-dollar corporations. My speakers included full- and part-time consultants, and both men and women.

So popular did this course become that it attracted not only business students from all disciplines but also psychologists, chemists, anthropologists, attorneys, and English majors. Many of those who took the course were older students from outside the university, including engineers, pilots, and many company executives and professionals who wanted to leave their corporate jobs or to consult part time. We even attracted a number of professors, who sat in on these lectures at various times to pick up what they could and some students from the prestigious graduate schools in the Los Angeles area.

Partially due to the success of the business consulting course, another program for which I had responsibility also prospered. This was the Small Business Institute at the university, for which I became the director. The Small Business Institute program, conducted at universities around the country under the sponsorship of the U.S. Small Business Administration, furnished consulting services to small businesses. Business students, supervised by professors, did the consulting. Over a period of years, we developed one of the largest Small Business Institutes in the country and several times won district, regional, and national awards for the top performance among all participating universities. The Small Business Institute program allowed students in the consulting course to do hands-on projects as a part of their education. Unfortunately, this fine program fell victim to budget cuts in the federal government in 1994. However, many universities continue it, asking small business clients to pay for the consulting work accomplished. I have to say, even when small businesses must pay, the program is still a bargain for the businesses that choose to participate.

Meanwhile, the success of our program led to many requests for help from outside the university. To make this program mobile, we developed a consulting seminar that I gave several times a year. These seminars were attended not only by neophyte and would-be consultants but also by many consultants with considerable experience in their professions. They generously shared their experiences and knowledge with other seminar students and with me. Eventually I taught the consulting course at other well-known universities, including the University of California, Los Angeles, and Drucker's School, Claremont Graduate University. Sometimes I taught the course as part of an MBA program and at other times in seminar form for the general public.

I left my first university to become president of a small graduate school, and eventually I decided to go full time to devote myself to the Institute of Leader Arts (www.stuffofheroes.com), into which my original consulting practice has evolved.

THE INFORMATION IN THIS BOOK

As a result, this book is based not only on my own experience but also on that of many others, including numerous guest lecturers, professors, and students who have accomplished more than 500 different consulting engagements for many different small businesses. It is also based on the face-to-face interchange of ideas from consultants in many different fields and geographic locations, and many consulting clients all over the world, some of whom are in the government or military.

Had I had this book in my hands when I first started out, I would have saved myself thousands of wasted hours and much frustration. I would have avoided countless blunders, including journeys down blind alleys, while I struggled to learn how to promote my practice, develop long-term client relationships, and, in one case, get paid for services already performed. This book contains the collective experiences of hundreds who have endeavored to earn their livelihood through the practice, either full or part time, of business consulting as well as ideas that I developed based on Drucker's concepts. Its aim is to help you to build a successful and rewarding business consultancy.

But the book is practical, not theoretical. If I have done it right, you should have all the tools necessary and know how to apply them to start and build a successful management consulting practice. I don't know whether you will make it big. As Peter said, "Without action, nothing gets done," and the action part is up to you. But in the almost 30 years since the first edition has appeared, literally thousands have used it to help build a successful practice—and you can, too. So let's get started!

NOTE

1. John A. Byrne, "The Man Who Invented Management," *BusinessWeek* (November 28, 2005), accessed at http://www.businessweek.com /magazine/content/05_48/b3961001.htm on November 19, 2007.

1

THE BUSINESS OF CONSULTING

INDEPENDENT CONSULTING has to be one of the most incredible businesses around, with advantages found in no other way of making a living. Consider working hours. You probably have some time of the day when you work best. Most people do. Some people work better early in the morning, others late in the evening, and a very few people work equally well all day, at any time. But in independent consulting, when you work doesn't make any difference because, except for the unique requirements of each consulting engagement, you can pick your own hours. You can decide when you work and when you do not. You can always work at your best time.

Are you in a job and don't like your boss? Are you working with people whom you just do not care to be around? In independent consulting you decide whether you wish to work with someone. Whether you work for a client or with collaborators on a project is entirely up to you.

Are you dissatisfied with your current income? Do you feel underpaid? In consulting, you set your own fees; you decide how much you're worth and how much you want to make. If you are worth more right now, today, you can immediately give yourself a raise.

Do you prefer to work at home? In consulting, you can make $100,000 or more working out of your own home without worrying about parking, driving, or the expense of an outside office. In fact, the office in your own home will probably be tax deductible. Peter Drucker is known as the Father of Modern Management and is arguably the most celebrated management consultant in history, and he worked out of his home his entire career.

Finally, are you concerned about taking the big plunge of going into your own full-time consulting practice? There's no need to risk your time, career, or a large dollar investment. You can start consulting part time and ease your way into full time. Many successful consultants have started part-time businesses after their full-time jobs, working nights and on weekends. And if you follow the instructions in this book, you will soon be able to build a successful consulting practice; you will not have to quit your full-time job until you are fully ready and certain that you will be successful.

WHAT IS CONSULTING?

Consultants operate in many, many different fields. Import-export, management, human resources, engineering, and marketing are some of the more common ones. There are consultants in archeology and consultants in clothes selection. There are even consultants to help authors overcome writer's block.

In my work and travels, I have met experts from all those fields and more. All had become or had the potential for becoming successful consultants. They had widely varying backgrounds and consulted in many different business areas. While I was writing the first edition of this book, my wife called my attention to an article in the *Los Angeles Times* that told the story of an enormously successful consulting business run by a young mother. She worked about six days every month, advising businesses on which records to keep and which to throw away.

A consultant is simply anyone who gives advice or performs other services of a professional or semiprofessional nature in return for compensation. This means that regardless of your area of interest or expertise, you can become a consultant. Everyone has a unique background, with special experiences and interests that are duplicated by few others and that are in demand by individuals or companies at certain times. There is a lot of emphasis on the individual in consulting, and personal consulting, sometimes referred to as coaching, has become enormously popular. Personal consulting has become such an important part of consulting that I've added a separate chapter on it.

I am frequently asked whether you need an advanced degree to be a consultant. The answer is definitely no. Although the orientation of a consultant is clearly professional, I have known many successful consultants with limited formal academic training. The important thing is that you have the necessary experience, qualifications, skills, and expertise to help with a task that an individual or company wants performed. Where you obtained such skills is of far less importance. I must add, however, that if you intend to work as a management consultant for a major consulting firm and not on your own, a master's of business administration (MBA) degree will probably be required as a minimum—and the more prestigious the university, the better. But to actually do the job and to become an independent consultant, an advanced degree is *not* necessary.

Sometimes those employed in large corporate consulting firms can be a little stuffy about being compared with independent consultants. When I wrote the first edition of *How to Make It Big as a Consultant*, I received a call from a consultant at one of the prestige firms who had read my book. "I consider consulting a profession, not an entrepreneurial opportunity," he said. I reminded him that his own multibillion-dollar employer was started by a single entrepreneur-consultant.

If you are on your own, whether you obtained your expertise from a university is not crucial. I know of a successful import-export consultant with no degree and of an expensive consultant to the top management of major corporations who has no MBA, only an undergraduate degree in sociology.

HOW BIG IS THE CONSULTING INDUSTRY?

Because consulting encompasses so many different aspects of work life, it is very difficult to measure precisely the total dollar volume for consulting services currently performed in the United States. Most people are able only to estimate the value of consulting services performed for business. One estimate indicates $300 billion involving just human capital in business.[1] If you include all types of consulting, I think you can at least double this estimate. The explosion in consulting has been fueled by technological advances like the Internet, which not only facilitates the consulting process but has created the demand for an entirely new class of consultants.

TYPES OF CONSULTING FIRMS

Characteristics other than the type of business may also define consulting firms, including their size, location, and type of client. These include:

1. **National General Management Firms.** These are large firms such as McKinsey & Company, Booz Allen Hamilton, and Arthur D. Little, which do millions and millions of dollars in consulting business every single year. How much is millions and millions? It is estimated that in one year, these firms can do a billion dollars or more in annual revenue.

2. **Major Accounting Firms with Consulting Divisions.** Most national CPA firms today, including all of the major firms, do management consulting in addition to their regular accounting activities.

3. **Functionally Specialized Firms.** These organizations specialize in particular areas of business. They might deal only in market research, in strategic planning, or—today, of course—in computers and the Internet.

4. **Industry-Specific Firms.** These are large national or international firms dealing only with certain industries or with certain types of operations.

5. **Public Sector Firms.** These firms specialize in consulting

primarily with the government (national, state, or local) or with nonprofit organizations such as universities or hospitals.

6. **Think Tanks.** These very large firms, such as RAND Corporation and SRI International, may have many or very few customers. The Aerospace Corporation, located in Los Angeles, consults mainly for the U.S. Air Force.

7. **Regional and Local Firms.** Numerous consulting firms operate in a single and limited geographic area, even though their annual sales may be quite large.

8. **Independent Practitioners.** Many new consultants seek to work in this area, and well they might. It represents a major opportunity for making it big working alone or with a minimum number of employees, at least to begin with. Starting up in this area is the focus of this book.

9. **Specialty Firms Outside of Business.** This may actually be one of the largest areas of consulting, although it is rarely counted because the focus is outside the area of business. Such firms may consult on health, etiquette, dress, or even personal behavioral management.

This wide variety indicates that the opportunities in the consulting business are tremendous. Many of the local or regional firms and even the larger firms started small with a sole practitioner and grew to be multimillion-dollar giants.

WHY DOES ANYONE NEED A CONSULTANT?

You may ask yourself why a large company hires a consultant, at some-times very high compensation, when it already has staffs of experts who, one would think, should be even more qualified than the consultant. In a television broadcast several years ago, a *60 Minutes* interviewer asked this very question about consultants to the government. After all, if the government employees themselves are qualified, why does the government need to hire consultants? And why pay them more than the employees are being paid on an hourly or daily basis?

Actually both the government and business organizations use consultants for a number of very good reasons. In fact, not only are consultants hired, they are hired again and again and held in considerable esteem. Because it is good business to find a need and then fill it, you have to understand the reasons for hiring consultants. Let's look at each of them in turn.

1. **The Need for Personnel.** Sometimes even the largest companies lack personnel during specific periods or for specific tasks. They may need assistance during a temporary work overload, or they may require unique expertise that is not needed on an ongoing basis every day of the year. Temporary assistance might be needed, for example, when a company bids for a government contract. During this period, a great amount of work has to be put out over a short period of time; the hired staff may not be available to handle the load without stopping other important projects, so consultants are hired. Or a company might need unique expertise on short-term projects, as in direct marketing, an area I once frequently consulted in. Even today, with the amazing growth in direct marketing and database management, excluding the Internet, some businesses use direct marketing only occasionally. So it does not make sense to hire a full-time employee whose salary could easily exceed $75,000 or more per year, in addition to benefits. Therefore, a company is perfectly happy to hire a consultant at fees of from $50 to $300 an hour or more to accomplish a specific task. The need for personnel also provides the motivation for the search consultant who is paid by client companies for finding executives or professionals with specific skills and experience. The large fees these consultants earn are an indication of the demand for their services.

The large revenue in executive search, another unique area of consulting, also demonstrates the need for personnel and their importance to a firm. The top firms routinely spend over $100 million in this area, and a few may do three times this figure.

2. **The Need for Fresh Ideas.** Not infrequently a company has a problem, and management believes that its employees are too close to it to understand all the ramifications. It makes sense, then, to bring in someone from outside the firm, someone with competent problem-solving skills but not necessarily a knowledge of the business. In fact,

sometimes the individual's very ignorance (assuming, of course, a talent for problem solving) helps to provide the answer. Peter Drucker has said that he brought to a problem not so much his knowledge about it, but his ignorance.[2] Drucker had a tremendous ability to penetrate through a confusion of factors, recognize the main issue, and then recommend ways to solve the problem. His services were well worth the fees he charged.

3. **Company Politics.** At times the solution to a problem may actually be known. However, for various political reasons, those who understand the problem cannot present it. For example, a division of a major company once proposed that the company enter a new market with one of its products, which would have required an investment of millions of dollars. The potential in this new market was highly controversial within the company. Because the new product would come from the division that proposed entering the market, the division's recommendations would be considered biased. However, by hiring an outside consultant to study the same issues, the division succeeded in accomplishing the same thing. The consultant was assumed to be more impartial and less likely to be influenced by company politics.

4. **The Need for Improved Sales.** No business can exist without sales. This is true no matter how knowledgeable its president and senior staff are, how skilled its financial people and accountants are, or how innovative its engineers are in developing or manufacturing new products. A company that needs to increase sales in a short time frame will sometimes look outside its own marketing or sales staff for help.

5. **The Need for Capital.** Every company needs money. The need for capital is extremely common in start-ups, but it is also very common in successful companies. In fact, the more successful a company, the more capital it needs. The need for capital is a continuing problem with many companies. An individual who has expertise in finding sources of capital will be in continuous demand.

6. **Government Regulations.** Government regulations, if not obeyed, can result in fines, imprisonment, or even the closing down of the business. No company is immune to government regulations, and all companies need to ensure that they fulfill these regulations in the

most efficient and effective manner. At the same time, a company needs to minimize the negative impact on its business and, if possible, use the regulations to help in its operation. These regulations may affect a variety of areas: equal employment opportunity, age discrimination, consumer credit protection, safety standards, veterans' rights, and numerous others. If you have knowledge in any of these regulatory areas or can become an expert in them, there is a real market for your consulting services. For example, as a university president, I approved large sums paid to a consultant who had worked in our state government and who understood the regulatory statutes governing our educational activities.

7. **The Need for Maximum Efficiency.** All organizations need to operate as efficiently as possible. An organization that operates at lower efficiency than it is capable of eventually has problems. More efficient competitors take away its market and drive it out of business. Inefficiency leads to high costs, making prices noncompetitive. Slippages, delays, and low productivity all result from inefficiency. If you know how to increase the efficiency of an organization, you have something important to sell as a consultant.

8. **The Need to Diagnose Problems and Find Solutions.** Businesses look for the MBA degree because graduates with these degrees are supposed to be very adept at diagnosing problems faced by business and developing appropriate solutions. Anyone who can do this is in demand. The more general problem solving you do and the better you become at it, the more your name will get around. Large consulting firms have capitalized on the need of businesses to have someone diagnose their problems and recommend solutions. For this reason, these firms have sought to hire MBAs from the top schools at extremely high starting salaries in order to build and maintain a reputation for problem solving. As noted earlier, some individual practitioners are nationally and sometimes internationally known for their problem-solving talents, and they are in great demand.

9. **The Need to Train Employees.** The operation of any business is becoming more and more complex, and today many employees are continually trained throughout their careers. Managers need differ-

ent types of training for leadership, organizational, and planning skills; computer operators need additional training in the latest equipment, techniques, software, and programming. In fact, developments are occurring so rapidly that virtually every single functional area of business needs continual training. If you are an expert and can teach skills in any area that is in demand, you have a niche in a type of consulting that commands large fees from industry.

10. **The Need for a Complete Turnaround.** A friend of mine, who made a worldwide consulting reputation as a workout specialist, often was called in by a bank or a group of investors to take over a company in danger of bankruptcy. He came in as president and did whatever was necessary to turn the company around. Sometimes he was president of several companies simultaneously, and he spent a great deal of time in flight, continually going from one distressed company to another. Once the company was sound again, off he went to the next project. Since many companies sometimes find themselves in extreme conditions, there is a need for a troubleshooting consultant who can pull off a complete turnaround (as long as the bank principals or investors are willing to put up a fight). Turnaround specialists command heavy-duty fees of as much as $2,000 per day or more.[3] William Brandt became a turnaround consultant while working on a doctorate in sociology. A friend asked him to help a failing coal mine. Once involved as a consultant, he never stopped. Brandt, only 39 years old, built Development Specialists, Inc., into a $4 million practice.[4]

11. **Computers and Data Processing.** Data processing specialists have been with us for a long time, but the technological advancement in this field has opened up opportunities at many levels for those who know their stuff. These consultants are earning big fees, too. For example, when my computer had problems, a business friend recommended a computer consultant. She turned out to be a young lady in her early twenties who had never entered college. She billed at $100 an hour and was worth every penny when every hour without my computer was costing me money. That was several years ago. Today's computer consultants make more, and many are not college graduates either.

Actually, the types of consulting are probably unlimited. While flying across the country some years ago, I picked up a copy of *American Way*. One article asked, "Are you losing ground at work? A personal coach can help you devise a game plan to regain your competitive edge." The article went on to describe personal coaching, also called executive coaching, which at the time was an unusual type of one-on-one business consulting that is frequently done over the phone or even over the Internet. The article stated that more than 10,000 coaches offered their services this way.[5] This type of consulting really has skyrocketed. Probably 100,000 personal coaches exist today. In fact, the number has grown so much that I have added an entire chapter (Chapter 20) on the subject.

SIGNALS INDICATING THE NEED FOR A CONSULTANT

James E. Svatko, former senior editor of *Small Business Reports*, came up with the following situations that signal the need for outside expertise from a consultant:

✦ Lack of a Written Business Plan
✦ Unexplained Low Morale
✦ Steady, Constant Increases in Costs
✦ Regular Cash Shortages
✦ Chronic Delays or Late Deliveries of Products
✦ Loss of Market Position
✦ Overworked Staff
✦ Excessive Rework Without Achieving Objectives
✦ Continual Supply Deficiencies
✦ Lack of Information About the Competition or Market[6]

Remember that these are only the reasons that businesses normally need consultants. There are also thousands of other areas in which both businesspeople and nonbusinesspeople may need assistance. For example, consultants are making millions of dollars today by teaching people how to manage their time, control stress, lose weight, and keep fit. If you have specific knowledge in almost any area—from handicrafts to hypnotism, mathematics to merchandising—you may have skills that are in demand by some segment of the population.

Fortune magazine wrote an exposé on consultants called "In Search of Suckers," in which well-known author and consultant Tom Peters was quoted as saying, "We're the only society that believes it can keep getting better and better. So we keep on getting suckered in by people like Emerson . . . and me."[7] I believe Peters was speaking somewhat tongue in cheek. After all, he included the world-famous nineteenth-century philosopher Ralph Waldo Emerson in the category of a huckster. Also, given the worldwide demand for consulting in all of these fields, I doubt that we Americans are the only ones seeking improvement.

HOW DO POTENTIAL CLIENTS ANALYZE CONSULTANTS FOR HIRE?

James Svatko's analysis of the consultant–client relationship led him to recommend that companies answer the following questions before deciding on hiring a consultant. You should answer these five questions yourself before submitting your formal proposal (which I'll show you how to do in Chapter 6) to a client:

1. Can you add something worthwhile to the company's total output?
2. Will your expertise bring the company any closer to its goals?
3. Can you make the company work more effectively?
4. Will you save the company time?
5. With the budget available, can you do a comprehensive and effective job?[8]

If your proposal doesn't prove that you can do these things for your client, either rework it or don't submit one.

WHAT MAKES AN OUTSTANDING CONSULTANT?

Being a consultant and being an outstanding consultant are two different things. After talking with many top-flight consultants around the country, I have identified seven areas that make the difference.

1. **Bedside Manner.** This is your ability to get along with your client. Here it's not so much what you say, but how you say it. Doctors with much knowledge but poor bedside manners often find that their patients prefer to go to doctors with much less experience or ability. Developing a pleasant bedside manner so that your clients have confidence in what you say can be as important as your technical knowledge.

2. **The Ability to Diagnose Problems.** In terms of the doctor analogy, we know that the doctor has access to all sorts of medicines to help cure a patient. But if he or she makes an incorrect diagnosis, the medicine may hurt more than it helps. Similarly, your ability to diagnose the problem correctly is extremely important. It is one of the most significant criteria of an outstanding consultant.

3. **The ability to find solutions.** Of course, having diagnosed a problem, you are expected to recommend the proper remedial actions. Chapter 11 is devoted entirely to problem solving. With practice, you will be able to solve complex problems consistently by suggesting the right course of action for your client to take.

4. **Technical Expertise and Knowledge.** You might expect that this would be the most important skill for a good consultant, and certainly technical expertise in a field is important. Expertise comes from your education, your experience, and your personal skills, but it may be in any one of a variety of areas, and it may develop in a variety of ways. G. Gordon Liddy, known primarily for his association with the Watergate break-in, commanded a six-figure income as a security consultant right after he got out of prison. So even a background that includes going to jail does not affect your ability to be a good consultant and to make a major contribution for the benefit of your client.

5. **Communication Skills.** Charles Garvin, from the well-known Boston Consulting Group, did extensive consulting in the area of business strategy beginning in the early 1960s. With 30 years' experience, Garvin identified three major attributes that every good consultant needs. The number one attribute is superior communication abilities. (Analytical skill is second, and the ability to work under pres-

sure is third.) You should read Chapter 14 of this book, devoted to making presentations, with particular interest.

6. **Marketing and Selling Ability.** Regardless of the technical area you are interested in, whether it is a functional area in business or something entirely different, you must learn to be a good marketer and a good salesperson. Not only do consultants sell an intangible product, they must also sell themselves. So I've devoted Chapters 2, 3, and 4 to explaining techniques for your consulting practice.

7. **Management Skills.** Last, but not the least in importance, is the ability to manage a business or a practice and to run projects. In my mind, an outstanding consultant must also be a good manager. As with other skills, the ability to manage can be learned. To assist you in this process, Chapter 17 will help you to manage your business efficiently. In addition, throughout the book I give step-by-step instructions for many processes that will help you perform as a skilled manager.

HOW MUCH MONEY CAN YOU MAKE AS A CONSULTANT?

No one should embark on a career as a consultant primarily to make money. Still, you need money to live, and it can provide the freedom to choose what one wishes to do in life and for whom. So this is a valid question.

More than 10 years ago, Albert Vicere and Robert Fulmer, two management professors at Pennsylvania State University, estimated that consultants were commanding daily fees that ranged as high as $10,000—and even higher.[9] Estimates today would be higher still. Of course, the higher fees tend to be charged by the large, well-known consulting firms, which are consulting to larger, better-known organizations. In fact, a very large consulting firm doing a major project may charge millions of dollars or more for its work.[10]

Another important variable is the field in which you are consulting and for whom you are consulting. If you are consulting for an individual in a field where your client isn't making much money, you can't charge very much either. But no matter what your fees are, you can make much more than you could doing the same work for someone else as an employee.

Recall that computer consultant with a high school education. If she is billing at $100 an hour, at eight hours per day, that's $4,000 per workweek—or well over $200,000 per year!

But wait. Though at $100 an hour you can sure make a lot of money over the course of a year, you have to realize that you will not be able to bill for every minute of every day. Some time must be spent in marketing your services. Therefore, consider the ratio of billable time to the unbillable time spent marketing.

Howard L. Shenson was an early pioneer who gave seminars on becoming an independent consultant. He estimated that new consultants should market their services at least one-third of their time during their first year in business and plan on only two-thirds in actual billable time. After the first year, marketing time can be reduced to 15 or 20 percent of the consultant's time. Other estimates for marketing time range as high as 40–50 percent. Many independent consultants note that, once established, they spend very little time marketing, because they either receive additional clients through referrals or spend all their available time on established clients.

When you are estimating how much you can actually make as a consultant, start with the assumption that in the first year you will spend about half of your time, or even more, marketing your services. You may not actually need that much, but it's safer than expecting to spend most of your time on work billed to your clients and then finding that you have grossly overestimated your first year's sales.

However, before you start billing based in what you can make, please read Chapter 7, which is all about pricing your services.

HOW DO PEOPLE BECOME CONSULTANTS?

Individuals get into consulting in many strange ways, and no two stories are exactly alike. You may be interested in hearing how some consultants got their start.

Howard L. Shenson was a PhD student at the same time he was teaching and serving as department head at California State University at Northridge. He received numerous requests from companies in the local area, and soon he was engaged in a variety of consulting activities in addition to his teaching and research. As the months went by, he realized he was spending more and more time consulting, and he was finding it more fascinating than his academic work. Finally he decided to devote himself entirely to full-time consulting, and he found not only greater job satisfaction but far higher compensation than he could ever earn as a professor.

Hurbert Bermont, author of the self-published *How to Become a Successful Consultant in Your Own Field* and a successful consultant in the publishing industry as well as a consultant's consultant today, got his start when his boss called him in one day and fired him. Bermont said he went through total shock at the time, but he later realized it was a favor in disguise. In desperation, Bermont called around and found a friend who agreed to let him use his office, secretary, and telephone for a nominal sum in exchange for training his friend's new secretary. He was able to acquire as a client the most prestigious and successful name in his business by working for the company at the right price: nothing. This door-opener eventually led to a paying contract with the company and, more important, gave him a major client with which to impress other prospective clients. At the end of six months, he was earning almost as much as it had taken him 20 years to reach in his previous career.

Phil Ross started out as an actor who worked as a salesperson with a manufacturing company between roles. Because of his unique abilities not only to sell but also to educate and motivate, he soon became national sales director. When he became dissatisfied with company policies, he began looking for another job, using a national executive search firm. In the process, he was recruited by that very recruiting firm to become an executive recruiter, or headhunter. Search consulting probably calls for more sales skills than any other type of consulting. This is because the consultant must be able to convince a company to become a client *and* persuade a fully satisfied employee to consider leaving his or her current organization and become a candidate for a job with a different company. Phil mastered these skills and excelled as a search consultant, and soon he was appointed national training director. After several years, Phil left to start his own executive search firm and eventually founded THE PROS, a consulting firm that assists corporations worldwide with their personnel and recruitment problems.

Luis Espinosa was born in Mexico and was my student at California State University at Los Angeles. He wanted to become a consultant for a major consulting firm. Using special job-finding techniques that got him face-to-face interviews with principals of top consulting firms, he was soon hired by Theodore Barry International. After only two years, he was recruited as a top-level strategic planner for a bank in Mexico City with $20 billion in assets. He then went on to a similar high position as an internal strategic planning consultant with an American bank and eventually became an entrepreneur in several industries.

This last story points out yet another advantage of consulting. Not infrequently, consultants who are highly visible to top management so impress their clients with their performance that they are catapulted immediately into senior executive ranks at extremely high salaries. Several years ago, *BusinessWeek* carried the story of Ilene Gordon Bluestein, who became director of corporate planning at the Signode Corporation in Glenview, Illinois, at age 28, only four years after leaving school—four years she spent consulting. Bluestein wasn't the only success mentioned. The article told of others who used consulting as a springboard to corporate success. All were young, held senior positions, and made large salaries. And every single one had been a consultant.

John Diebold opened a consulting operation in his parents' house in Weehawken, New Jersey. Had he prepared a resume, the most recent item would have been the fact that he had been fired from another consulting group because he had tried too hard to convince a company to buy a computer. That was in 1954. Three years later, he bought the company that had fired him. Eventually, his firm, The Diebold Group, had branches around the world, and he was called The Prince of Gurus.[11]

I've already told you how Peter Drucker became a consultant, and here's my own story. I left the U.S. Air Force where my primary duties had been flying. However, after a tour of duty in Vietnam, I was put in charge of the development of personal body armor systems for aircrew in the Air Force. After leaving the Air Force, I wrote an article about personal body armor for a magazine called *Ordnance*. Meanwhile, I had been abroad for three years, and a company that made pilots' helmets and oxygen masks hired me to direct its research and development activities.

One reader of my article was the vice president of a large aerospace company in California. His company had developed a lightweight infantry helmet and wanted help in marketing it. He asked me to lunch and offered me a full-time job on the spot. I explained that I was happy in my current job. He then asked whether I would do the work as a consultant, because it did not conflict with my company's product line. I got permission from my regular boss, and thus a new consultant was born. I didn't know anything about consulting then. I learned the hard way. I certainly wish *How to Make It Big as a Consultant* was available then!

SUMMING UP

In this chapter, I've supplied an overview of the entire consulting business. I hope I've opened your eyes to some of the potential, both in the lifestyle of a consultant and in the compensation you might receive, as well as to the different consulting areas that you might enjoy. Finally, although I've mentioned stories of several individuals who have become consultants, you should realize that how you become a consultant is not as important as *that* you actually become one. There are many routes to becoming a consultant, but what counts is that you become a successful consultant. The process of making it big as a consultant starts in Chapter 3 with your learning how to get clients using direct marketing methods, because they don't always fall into your lap as my first client did.

NOTES

1. Gautam Ghosh, "Human Capital Consulting Pyramid, *Slideshare*, accessed at http://www.slideshare.net/gautam/human-capital-consulting-market -pyramid, on July 1, 2008.

2. William A. Cohen, "Peter Drucker on the Value of Ignorance," *Performance and Profits*, accessed at http://www.amanet.org/performance-profits/editorial.cfm? Ed=609, November 20, 2007. You can read more about that in Chapter 6, "Approach Problems with Your Ignorance—Not Your Experience," in *A Class with Drucker: The Lost Lessons of the World's Greatest Management Teacher* (AMACOM, 2008).

3. Susan Carey, "Turnaround Consultants Make a Living Fighting Fires," *Wall Street Journal* interactive edition, accessed at www.collegejournal.com/ SB95193512839781581-consultingcareers.html, December 9, 2000.

4. Lois Therrien, "William Brandt: Putting Small Businesses Back in the Black," *Business Week* (August 21,1989), p. 99.

5. Janet G. Sullivan, "Kick the 'Buts,'" *American Way* (May 1999), p. 58.

6. James E. Svatko, "Working with Consultants," *Small Business Reports* (February 1989), p. 61.

7. Tom Peters quoted in Alan Farnham and Amy Kover, "In Search of Suckers," *Fortune* (October 14, 1996), accessed at www.pathfinder.com/fortune/1996/961014/gur.html.

8. Svatko, p. 59.

9. Farnham and Kover.

10. Howard P. Allen, "Are Management Consultants Worth Their Hire?" *Business Forum* (Fall 1988/Winter 1989), p. 31.

11. Frank Rose, "The Prince of Gurus," *Business Month* (April 1989), p. 67.

2

How to Get Clients: Direct Marketing Methods

MARKETING IS one of the most important areas in consulting, because without it you have no clients and therefore no sales. Without sales there can be no consulting practice. It makes no difference how expert you are or how much demand there is for your field of expertise. Without clients, the business and the practice cannot exist.

In this chapter, we'll cover the direct methods, and we'll cover the indirect methods in the next chapter. Both the direct and the indirect methods of marketing your practice and obtaining clients are important. The indirect methods take longer, but they can greatly expand your practice. To build a dynamic practice, you should integrate both methods into your marketing program. Finally, in Chapter 3, we'll discuss a special case: marketing your services to government.

DIRECT METHODS OF MARKETING

You can approach potential clients directly and let them know that you are available using up to seven direct methods of marketing:

1. Direct Mail
2. Cold Calls
3. Direct Response Space Advertising
4. Directory Listings
5. *Yellow Pages* Listings
6. Approaching Former Employers
7. Using the Internet

You'll find the first six methods in this chapter. The Internet is useful to a consultant in so many ways that this relatively new technology requires a chapter of its own (Chapter 16). In this chapter, I will also cover brochures, which are an important tool in marketing that may be used with any of the seven methods.

DIRECT MAIL

With direct mail, you send potential clients a letter, a brochure, or both to advertise your services. An example of a direct mail piece is shown in Figure 2-1. Note that this letter talks directly to the client's needs and tries to avoid sounding pompous or distant. The key is to establish personal communication with the potential client. By suggesting the firm's past accomplishments, the direct mail piece describes the kinds of things that can be done for the potential client. Finally, the piece doesn't leave things hanging; at the very end, the prospective client is asked to call at once for additional information or to set up a consulting appointment.

Direct Mail Letters

Writing direct mail letters for any purpose is an art. Not everyone can write compelling copy for direct mail letters, but you don't have to be able to do so. There are plenty of good copywriters around who make

Figure 2-1. Example of an effective direct mail letter.

William A. Cohen, PhD, Major General, USAFR, Ret.
1556 NORTH SIERRA MADRE VILLA ~ PASADENA, CALIFORNIA 91107
Tel. (323) 343-2972/Fax (626) 794-5998
Email: wcohen@calstatela.edu
Website: www.stuffofheroes.com

January 10, 2002

Mr. James W. West, President
Consolidated International, Inc.
3456 Avenue of the Americas
New York, New York 10158

Dear Mr. West:

"Our productivity increased 35% in less than three months after your one-day 'Stuff of Heroes' workshop for our general managers. This is the most significant increase I've witnessed since I became president." That's what the CEO of the Albright Corporation wrote me after a one-day leadership seminar we gave last month.

I'm writing to you because you may be looking for a way to dramatically increase your company's productivity, or customer service, or sales. I have had the privilege of helping some of the finest organizations in America, such as the Cheesecake Factory Restaurants, Hobart Corporation, FBI, U.S. Marine Corps, National Management Association, Hughes Aircraft Company, the National Association of Accountants, American Business Women's Association, Boeing Aircraft Company, Contel Corporation, and many more.

Why do such prestigious organizations engage us? Because, quite frankly, we produce for them. These speeches, seminars, and workshops are not ordinary:

- Every presentation is individually tailored especially for the organization and it's individual needs.
- As a university professor of both leadership and marketing, I combine research from both of these disciplines and present it in a dramatic way for maximum impact.

- Backed by hard research, our concepts have been endorsed by world famous individuals like Senator Barry Goldwater; General H. Norman Schwarzkopf; astronaut Frank Borman; Secretary of State Alexander Haig, Jr.; Barry Gordon, the longest serving president of the Screen Actors Guild; management thinker Peter F. Drucker; and CEOs from around the country.

For complete information, call me at my personal number at (323) 343-2972.

Sincerely,
William C. Cohen, Ph.D.
Consultant

P.S. I am the only consultant I know of who offers a money back guarantee if you are not satisfied, no questions asked. Call me right away, the number of dates available is limited. You have nothing to lose and everything to gain.

WAC

---

this their business, as well as plenty of very successful consultants who have someone else write their advertising copy. The cost may be several hundred to several thousand dollars, but for a good direct mail letter, the investment is well made.

To find a good copywriter, look for one who already has a track record in direct response work. He or she knows how to write copy for direct results, and that's what you're looking for. Where can you find someone like this? Try the English or advertising department of your local college or university. Sometimes you'll find outstanding freelancers masquerading as professors or graduate students. Direct marketing clubs or copywriter associations can sometimes recommend candidates for you to check out; check the associations in your telephone book. You can also consult the *Yellow Pages*; look under Copywriters. Other good sources are direct marketing professional magazines, such as *Direct Marketing, DM News,* and *Target Marketing.* Their classified and space advertisements contain listings of many freelance copywriters.

Your local library either has or can get these publications for you. You can also go to the Internet search engines. Search "direct marketing copywriter." You'll get thousands of hits. In all cases, ask for some references and samples of the copywriter's work before you contract for any job.

Writing Your Own Direct Mail Copy

You can write your own direct mail copy, but you must be a competent writer and be willing to work at doing this special type of selling in print.

There are numerous formulas to help you write effective direct mail copy. My own formula consists of four steps:

1. Get attention.
2. Develop interest and demonstrate benefits.
3. Show credibility.
4. Deliver a call to action.

Write in the first person. Write simply, with your potential client in mind. And keep it personal. Define your target audience exactly. Focus on that individual reader as you write your copy.

Let's say you are consultant John Smith. We'll create a direct mail piece and go through it step by step.

1. **Getting Attention.** You can get attention with a headline, but usually it isn't written as a headline. Instead, make it the first paragraph in your letter. It is an extremely important paragraph because it must hook your prospective client instantly. If it fails to do so, your letter goes right into the trash can unread.

To construct a headline/paragraph, try to think of the most significant thing you've done that would be important to your target audience. Let's say you're a marketing consultant specializing in increasing sales for small to medium-sized companies. Think through the assignments you've had and what happened as a result of your work. Look for five to ten great accomplishments, and then pick the most important. If you are a new consultant, consider what you did while working for someone else. Whether these accomplishments were achieved for a client, for a boss on a full-time job, or for no pay in a volunteer organization does not really matter. What is critical is that you brought about good results.

Finally, craft your attention getter. Keep reworking the paragraph to minimize the number and complexity of words and to maximize their dramatic effect.

Let's assume that you can honestly write the following letter. (Of course, be certain that your claims are accurate. Not only is lying unethical, but lying when using the mails constitutes mail fraud.)

> A few weeks ago, a client called to thank me. He's the president of a $5 million export company. The sales plan I put into effect for him caused his sales to increase by 541 percent in 2 months. And he told me that this increase in sales came with no increase in costs. No wonder he was so excited!

Can you imagine the president of a small company throwing that letter away without reading further? I can't. Especially if it is written on high-quality bond paper, has an impressive letterhead, and is addressed to the recipient by name. Every company of that size wants to increase sales. If you've increased a similar company's sales by 541 percent at no extra cost in such a short time, maybe you can do the same for the prospect's company. The owner would have to be a fool not to read on. However, the fact is that most consultants never stop to consider the benefits to their clients in quantitative terms. When you take the time to make those benefits clear in terms of dollars and cents, you will frequently be amazed at what you have accomplished.

Now that you have your prospective client's attention, the next step is to develop interest.

2. **Developing Interest and Demonstrating Benefits.** You can develop interest and demonstrate benefits at the same time. All you need to do is to state the reason for your letter and list some more of your accomplishments from the five to ten that you selected earlier.

I am writing to you because I am a marketing consultant specializing in increasing sales for companies like yours. If you are interested in increasing your company's sales dramatically at low cost, you may be interested in some other things I have done:

- Trained 7 salespeople of a $20 million clothing manufacturing company. Sales increased by an average of 46.3 percent after 6 months.

- Conducted a marketing audit for a $2 million company making small industrial parts. This company increased its sales by $441,000 the first year and cut selling costs by 4 percent at the same time.

- Developed and helped implement a marketing plan for a new product for a $75 million pharmaceutical company. First-year sales were $11 million—twice that of new products introduced in the past.

- Created a sales and promotional plan for a start-up newsletter for a small publishing company. The newsletter was profitable after only 8 months. Second-year profit objectives set prior to my plan were exceeded by 111 percent.

Take note of a couple of things:

✦ There are few adjectives but a great many numbers. Numbers add credibility even as you develop interest and show your prospective client some of the benefits he or she can expect.

✦ You use Arabic numerals; you don't spell out the numbers. You're not looking for an A in English. You want an A in response rate so that you can turn prospects into clients. Using Arabic numbers lets your figures really stand out.

These accomplishments are like your attention-getting paragraph in that your prospective client knows that if you can do such things for other organizations, you can probably do them for his or her firm. Again, the accomplishments must all be true, but take the time to work out the percentages of increases and other relevant numbers.

3. **Showing Credibility.** Up to now, everything you've stated consists only of your words. So having a third party confirm your abilities is important. The best way to do that is to quote from letters from clients, from former clients, or even from former bosses if you are a new consultant. After you have been a consultant for a while, you're going to get letters of thanks. Then all you need to do is ask whether you can quote the writer in your sales literature.

How do you get endorsements when you are just starting out? The best way is simply to ask for them. If you've done a good job for someone, telephone and ask what the client thought about your work. Was the client happy with the results? Did anything good happen? If your client was pleased, ask, "Would you be willing to write a letter from which I can quote?" You might even offer to supply ideas and figures that would help in writing it. Once you collect four or five good quotes, you are ready to confirm your credibility in your sales letter:

> Here is what some of my clients have said about my work:
>
> John Smith is the World's Best Consultant for small and medium-sized companies. — *George Able, president, ABC Service Company*
>
> You tripled my sales in three months and saved my company. — *Hugo Mondesto, president, Q. T. Limousine Service*
>
> Your sales training really did wonders. Now all of my salespeople are superstars. — *Joe Fine, The Cutting Edge, Inc.*

In some cases, you may not be able to get permission to extract from a letter for your direct mail. In that case, use initials only and disguise the company name like this:

> The ROI for your services was 500 percent plus. Thanks. — *A. A. president, a medium-size travel agency*

Another way of showing credibility is with a brief statement of your educational and technical or consultant experiences:

> I have a BS in engineering from California State University at Los Angeles and an MBA from the University of Michigan.

I have managed marketing activities and consulted in marketing for 12 years.

4. **Issuing a Call to Action.** Research has demonstrated conclusively that a prospective client who does not act immediately to contact you will probably never do so. So the final part of your direct mail letter should be a call for immediate action. To do this, be very clear and explicit about what you want your prospective client to do. Usually you want the prospect to call or write you to set up a face-to-face interview. You can call your prospective client to action like this:

> Please call, write, or e-mail me for a no-cost-or-obligation, face-to-face interview so that you can judge for yourself whether I can help you. One cautionary note: Please do this right away. The majority of the work I do is done by me personally; I believe that's one of the secrets of my success. But I get booked early. Even if your ideas are not firmed up yet, I recommend contacting me now. That way, it is more likely that I will have the time available to help you.

I recommend using a PS as well because a PS is almost always read. Some people read the postscript even before they read the rest of the letter. Use the postscript to stimulate the action you want. If you can, offer something free in return for action:

> PS: I have prepared a special booklet, *How to Get the Most Out of Marketing Consultants,* for my clients. If you call or write, I will send you a copy with my compliments, while they last.

The "while they last" phrase and the free offer provide additional incentives for your prospective client to respond right away.

Of course, there are many ways of writing a direct mail letter to get clients. The following books on copywriting can help:

Teach Yourself Copywriting by J. Jonathan Gabay (McGraw-Hill)

The Copywriter's Handbook by Robert W. Ely (Holt)

Persuading on Paper by Marcia Yukin (Infinity Publishing)

Locating the Right Mailing List

Producing your letter, your brochure, and the envelope is not inexpensive. Postage costs have increased astronomically in recent years. You can expect to spend as much as $1 or more including postage to get each direct mail package to a potential client. So you do not want to waste your mailing on individuals who might be only slightly interested in your services. You want to reach those who are real potential customers, who have the authority to hire you, and who would probably be interested in the services you have to offer.

Some sources of help are professionals who handle mailing lists: list brokers, managers, or compilers. These experts can be found in most *Yellow Pages* under the heading "Mailing Lists" or located through the Internet. They will discuss your needs with you and help you rent lists of potential clients interested in the services you offer. Usually you pay nothing for this advice. The list broker is paid a commission by the list owner when you rent the lists.

If you are located in a small town, the potential size of your market, depending on your specialty, may be so small that a direct mail campaign is not advisable. On the other hand, you could conduct a direct mail campaign or use the Internet to promote a national or even international business. You may not even have to travel, depending on the type of consulting you do and whether clients find communication by telephone, mail, or e-mail acceptable.

Large consulting firms may spend a lot of money every year on a direct mail campaign like this. These companies, with client lists numbering in the thousands, stay in touch by mailing out multiple packages (each containing a letter, a card, and a small brochure) within the span of a single year. But the investment can bring back big returns. Even a response rate of less than 1 percent can result in hundreds of thousands of dollars in consulting fees.

If you would like additional information or catalogs of lists, here are some companies that can supply them:

All About Lists
http://www.all-about-lists.com/?source=goto/
877-792-1116

Buyer Zone
http://www.buyerzone.com/marketing/mailing_lists
/qz_questions_758z.jhtml?_requestid=160728
888-393-5000

Marketing Comparison
http://www.marketingcomparison.com/mailinglist
.jsp?id=1178802302454003027
866-461-0519

COLD CALLS

Cold calls are calls you make to prospects with whom you have had no prior contact. This method can be extremely effective in aquiring clients. However, it is time-consuming, and it involves a significant amount of rejection, which you must learn to cope with if you are to use this method.

Let's say you've decided to devote a single day to obtaining clients by cold calling. That means you should make 25 to 30 contacts with individuals who have the authority to hire you. If even half this number retain your services, you would soon be extremely wealthy from consulting. As a matter of fact, you would have more consulting work than you could possibly handle. But the reality is that if a single call leads to even a one-time engagement worth $3,000 to $5,000, the day of calling is well worth your time. And if the client is satisfied and hires you again and again, this single success out of many calls is really worthwhile. However, 25 to 30 calls with one success usually means 24 to 29 rejections, some of which may be rude and abrupt. Therefore, if you wish to use cold calling, you must train yourself to be prepared for the rejection that comes with it.

You can maximize your success in using the cold call method by doing the following:

1. **Write out exactly what you want to say ahead of time.** Usually you should follow the outline of a good direct mail letter. That is, speak about benefits to your potential client, and sell yourself by describing past accomplishments. (These can be things you did while employed full time, as long as you were the one responsible and actual-

ly did whatever it is you claim.) While planning what you are going to say, never forget that the object is not to make a consulting sale over the phone, which is almost impossible, but to get a face-to-face interview in which you can get the assignment finalized. (I show you how to do that in Chapter 5.) So now you know how to tell when you have made a successful cold call: It always ends with an appointment for a face-to-face interview.

2.   **Use creative ways to get around the secretary.** One of the most bothersome aspects of the cold call method is that frequently secretaries are in place between you and the executives who may wish to hire you. Part of a secretary's job is to screen out job seekers and salespeople. Therefore, getting past the secretary is essential. One method is simply to avoid the secretary altogether. Call before 8:00 A.M. or after 5:00 P.M., and chances are that the executive will answer the call directly. Another technique is to identify yourself by name and ask for the executive, using his or her full name. If you do not have the name, call the company and ask the receptionist for the individual's full name. What you are looking for is not "Mr. Smith," but "Don Smith."

When the receptionist connects you with his secretary, say firmly, "This is Jim Black for Don Smith. Would you connect me, please?" Or you can say, "This is Jim Black, president of the XYZ Consulting Group, for Don Smith. Would you connect me, please?" If the secretary asks about the nature of your call, say that it is a private business matter. If she refuses to connect you without an answer, ask her to give the information to her boss and leave your number for a callback. The chances of getting through are better this way than if you say that you are calling to see whether Mr. Smith is interested in hiring you as a consultant.

3.   **Combine your calls with a direct mail campaign.** This one-two combination punch can work very well. Do the direct mail campaign first, and then wait several weeks, giving the executive time to call you directly. If this happens, you have a better chance of setting up an interview. After several weeks have gone by, call those who have not responded to your mailing. Now if the secretary asks why you are calling, you can say that it has to do with a letter you wrote to Don Smith.

I recommend that you do not state in the letter that you will call. For one thing, indicating that you will call may stop the executive who may otherwise have called. (It's always much better if he or she calls you.) Second, consulting work can be irregular. You can have little to do for a period, and then get extremely busy with contracted work. You may then delay calling when a call is expected, and you could be viewed as unreliable.

The direct mail campaign, combined with a follow-up call, works well because some executives who desperately need your services may not be completely convinced by your letter. In a personal conversation, they may recognize that you can fulfill their need and will make an appointment for an interview.

DIRECT RESPONSE SPACE ADVERTISING

At one time the advertising of consulting services was uncommon. It was looked down upon in the same way as advertising by a doctor, dentist, or lawyer. Today all these professionals advertise, and you should too. Executive search consultants, for instance, advertise in magazines or trade journals in their areas of specialty. Because potential clients in certain industries prefer to deal with specialists, these ads are often successful.

Direct space advertising is expensive, so make it count. For one thing, be certain to place your ad in a medium likely to be read by your target audience. Don't be fooled by the total number of people reached by your ad. Only likely clients count. For this reason, don't advertise in your local newspaper unless everyone in the general population is a potential client for the services you offer. Let's face it, that's simply not true.

Also, if you decide to advertise, the ad must be well written, that is, written with your potential clients in mind. Learning how to write copy that makes such advertising work is not easy. The type of advertising that you are interested in is *direct response space advertising.* Like a direct mail letter or cold calling, this type of advertising is intended to bring a direct response. At the very least, such an ad should result in inquiries that will lead to consulting engagements.

Even some professional writers cannot write this kind of copy, which must be so compelling that prospective clients needing your services would be foolish not to contact you. Most such advertisements use the AIDA formula: attention, interest, desire, and action.

- ✦ A dramatic headline is used to attract people's attention.
- ✦ Their interest is immediately aroused in the lead-in paragraphs stating specific benefits.
- ✦ The copy states and talks about additional benefits until readers' desire to respond to the ad is at a peak.
- ✦ At this point, the ad calls upon them to respond at once by taking specific action.

Here are two books that can help:

Tested Advertising Methods, 4th ed., by John Caples and Fred E. Hahn (Prentice-Hall)

How to Write a Good Advertisement by Victor O. Schwab (Wilshire Books)

DIRECTORY LISTINGS

Many directories list consultants and their services. Some are free; some charge for listings. Usually this method of advertising is not very effective for a simple reason: Few potential clients use directories when seeking consultants. As a test, I once paid several hundred dollars to be listed in a directory. Over the period of a year, I received numerous letters about my listing, but every single one was from someone who was seeking to sell *me* something and who was not interested in using my consulting services! Directory listings are not recommended unless the listing is free.

YELLOW PAGES LISTINGS

Listings in the *Yellow Pages* may be effective for certain types of consulting practices. Clients who have never used a consultant before may turn to the *Yellow Pages* in search of services. If you decide to advertise this way, buy a large ad. The rationale is simple: A large ad attracts readers' attention more than a competitor's small ad. Second, many people assume that only large companies place large ads. As a result, a large advertisement for a small business may actually outpull a small ad placed by a multibillion-dollar organization. Try such an ad for one year. If it brings in clients, continue to use it. If not, simply maintain a listing in the *Yellow Pages* with no ad.

APPROACHING FORMER EMPLOYERS

Many consultants get their initial cash flow going by contracting their services to former employers. No matter what the circumstances of their departure (unless they were fired for incompetence), they have something to offer their former company in expertise and experience. By retaining you as a consultant, your former employer uses that expertise without the overhead of an annual salary and benefits, even though as a consultant you may get a much higher hourly rate than when you were an employee. A former employer may also wish to hire you simply to ensure that you will not go to work for a competitor, either as a consultant or as a full-time employee. In any case, approaching former employers is certainly worth exploring; explain that you are now going into full-time consulting and that you would be happy to do for the company what you did in the past, as well as other related work.

BROCHURES

The basic purposes of any brochure are first to advertise your type of work and second to convince the reader that you are the most capable individual available to do this work. Therefore, if you are going to develop your own brochure, write it to answer two questions: (1) What is it that I do? and (2) Why am I the best one to do it? Answering these questions may require that your brochure have different sections, such as:

- ✦ Descriptions of the kind of work you do
- ✦ Specific examples of problems you have solved for clients in the past, along with the benefits to them from using your services

✦ Reasons why your services are better than those offered by competitors

✦ Your experience, background, and special qualifications that make you unique

✦ A list of previous clients (if available)

✦ Testimonials from previous clients

With regard to this last section, if you haven't done any previous consulting, you can write down accomplishments that you attained when you were an employee working for someone else. As long as these accomplishments are in your area of consulting expertise and benefited whomever you were working for at the time, whether the beneficiary was an employer or a client, is unimportant. Of course, you may not use actual names unless you have permission to do so.

A number of good books are available to help you in preparing your own brochure. Here are a few:

> *The Ultimate Marketing Toolkit: Ads That Attract Customers. Brochures That Create Buzz. Websites That Wow* by Paula Peters (Adams Media)
>
> *Better Brochures, Catalogs, and Mailing Pieces* by Jane Maas (St. Martin's Press)
>
> *The Perfect Sales Piece: A Complete Do-It-Yourself Guide to Creating Brochures, Catalogs, Fliers, and Pamphlets* by Robert Bly (Wiley)

DESIGNING YOUR BROCHURE

Consultant brochures can have very different objectives. One consultant whose area is strategic planning wanted her brochure to continually remind her clients and prospective clients of her expertise. Her brochure was a 20-page manual on strategic planning, printed on glossy paper. It cost a fortune, but she maintained that it was well worth the investment.

Another consultant I knew years ago produced a multicolor glossy brochure with numerous photos. At that time, it cost him $20,000 for only 1,000 copies. He told me that most of his prospective clients barely looked at his brochure and few read it through. Yet he was entirely satisfied. His consulting practice was in a highly technical area of composites and composite structures. The brochure demonstrated conclusively that he was a force in the industry, and he said that the brochure enabled him to capture significant business that he previously could not obtain.

Before you even begin to design your brochure, decide what it is supposed to do. Most of us want something simple that we can use with our direct mail letter or to get to prospective clients in other ways. We want a brochure to help us get in the door for a face-to-face interview, to reinforce our capability, and to help close the sale of the engagement during or after the interview.

Deciding on the target market is also important. An expensive brochure says that you are high-priced. That's fine if your market has the money, and that's why the big consulting houses have fancy and expensive brochures. But if your clients are small businesses, even if your pricing is anything but high, you may scare off prospective clients.

Deciding on the objective for your brochure as well as your target market helps you to decide on the type of printing, paper, size, and other factors. It also helps you to decide what should go into your brochure.

The brochure usually consists of the following sections:

- ✦ **Who You Are.** This can be handled by your qualifications and a photo. I like to include a photo because it lets people know that a real person is behind the name.

- ✦ **What You Do**. A list of the kinds of things you do gives your prospective clients some idea of how they can profit from using you.

- ✦ **How You Work.** This can take the form of a case history of an assignment, or it can be just a description of your method of operation from initial meeting to assignment completion.

- ✦ **What You've Done.** Here you can list your accomplishments as described in your direct mail letter. Remember to use few adjectives and a lot of numbers, dollar figures, and percentages. You can also include a client list and a page with quotes regarding your performance, as in your direct mail letter.

✦ **How to Contact You.** Finally, make certain to include your address and phone number.

Your direct mail letter should accompany your brochure.

Once you know what your brochure is going to contain and its approximate size, you can begin to work out a rough layout. Do this before you begin to write copy. If you have the equivalent of only two sides of an $8^{1}/_{2}$ x 11-inch sheet of paper, you may not have enough space for everything you want to include. Do a rough layout and you'll know.

Only after the layout is done should you begin to write copy. Again, you can get a professional designer and copywriter to do all of this for you, or you can do it on your own. In the early days, I did everything myself except the final typesetting. Nowadays, with the numerous computer software programs and printers available, you can probably do everything yourself and make your brochure look very professional.

The format of your brochure can be anything: a simple, one-page flier to a slick, many-paged booklet, or something in between. Small consulting operations often get good results with a modest brochure, perhaps one $8^{1}/_{2}$ x 11-inch sheet folded twice that describes the background of the company, the type of work it does, and the qualifications of the principal or principals. Many of the very large firms produce quite elaborate brochures covering all aspects of their practices, which are designed singlehandedly to impress clients with the stature, size, and accomplishments of the firms.

I have included an example of one of my own brochures in Appendix B. In recent years, the emphasis of my work has been on my speeches, seminars, and workshops. So my brochure is really a media kit. The one in Appendix B emphasizes my background for leader development. The front describes what I offer, and the back presents my testimonials under the title "Kudos from Very Important People for Dr. Cohen's Seminars, Books, and Speeches." Inside, on the left-hand folder pocket, I put articles that have been written about me or that I have written for newspapers or magazines. In the right-hand pocket, I put a description of my background, the various services I offer, letters I have received from satisfied clients, a list of my clients, and a 5x7-inch black-and-white photograph.

What I particularly like about this is that I do everything on my own computer using desktop publishing hardware and software. So my brochure is never out-of-date, nor do I waste money in printing copies that I never use.

SUMMING UP

Clients will not automatically come to you. You must market your consulting service. But if you do your marketing well, in accordance with the guidelines in the next two chapters, you will soon build a successful consulting practice. In the next chapter, we look at indirect methods of marketing your consulting practice.

3

How to Get Clients: Indirect Marketing Methods

INDIRECT SELLING METHODS must be a significant part of your overall marketing program. They usually do not bring in clients as quickly as can direct marketing methods. However, in the long run, the benefits of indirect methods are considerable. Many times you are so busy consulting that you may have less time to spend on your marketing. That is when the benefits of indirect methods are really clear, because they go on working, even when you may have let the marketing part of your business slip. So make no mistake about it: Indirect methods may not work instantaneously, but they are necessary for any consulting practice over the long haul.

THE BASIC INDIRECT METHODS

Indirect methods of getting clients include:

1. Speaking Before Groups
2. Sending out Newsletters

3. Joining and Being Active in Professional Associations
4. Joining and Being Active in Social Organizations
5. Writing Articles
6. Writing a Book
7. Writing Letters to the Editor
8. Teaching a Course
9. Giving Seminars
10. Distributing Publicity Releases
11. Exchanging Information Leads and Referrals with Noncompeting Consultants

Let's look at each of these in more detail.

SPEAKING BEFORE GROUPS

Speaking in public is an excellent way of building your consulting practice. In almost any community, numerous groups use guest speakers, sometimes on a monthly or even a weekly basis. If the type of consulting you do is associated with the needs of these groups and is of interest to their members, you can benefit from speaking to them.

Dr. Pedro Chan, an immigrant to the United States from Macao, China, used this method to build his acupuncture consultancy for physicians. You can do the same thing. Simply pick a topic having to do with the services you offer, whether it's tax consulting, starting a new business, direct response marketing, or some other subject of potential interest. Then prepare a 45-minute talk that would be of interest and value to your audience. If you consult in direct marketing, you could speak on the topic, "5 Ways to Increase Direct Mail Response." If you consult in personnel matters, you might choose "How to Decrease Personnel Turnover."

Now go to your telephone book and look for local organizations that appear to have meetings and therefore may use guest speakers. Call and ask to speak to the program chair. Explain what you have to offer and how the membership can benefit from your presentation.

After your speech, let your listeners know how to contact you for additional information. A business card is good, but even better is a prepared handout with useful information pertaining to your presentation, your telephone number, and your address. An example of such a handout is shown in Figure 3-1.

Figure 3-1. Example of an effective handout.

•30 WAYS•
TO INCREASE YOUR LEADERSHIP EFFECTIVENESS 1000%

William A. Cohen, PhD, Major General, USAFR, Ret. © 1990
www.stuffofheroes.com; wcohen@stuffofheroes.com

• 7 WAYS •
TO ATTRACT FOLLOWSHIP

1. *Make others feel important.* People will follow you when you make them feel important, not when you make yourself feel important.

2. *Promote your vision.* No one will follow you simply because you decide you want to lead. You must have a clear idea where you want to take the group you lead. Then you must promote the goal and convince those you lead that it is worthwhile.

3. *Treat others as you would be treated yourself.* You wouldn't want to follow a leader who treated you poorly, and neither would anyone else.

4. *Take responsibility for your actions and the actions of those you lead.* If you don't, you are no longer the leader.

5. *Praise in public, criticize in private.* If someone has earned your praise, let everyone know about it. If someone has earned your ire, let only that person know about it.

6. *See and be seen.* You've got to get around to really know what's going on, to fix what's wrong, and to capitalize on what's right. It's also the only way those you lead can be sure you're for real.

7. *Use competition to make striving a game.* People love to compete. It is the secret of successful products from professional sports to video games. It is the secret of unbelievable achievements in

all activities. Use competition as a positive force to reach your objectives.

• 7 WAYS •
TO TAKE CHARGE IN A CRISIS OR HIGH-RISK SITUATIONS

8. *Establish your objective at once.* You can't lead anywhere until you know where you want to go.

9. *Communicate what you want done.* Do this in a way likely to get the attention of those you lead.

10. *Act boldly.* This isn't the time to be cautious. This is the time to take risks.

11. *Be decisive.* Don't put off making decisions. Do it now!

12. *Dominate the situation.* Do this by taking the initiative. If you don't, the situation will dominate you.

13. *Lead by example.* Make your credo "follow me." Live by it.

14. *Dump people who can't do the job.* Hire replacements fast...but do a thorough job of interviewing to minimize risk.

• 7 ACTIONS •
TO DEVELOP YOUR CHARISMA

15. *Show your commitment.* Charismatic leaders are committed to their missions.

16. *Look the part of your vision.* If you don't, you start out with a disadvantage. If you do, it reinforces your commitment.

17. *Dream big.* Important leaders have important dreams.

18. *Keep moving toward your goals.* He who hesitates is lost...and so is everyone in the group.

19. *Do your homework.* You keep ahead by working while others rest.

20. *Build a mystique.* Magicians have power because of the mystery they create. So do charismatic leaders.

21. *Use the indirect approach.* Direct assault produces resistance. An indirect approach produces agreement.

• 4 WAYS •
TO BUILD LEADERSHIP SELF-CONFIDENCE

22. *Become an uncrowned leader.* Become the leader in situations where others don't want to lead.

23. ***Be an unselfish teacher and helper of others.*** Help and teach others whenever they need your help and are ready to accept it.

24. ***Develop your expertise.*** Leaders don't know everything, but they need to know something, and expertise is a source of leadership power.

25. ***Use positive imagery.*** Simulations in the mind are rehearsals for success.

• 5 ACTION STEPS •
TO MOTIVATE THOSE YOU LEAD

26. ***Work on the important things first.*** High pay, top benefits, and ironclad security are nice, but they are not the most important.

27. ***Treat others with respect.*** They won't respect you if you don't respect them.

28. ***Make the work interesting.*** No one wants to get bored to death while working.

29. ***Always give recognition for good work.*** It's more than the right thing to do—it is a leader's duty.

30. ***Give those you lead an opportunity to develop their skills.*** Skill builds pride. More important, others have dreams. A leader helps followers to achieve their dreams.

In the biography that you give to the organization to promote your presentation and to be used when the host introduces you, include the fact that you are a consultant. In some cases, you will actually get paid for your presentation, but this is only a bonus. Your major objective is to gain exposure and eventually to get additional clients.

Here are three books that will help you:

Presenting to Win by Jerry Weissman (Prentice Hall).

10 Days to More Confident Public Speaking by Lenny Laskowski (Grand Central Publishing)

101 Secrets of Highly Effective Speakers by Caryl Rae Krannich (Impact Publishing)

You may also want to join the National Speakers Association and participate in their many programs for helping speakers. The association even has a professional emphasis group for consultants. For membership information, contact The National Speakers Association, 1500 South Priest Drive, Tempe, AZ 85281 (480-968-2552, http://www.nsaspeaker.org).

SENDING OUT NEWSLETTERS

Let me tell you a story about the effective use of a newsletter. I was the head of a rapidly growing organization and had been hiring new people every few months, mostly through advertisements in the *Wall Street Journal*. Every time one of my ads appeared, headhunters would call offering to find the needed candidate for me. Since I had never dealt with headhunters but knew that they were expensive (with fees up to 30 percent of an executive's annual salary), I turned them all down. However, one day I received a friendly letter from a recruiter, along with a free subscription to his newsletter. Over the next two to three months, I continued to receive this newsletter, which I found useful. When I next needed to recruit, I hired this headhunter to help me. That newsletter helped earn the headhunter a large fee on that one placement, not to mention the potential for future business.

To get clients, your newsletter should not only dispense news; it should dispense news of interest and value to potential clients and remind your past and current clients that you are still around. Every time clients or potential clients receive one of these newsletters with your name on it, they think of you.

One time-saving method is to use newsletters written by someone else. These syndicated newsletters are mailed out with your firm's imprint on each copy. Here are a few organizations that can provide this service:

> Company Newsletters, 18593 Jasper Way, Lakeville, MN 55044-9681 (612-892-6943, http://www.companynewsletters.com).
>
> The Newsletter Company, 703 McKinney Avenue, Suite 200 Dallas, TX 75202 (800-828-7198, http://www.thenewslettercompany .com).

The Newsletter Guy, 1517 Buckeye Court, Pinole, CA 94564 (877-588-1212 or 510-724-9507, http://www.thenewsletterguy.com)

A sample of a generic newsletter is shown in Figure 3-2. Of course, you can write your own newsletter with specialized information pertaining directly to your services. It doesn't have to be elaborate; you can type a master directly onto your business letterhead and have it reproduced by a quick printer. If the material is of value to your readers, you can be sure it will increase your credibility and help to build your practice.

With the advent of the Internet, you can easily develop your newsletter and distribute it by e-mail. That way, you save all sorts of printing and mailing costs. Or you can use both print and Internet forms for increased effectiveness.

E-Zinez.com publishes a free handbook on how to publish an e-mail newsletter (http://www.e-zinez.com). Also see the E-zine Articles Web site at http://ezinearticles.com/?Creating-Demand -With-Email-Newsletters&id=17354. You'll find all sorts of good information.

For an example, look at my Internet-based newsletters. The link for one is at http://www.stuffofheroes.com/Vol.%206,%20No.7.htm. If you are interested in leadership, you'll also find more than 30 articles on leadership, which can be accessed from the Home page or the Journal Archives.

We talk more about using the Internet for promotion in Chapter 16.

Here are some other excellent sources on newsletters in general:

Home-Based Newsletter Publishing: A Success Guide for Entrepreneurs by William J. Bond (McGraw-Hill)

Marketing with Newsletters: How to Boost Sales, Add Members & Raise Funds with a Print, Fax, or Web Site Newsletter by Elaine Floyd (EF Communications)

Producing a First-Class Newsletter: A Guide to Planning, Writing, Editing, Designing, Photography, Production, and Printing by Barbara A. Fanson (Self-Counsel Press)

Figure 3-2. Example of a generic newsletter.

It Used to Be Bonds For Income But Take a Look at This Idea

Historically, if you desired income, you purchased income investments such as bonds or preferred shares. However, the data suggests that stocks may be a better source of income. Although most stocks do not have very significant dividends (the average dividend on the S&P 500 stands at 1.28%), their appreciation over time can be used as a substantial source of income.

A study published in the AAII Journal (February 1998) indicated that a portfolio heavier in stocks provided a better chance of a retiree meeting their income needs than a portfolio of bonds.

For the period analyzed of 1926 to 1995, the data showed that if an investor wanted to draw 7% annually on their portfolio for 20 years after retiring, a 100% bond portfolio would have been successful in delivering the necessary income only 47% of the time. On the other hand, a portfolio of stocks would have been successful at delivering the required income 92% of the time.

If we look at the same data but only for the period since World War II, stocks show up even better than bonds as a retirement income source. Stocks would have been successful 100% of the time in producing a 7% annual income while bonds would have been successful only 42% of time.

The best part about this study is that it takes into account that stocks can be more volatile than bonds. The study accounted for the fact that a retiree would need to take their 7% income even in years when their portfolio was declining in value and thus tests these hypothetical portfolios under a real life scenario.

If you've been staying away from the stock market, worrying that it's "too high" and relying on income investments to supply your retirement income, this article suggests that you are taking the more financially risky path. I know that stocks seem more risky because many investors focus on the *short term*. But when you look at the *long term*

as this article does, you can more clearly see that bonds have been the more risky income alternatives as they *have failed to deliver a 7% income more than half of the time.*

If you'd like details on how to design a stock portfolio that has provided an investor's income needs comfortably at 8% annually for the past 25 years, please check off the attached coupon.

Health-adjusted SPIAs—Poor Health Can Be a Factor in Producing More Income

There's a type of annuity that pays you more if your health profile is not good. This may sound strange, but here's how it works:

SPIA, which stands for Single Premium Immediate Annuity, has long been a popular investment for obtaining a fixed income which cannot be outlived. With the life option, a SPIA pays you a fixed monthly income for life. Insurance companies calculate the size of your monthly payment based on standard life expectancy tables. Once calculated at the beginning, you continue to receive the same monthly amount, regardless of how long you live. It's almost like getting a second social security check.

Some companies take into account your individual health condition and use that information to calculate your life expectancy. If your health records indicate conditions that could lower your life expectancy, this is factored into the monthly payment you receive and increases the monthly payment. You then receive this fixed monthly amount no matter how long you live.

Take this hypothetical example. A man age 70 decides to obtain a SPIA. He deposits a $100,000 premium and based on his standard life expectancy of 16 years, his monthly payment is $871.05 (a 10.4% annual payout rate). He will receive this fixed monthly amount regardless of how long he lives.

Your Office Address and Phone Number Here

(continues)

Figure 3-2. (continued).

However, if he has a negative health profile and the insurance companies calculate his life expectancy at only 10 years, his monthly payment will jump to $1393.68. Because of the negative health history, this annuitant receives more income.

SPIAs have been most popular with single individuals who are not concerned with leaving an inheritance. That's because, once the initial premium is paid, the SPIA cannot be surrendered for value. Rather, you receive a fixed monthly income for life. For those people who like the idea of increasing their monthly income and do want to leave funds to heirs, remember that you would use only a part of your assets for a SPIA and other assets can be designated for heirs.

If you would like a quote on how much monthly income you could get from a SPIA, complete the attached coupon. If you have poor health history, please call to make an appointment, as we will need your written permission to release this information to insurance companies in order to obtain quotations.

Additionally, if you've been relying on municipal bonds for tax sheltered income, please call for an appointment and we'll show you how some previous mini-bond investors use SPIAs to increase their monthly tax sheltered income.

What About Asia (and Other Investor Mistakes)?

In the October 1998 issue of this newsletter I wrote an article explaining the difference between the rich and the not-as-rich. The not-so-rich people tend to focus on the next few days or weeks, while wealthier people tend to have much longer time horizons. They invest in real estate and stocks and wait until they rise.

Similarly, it's my observation that investors with short time horizons do not do as well. They tend to buy items when popular (like Internet stocks) and sell items that are unpopular. I suggest rather that buying low and selling high is a much better method of making money. In this light, I wrote in October of 1998,

"If you were to adopt such a strategy with some of your funds, where would you put money to work now? Into Asia, into gold, into beat-up technology stocks and into Eastern Europe."

In fact, for the first part of 1999, the best performing mutual funds according to CDA/Weisenberger

were emerging growth funds, reflecting rapid increases of stock prices in Asia and Eastern Europe (Emerging Market Equity 33.23). The second best sector was technology/communications (up 30.7%). Please note that the price of gold is still very weak and this "buy low sell high strategy" is not for someone with a short time horizon and is not guaranteed to produce profits.

But these results do indicate as they have many times in the past, that if you listen to the current news of the day, you're likely to make poor investment decisions. In fact, a recent example would be the rising of interest rates. Many investors believe or have been taught that when interest rates rise, stocks go down. In fact, the Dow Jones average hit a new high after the recent increase in interest rates by the Federal Reserve. This provides yet another lesson not to invest based on today's news.

If you like the idea of a buy low/sell high system, on which we base our client's portfolios, we're happy to show you how to use a system to do that. Not only have we found it more lucrative, but it frees up the time you otherwise waste listening to the latest forecast on CNBC, CNN or your other favorite financial show.

Check off the coupon for details.

Space for your individual announcement or paste in another article from our web-based article database accessible by newsletter subscribers

JOINING PROFESSIONAL ASSOCIATIONS

Membership in professional associations can be an excellent way to obtain clients over the long term, for two reasons. First, your participation lends you the credibility of the association, even if you yourself are unknown. Second, professional associations are excellent for making contacts, especially if you take an active role. Plan to participate actively in programs, such as holding an office. Over the years, many clients have come to me because of my active role in associations.

JOINING SOCIAL ORGANIZATIONS

Social organizations are more for contacts than credibility. They include alumni associations, tennis or bowling clubs, or health studios; I have even obtained clients from fellow members of a martial arts club! When a social relationship is established, a client relationship often follows. Individuals see you, get to know you, and come to trust you. If they happen to have a need in your area of consulting, they may well think of you. With very little direct effort, you may acquire a client.

Like professional organizations, social organizations are a basis on which you can build long-term relationships. It's no wonder that so-called relationship marketing is considered such an important idea for all businesses.

WRITING ARTICLES

Naturally, if you are going to write an article, it must pertain to your type of consulting, and it must be interesting and valuable to the reader. Perhaps most important of all, the biographical information that you include with the article should note that you are a consultant.

The first consulting assignment I ever received, as explained earlier in the book, resulted from an article I had written for a magazine called *Ordnance.* The executive vice president of one of the largest aerospace companies in the country saw my article and found it particularly interesting, because he had headed a project having to do with the very product that I wrote about. He contacted me immediately, and a consulting engagement resulted.

Management consultant-trainer Howard L. Shenson used to tell the story of a consultant who wrote a single article and syndicated it to 90 different in-house publications. It resulted in so many requests for his services that he had to go into business as a consultant broker, brokering the offers that came his way because he simply could not handle so much business on his own.

I've used this marketing method to promote not only my consulting services but other activities as well. One example concerns a book that I wrote in 1982, *Building a Mail Order Business*. To assist in the promotion of the book, I wrote an article entitled "Can Anyone Make a Million Dollars in Mail Order?" and self-syndicated it around the country to magazines and newspapers, offering each an exclusive in its geographic area or industry. (As long as the publications know what kind of rights you are offering, this is entirely legal and ethical.) In this manner, I multiplied my readership for this one article many times over.

One day my publisher called and asked whether I would be willing to go on radio station KLBJ in Austin, Texas, the station started by President Lyndon B. Johnson. Naturally I agreed. This radio appearance, which was actually done from my office in California through a telephone hookup, led to additional radio and television appearances around the country and in Canada. But the interesting thing is that this first appearance resulted from the one article. Someone in Austin had read the article, requested a copy of the book, and felt that it might be an interesting subject for a half-hour talk show.

Another technique you can use is to rewrite articles on the same subject matter. I learned this from a very famous individual in his field: Captain P. V. H. Weems, USN retired, who is considered the father of aerial navigation. When I was a young Air Force officer, I had the good fortune to have caught the attention of Captain Weems, who invited me to his home during my vacation. During this visit, Captain Weems taught me to rewrite a single article many times to gain increased publicity for my ideas. "If you just write about your topic once, you will miss a good deal of your potential readership," he told me. I have also used this technique. A recent example is in Figure 3-3, which was published in eight different magazines and journals in various forms to promote one of my books on leadership.

Three books that may be helpful in the area of marketing and publishing articles are:

Sell & Resell Your Magazine Articles by Gordon Burgett (Communication Unlimited)

The Complete Idiot's Guide to Publishing Magazine Articles by Sheree Bykovsky and Jennifer Sander (Alpha)

A Complete Guide to Marketing Magazine Articles by Duane Newcomb (Writer's Digest Books)

WRITING A BOOK

Writing a book is much like writing an article except that there is more to it. Having your book published demonstrates expertise in a certain area because the reader knows that your writing has passed a rigorous screening by the publisher. Publication gives you a credibility edge over your competitors who do not write. I continue to receive a considerable number of requests for consulting that result from my books.

For more information about writing books, see:

The Art of Creative Non-fiction by Lee Gutkind (Wiley)

How to Write Books That Sell by L. Perry Wilbur and Jon Samsel (Allworth Press)

Writer's Market (Writer's Digest Books) (This book comes out once a year, so you want to get the latest edition.)

WRITING LETTERS TO THE EDITOR

Letters to the editor can have the same result as other types of writing: building credibility. Some letters may be printed as so-called op-ed pieces (i.e., they run opposite editorials in the same newspaper). You can also submit letters to magazines, especially those that have a specific focus of interest to potential clients. To be effective as a marketing tool, the letter should contain comments resulting from your expertise

Figure 3-3. Example of an article promoting a book on leadership.

WILLIAM A. COHEN

Laws of Leadership

If you don't maintain your integrity, you will never be fully trusted by those you lead.

I HAVE TRIED TO IDENTIFY principles of leadership that are universal in all situations. The basis of my research was a survey sent to more than 200 former combat leaders and conversations with hundreds more. I sought those who had become successful in other organizations after leaving the armed forces. I asked them to list what they considered to be the three most important principles.

Their responses confirm there are universal principles that successful leaders follow to boost productivity and achieve extraordinary success.

The strength of the results of my investigation motivated me to name these principles the *eight universal laws of leadership.*

1. Maintain absolute integrity. Without basic trust between leader and followers, the leader is forever suspect. Integrity means doing the right thing. Lack of integrity can have terrible consequences. Even if a leader loses a fight, by maintaining absolute integrity, he or she retains his or her mandate to lead. Others will still follow, while leaders who violate this law are never fully trusted, no matter their abilities or accomplishments.

2. Know your stuff. Those who follow you want to know whether you know your stuff. Followers want you to be good at what it takes to get the job done.

3. Declare your expectations. This law includes planning, goal setting, and communicating. You can't get "there" until you know where "there" is, and let your followers know.

4. Show uncommon commitment. To show uncommon commitment, you've got to take risks. "No guts, no glory." Ask yourself, what is the worst that can happen? Accept that, and press on. If you aren't committed, no one else will be.

5. Expect positive results. The higher your goals, the higher goals you will achieve. There is a direct relationship between the goals you expect and what you get. Successful leaders expect positive results and maintain a positive attitude regardless of external realities. If you expect to succeed or expect to fail, you're right. So, although it makes sense to be ready for the worst, expect the best.

6. Take care of your people. If you take care of your people, they will take care of you. Loyalty is a two-way street. You cannot expect others to support your interests if you ignore theirs. J.W. Marriott once said: "We take care of our people, and they take care of our guests."

7. Put duty before self. If you are a leader, your duty encompasses accomplishing your mission and taking care of your people. Usually, the mission must come first. Sometimes, you must take care of your people first, or you may never accomplish your mission. All leaders must put the interests of the mission and their followers before their own. If your mission and your people don't come before you, you are not the leader.

8. Get out in front. The only way to lead is to get in front. You lead by pulling, not pushing. Get out where you can see and be seen. That way, not only will you know what's going on, but those who follow will know you are committed.

Review these eight laws of leadership every morning and look for opportunities to implement them. At the end of the day, review your actions. Note where you succeeded and where you did not. When you fall short, replay the events in your mind. See the new outcome as a result of applying these concepts. The success you will achieve will be dramatic.   EE

> *Get out in front where you can see and be seen.*

William A. Cohen is professor of marketing at Cal State University, Los Angeles and author of The Art of the Leader. *323-343-2972.*

Excellence in Action: Start thinking today about ways in which you can apply these eight concepts.

in a certain field, and you should identify yourself as a consultant in the area on which you are commenting. However, you should understand beforehand that the editor makes the decision on whether to publish your letter. Far more letters are received than could ever be published. To maximize your chances, make sure your letter is timely and well written.

When this technique works, it really works. A colleague of mine recently said that he received 110 letters of inquiry after his recent op-ed piece in the *Wall Street Journal.*

TEACHING A COURSE

Teaching a course at a community college or a university can also lead to consulting assignments. Naturally the course must be in your area of expertise. Also make sure you teach this course at night, because this is when business executives are more likely to be continuing their education. My own teaching has led to major consulting assignments with large companies, locally as well as internationally.

My only cautionary note is that you normally do not consult with individuals while they are your students because doing so is considered a conflict of interest. When I am asked about consulting while I am also serving as an instructor, I indicate that I would be happy to talk about the student's becoming a client after the course is over.

GIVING SEMINARS

Giving seminars is much the same as teaching a course. Attendees at seminars tend to be responsible individuals with companies interested in the topic. If your seminar has to do with the area of your consulting services, this can easily lead to additional assignments. I know of several consultants who depend solely on this method to promote their practice; the fees they receive for giving the seminar are only a secondary consideration. You don't even need to do the administrative work of setting up your own seminars. Contact any local community college or university. Many offer seminars and are always on the lookout for new talent. They will require an outline of the seminar that you wish to give, its target market, the hours of attendance, the price, and a strong description of your background and expertise for giving the seminar.

Here are some books that can help you:

How to Develop and Promote Successful Seminars and Workshops by Howard L. Shenson (Wiley)

How to Run Seminars and Workshops by Robert L. Jolles (Wiley)

Marketing with Speeches and Seminars by Miriam Otte (Zest Press)

DISTRIBUTING PUBLICITY RELEASES

Newspapers, trade journals, magazines, and other publications all depend on a constant flow of news. They are interested in what you have to say, as long as what you have to say is of interest to their readership. Anytime something of importance happens in your field, there is probably a story in it for some publication. Many times you will be surprised that what you consider common knowledge is new and quite interesting to many people, including potential clients.

It is easy to write a publicity release. Just tell your story in a terse, straightforward style like that used in a newspaper article. A potential mailing list for your publicity release should include newspapers and other media such as trade journals whose target readership contains potential candidates for your services. Directories that list such media are available in your local library, and your librarian will be happy to help you find what you need.

Here are some additional sources of information that will help you:

Bulletproof News Releases by Kay Borden (Franklin Sarrett)

The Consultant's Guide to Publicity by Reece Franklin (Wiley)

The Publicity Handbook by David R. Yale and Andrew J. Carothers (McGraw-Hill)

EXCHANGING INFORMATION WITH NONCOMPETING CONSULTANTS

Once you have established your area of expertise in consulting, you will find that there is a noncompeting-consultant network made up of other consultants who provide different services, much like doctors who deal in only one specialty and refer their patients to other specialists. Let's say that you specialize in organizational development and that a potential client or one of your established clients is seeking marketing consulting. You can recommend another consultant who will be able to help your client. In turn this marketing consultant can recommend your organizational development services to his or her clients when needed.

To participate in this kind of network, use the cold calling or direct mail techniques described in Chapter 2, only this time target noncompeting consultants. Offer these other consultants an exchange in which you will recommend their services to your clients or potential clients if they will do the same for you. Make certain that they have a good supply of your business cards and brochures, and ask for the same from them.

Of course, before you make such an arrangement, you must be sure that this consultant will do a good job when you refer clients. You won't build much of a practice by referring people to consultants who fail to do a good job.

When clients contact you, always find out how they got your name. In many cases, the contact is the result of a referral, and referrals are a sure sign that you are well on your way to a successful practice. But in order to know which of the direct methods or indirect methods to continue and which to eliminate, you should always ask the question, "Can you tell me how you got my name?"

SUMMING UP

You may be tempted to ignore the indirect methods of marketing your consulting practice, especially when your direct methods start to pay off and you feel you have more than enough work to last for the foreseeable future. Be forewarned. The workload can change very rapidly in consulting. A client's sales may suddenly fall off, forcing him to delay work you had anticipated. Other prospective work—that you thought was a sure thing—can suddenly disappear. In a blink, you are finished with your current work and no other engagements are scheduled. It is then, while you are just beginning to reinstitute your direct campaigns, that you'll be glad you implemented and continued the indirect methods.

In the next chapter we are going to look at a somewhat different market: consulting in the public sector. There are tremendous opportunities for consulting with local, state, and the national government, and you'll see exactly how to approach these markets and take advantage of the opportunities they offer.

4

MARKETING CONSULTANT SERVICES TO THE PUBLIC SECTOR

THERE IS A TREMENDOUS OPPORTUNITY for consultant services in the public sector. For the same reasons that large businesses use consultants, federal, state, and local governments have a real need for external consulting services and will probably continue to spend millions or even billions of dollars to obtain them. During my career, I have consulted for the Federal Bureau of Investigation, the United States Postal Service, the Air Force, the Army, the Navy, the Marine Corps, a number of public universities, various police departments, and other public sector clients. No consultant should dismiss the public sector market, for the potential is big.

THE GOVERNMENT REQUIRES ALL SORTS OF CONSULTING SERVICES

Consulting services used by the government include:

- Advice on, or the evaluation of, agency administration and management in such areas as organizational structures and reorganization plans.
- Management methods.
- Zero-based budgeting procedures.
- Mail-handling procedures.
- Record and file organization.
- Personnel procedures.
- Discriminatory labor practices.
- Agency publications.
- Internal policies, directives, orders, manuals, and procedures.
- Management information systems.
- Program management such as program plans.
- Acquisition strategies.
- Regulation development.
- Assistance with procurement of solicited or unsolicited technical and cost proposals.
- Legal questions.
- Economic impacts.
- Program impacts.
- Mission and program analyses.

External consultants also conduct various research and development and technology assessments, even though the government officially does not classify these areas as consulting services.

CONSULTING FOR THE GOVERNMENT

Consulting has grown in such importance that the U.S. government has its very own consulting agency that does a good deal of consulting. On the agency's Web site are 28 different areas in which it has consulted for the government:

1. Career Development/Mentoring

2. Change Management
3. Classification Studies (Includes Survey and Design, Job Analysis)
4. Conflict Resolution and Intervention
5. Employee Relations
6. Employee Screenings/Background Checks
7. Ethics Training
8. Executive and Leadership Coaching
9. Executive Performance Review and Compensation Analysis
10. Executive Search
11. Facilitation and Partnering Services
12. Governing Board–Executive Manager Goal Setting
13. Investigations (Includes Fact Finding)
14. Management and Organizational Reviews
15. Organizational Assessment, Development, and Redesign
16. HR Outsourcing
17. Performance Management (Includes 360 Review Assessment, Performance Appraisal System Design and Development)
18. Policies and Procedures Review and Development
19. Recruitment and Staffing
20. Salary and Compensation Studies
21. Selection and Assessment Services
22. Strategic Planning
23. Succession Planning
24. Surveys (Includes Employee Attitude Surveys, Client Surveys)
25. Temporary HR Professionals
26. Training Products and Services (Includes Ethics Training, Workplace, Employment Law, and Other Training)
27. Work Process Redesign and Reengineering
28. Workforce and Human Capital Planning[1]

However, even thought this agency has done a lot of consulting, there still is room for you to do business. There are plenty of opportunities on the government bandwagon.

HOW DO YOU GET ON THE GOVERNMENT BANDWAGON?

FEDERAL AND STATE BIDDING PORTALS

Since the third edition of *How to Make It Big as a Consultant* was published, Federal Business Opportunities (FedBizOpps.gov, or FPO, available at http://www.fedbizopps.gov) has been designated as the single government point of entry (GPE) for federal government procurement opportunities over $25,000. Government buyers are able to publicize their business opportunities by posting information directly to FedBizOpps via the Internet. Through this one portal, commercial vendors seeking federal markets for their products and services can search, monitor, and retrieve opportunities solicited by the entire federal contracting community. So this is now the basic method of locating opportunities to sell to the government, replacing the once omnipresent *Commerce Business Daily (CBD)*, a newspaper published by the U.S. government five days a week and later available online.

Many states also publish business opportunities periodically (for example, California provides the *California State Contracts Register*). Contact the contracting office of the state you would like to do business with to see whether such a publication is available.

With regard to either federal or state methods of advertising work opportunities, I recommend that you not bid directly on consulting opportunities unless you have had prior contact with the government agency. Simply responding to an advertisement usually produces nothing but the wasted time and money in putting the proposal together. You need face-to-face contact with your prospective customers to convince them that you are better than the competition, and rarely can you do this with a proposal alone. The way to use these publications effectively is to consider the advertisements as a source of future clients and to make appointments for face-to-face meetings so that a later request for proposal will find you well prepared.

SMALL BUSINESS ADMINISTRATION

Another method of locating opportunities in government is to contact the Small Business Administration (SBA) in your area. Almost every government agency needs some type of consulting service. Whether it needs your services is another story. That you must investigate, and your local SBA office can help. Let it know that you are a business consultant and explain your area of expertise. Frequently it can refer you to someone within the agency who can help you find government contracts. The SBA also hires small business consultants to help counsel its own small business clients.

THE BUYING PROCESS

The government buying process usually begins with an invitation for bid (IFB) or request for proposal (RFP). With an IFB, usually you just state a price for whatever is wanted; with an RFP, in addition to a price, you must submit a technical proposal documenting your method for providing the requested services. It is important to recognize that submitting an IFB or an RFP does not guarantee you a contract. Usually other firms are competing for the same work. Low price is always of importance; in fact, with the IFB, low price determines who wins the contract, assuming that the firm is otherwise qualified. With the RFP, however, other factors may be of equal or even greater importance. This is the reason that preproposal marketing is so important.

THE IMPORTANCE OF PREPROPOSAL MARKETING

Some years ago, I completed several research projects seeking the primary factors that influence the winning of small ($2 million or less) government research and development contracts. Two popular theories seemed to indicate that marketing was more important than technical approach or even than the price attached to the proposal. One of these theories was consumer acceptance theory.

According to consumer acceptance theory, the consumer may achieve three levels of intensity in a relationship with any product or service: acceptance, preference, and insistence.

- ✦ Consumer *acceptance*, the lowest level of intensity, means that the customer may have had some contact with the product or with some promotional effort. This contact leads to a decision on acceptability.
- ✦ Customer *preference* suggests a more satisfactory experience, compared to that of a competing product, and implies that the product will be favored over the competition's.
- ✦ *Insistence*, the highest level of intensity, is the stage in which the customer takes the product almost regardless of price or hardship and brooks no substitution. This stage, according to the theory, can be reached by a full knowledge of the product based on considerable experience.

The other idea that was important to this application of marketing was the merchandising theory. *Merchandising* in this context means fitting the product to the potential customer's wants and needs. According to the main aspect of this theory, merchandising must be the central part of any marketing program. The market must be segmented in order to zero in on a specific customer, and the approach must accommodate the fact that this customer has a number of sometimes conflicting wants and needs that must be satisfied. These wants and needs are influenced by the customer's physical or mental state, by individual background or conditioning, by the immediate situation, and, most important, by what the customer knows about the product, either directly through its use or vicariously through communication with others. These wants and needs are also of different relative values and may change. The desire for a particular product is influenced by its accessibility, including such factors as price, the customer's available funds, and the effort required to get it. Suppliers are likely to see a product from an entirely different perspective than the customer's. Yet the potential exists for presenting the product in such a fashion that it satisfies the most important of the customer's wants, needs, and desires, or for altering the product within certain limits to accomplish the same purpose. To do this requires presentation to the customer; feedback from the customer; analysis of the customer's wants, needs, and desires; and calculation of the best way to satisfy them.

Thus, both theories, based on practice in the consumer-industrial world, argued for heavy investment in preproposal marketing for small government research contracts. And, in fact, actual research with several different companies indicated the tremendous importance of the marketing done before the proposal was ever submitted. During this preproposal marketing, not only would the product or service be sold, but also critical information would be learned and ideas shared between the company and its potential government customer. The information included how much the customer had to spend, the scope of the activities, and the kind of product or service customers expected and thought they would receive. In some cases, win ratios increased from 0 to 100 percent by the simple influence of preproposal marketing. Preproposal marketing activities are absolutely critical for selling consulting services to any organization. Unfortunately, many consultants forget this when attempting to deal with the government.

THE MARKETING SEQUENCE FOR GOVERNMENT CONSULTING

The sequence of marketing to the government involves six steps, all of them built around the notion of preproposal marketing.

1. Locate potential clients.
2. Screen.
3. Visit and make presentations.
4. Maintain contact and gather intelligence.
5. Prepare the proposal.
6. Negotiate the contract.

LOCATING POTENTIAL CLIENTS

Potential clients can be located through FedBizOpps, the state register of opportunities, the SBA, or other government directories, and through government sources on the Internet. You should use all of these sources to develop a list that includes every potential client in the government.

SCREENING

Accomplish the initial screening by telephone. Go right down your list and call each potential client one after the other. Indicate what types of consulting services you provide and try to pinpoint the interests of the potential client. If there is no interest, it is better to establish this now, when the only cost is a telephone call. Finally, try to establish an appointment for a face-to-face presentation. If this must be done at some other location, such as out of state, coordinate the visits so that you can make several on one trip.

VISITING AND MAKING THE INITIAL PRESENTATION

For the initial presentation, organize yourself ahead of time and know exactly how much time you have. If you have 30 minutes or 45 minutes or an hour or two hours, you should know this ahead of time and limit your presentation to these requirements. Also ask your contact how many people will be present. This will help you to plan your presentation and to know how many handouts or brochures to bring. I cover presentations in more detail in Chapter 14; for now you should understand that you must organize ahead of time and take enough brochures and other handouts so that all your potential clients can have a copy.

MAINTAINING CONTACT AND GATHERING INTELLIGENCE

Probably the most important part of preproposal marketing is not only to continue to sell at every meeting, but also to learn about forthcoming contracts before they are published in FedBizOpps or elsewhere. Also try to learn the scope of activity and how much money is available for these forthcoming contracts. Tell your potential client the approach you would recommend and why. In some cases, these approaches can be incorporated into the RFP. This may seem like giving away ideas to competitors, but actually it's not necessarily bad because you should be better prepared than they to do whatever you proposed. At the same time, you should be honest and forthright in selling your ideas and disagreeing (tactfully) with your potential client when information stated is at odds with facts as you know them or if the cost will be more or less than the agency anticipates. In this way, by the time you respond to the proposal, both you and your potential client should understand exactly what is going to be requested, what you are going to propose, and approximately what the services should cost.

PREPARING THE PROPOSAL

The proposal should contain no surprises. It is a sales document, one that confirms your outstanding ability, not a vehicle for presenting something new that you haven't yet discussed with your potential client. This is true even though you may think of something at the last minute. The reason is that no matter how lengthy or short your sales document (and some proposals are no more than a single-page letter), you do not have sufficient space to explain everything in detail. You will probably not be permitted additional verbal discussions once a proposal has been requested, so you may not be able to explain a new idea sufficiently. Any question that goes unanswered could work to your disadvantage in a competitive review process. Also, no matter how unique and advantageous your new idea might be, time is needed for your potential clients to sell the ideas to their bosses or to other agencies that may have an influence on the work to be done. Remember that any bureaucratic organization, including the U.S. government, tends to avoid and minimize risk. New ideas that have not been previously sold during the preproposal marketing phase run a high risk in the eyes of potential clients. Restate what you have already sold, and bid in accordance with the funds and scope of the effort as you uncovered them during your prior contacts.

NEGOTIATING THE CONTRACT

Negotiating is a basic skill that is part of your stock in trade as a consultant. You will negotiate with clients, subcontractors, members of your client's organization, other consultants, vendors, and many others. So don't assume that negotiating a public service contract is simply a matter of signing a contract for a proposal. Rarely is any proposal accepted exactly as made. There may be considerable discussion and give-and-take regarding terms, price, delivery, and performance. See Chapter 10 for more help with negotiating.

Recommended books on government contracts and business opportunities are as follows:

> *Federal Contracting Made Easy*, 3rd ed. by Scott Stanberry (Management Concepts)
>
> *Selling to State and Local Government: Understanding the Government Buyer* by Charles A. Harris (AuthorHouse)
>
> *21st Century Complete Guide to Federal Business Opportunities—Government Procurement, Selling Products and Services to the Federal Government, Contacts, Regulations, Solicitations* (Four CD-ROM Set) (CD-ROM) by the U.S. Government (Progressive Management)

You should also take a look at the following government Web sites for reference:

> *Business.Gov Government Contracting*, accessed at http://www.business.gov/topic/Government_Contracting
>
> *Getting Government Down to Business*, accessed at http://www.aptacus.org/new/
>
> *U.S. General Services Administration Quick Links*, accessed at http://www.gsa.gov/Portal/gsa/ep/contentView.do?bodyOnly=true&contentId=18174&contentType=GSA_BASIC

SUMMING UP

This chapter completes your preparation for marketing. After applying the methods in the last three chapters, you are ready for your first interview with your prospective client. In the next chapter, we look at this first interview and how you should manage it.

NOTE

1. CPS Human Resource Services, Consulting Services, accessed at http://www.cps.ca.gov/ConsultingServices/listservices.asp, July 2, 2008.

5

MAKING THE INITIAL INTERVIEW A SUCCESS

IN THIS CHAPTER you are going to learn how to prepare for and conduct the initial interview with your prospective client. Along with general instructions about how to dress and how to act, I will give you the essential questions that you must ask to learn all you can about the potential assignment, eventually enabling you to confirm your understanding of the engagement. In addition I will point out nonverbal signs to look for and explain what each means, and I'll give you listening techniques that will help you to understand your client's feelings and intentions. Finally, I will show you psychological techniques for building empathy with your prospective client, thus helping you land a contractual relationship.

LOOKING AND ACTING LIKE A PROFESSIONAL

The first impression you make with your client should be the very best. In some cases, you can never overcome the effects of a questionable image in your client's mind. In large part, this initial image is made up of your appearance and your behavior. You want to look and act like the professional you are.

Dress is extremely important in making a good first impression. There are only two rules: Dress as neatly as possible, and try to look as much as possible like your client. For most business consulting, a conservative suit and tie for men and a suit for women are appropriate. However, if after several engagements you observe that in your client's industry a different type of dress is common, follow the second rule and dress like your client. Here are two good books on the subject:

> *Image Matters for Men: How to Dress for Success!* by Veronique Henderson and Pat Henshaw (Hamlyn)
>
> *John T. Molloy's New Dress for Success* by John T. Molloy (Warner Books)
>
> *New Woman's Dress for Success* by John T. Molloy (Warner Books)

Your demeanor is important too. In this first interview, be professional but not pompous. Always strive to be friendly, to understand your potential client, and to build empathy. Think back to the different medical doctors you have met over your lifetime. Some are professional and friendly, and you feel you can place trust in them. Other doctors, who may be of equal if not greater competence, somehow build a wall between you and them, and you trust them less. The same is true with the business doctor: the consultant. You must maintain a professional attitude, at the same time remaining tactful, friendly, and empathetic.

HOW TO BUILD EMPATHY WITH YOUR POTENTIAL CLIENT

Psychologists discovered some time ago that we act more favorably toward those with whom we have rapport. The usual way of gaining rapport is finding some common background, experience, or interest. Although you can try to establish rapport this way, some years ago researchers John Grinder and Richard Bandler discovered a faster, more powerful means. They called the body of their research neurolinguistic programming. The part we are concerned with in building rapport is what they called mirroring and matching.

Mirroring and matching requires following your client's voice, speech tempo and patterns, word usage, breathing, postures, and movements. You do not mimic in an obvious way, but you do watch your client. If he or she speaks in a rapid staccato, you ease slowly into the same speech pattern. If your client speaks more slowly, you do the same. If your client crosses a leg, follow their lead. In other words, mirror and match—without mimicking instantaneously. Follow the person you are matching gradually as you continue with the interview.

To master this technique, practice with a friend or spouse until you can do it naturally. Once you are able to do it naturally, you have an amazing tool for developing instant rapport. You will have the feeling that you have known the person you are mirroring for years, and the client will have the same feeling about you.

Scientists do not know exactly why mirroring and matching works. They do know that people who are already in rapport practice mirroring and matching without thinking about it and without any conscious effort. You can verify this yourself by watching two old friends converse. It is as if the brain were saying, "I must like this person because he is exactly like me." And the power of liking—of rapport—is usually more important than any rational, technical argument you can make for coming to an agreement.

SEVEN ESSENTIAL QUESTIONS

Asking questions is essential. Peter Drucker helped his clients mainly through asking questions. During the first interview, you absolutely must ask seven questions. By asking them, you will better understand the client's problems, and the answers will help you to decide whether to accept the assignment.

1. **What problem needs solving?** Whether the client contacted you or vice versa, find out exactly why the client is seeing you. Something is bothering the client. Some clients will blurt it out immediately; others will say very little, not wanting to reveal the full story until they know more about you. Nevertheless, you must draw them out and understand exactly why they are seeing you.

2. **Exactly what does the client want you to do?** What are the specific objectives of the assignment? Even though your primary purpose is to gain information in this first interview, you need to have the objectives explained explicitly once the reason for the assignment has been determined and you have talked to your potential client at some length about the task. For example, maybe this is a personnel problem—does she wish to decrease employee turnover? Does she wish to increase sales? Is there a problem in new product development, with too many unsuccessful products? Whatever your client's objectives might be, you have to know exactly what they are.

3. **How will you know whether the objectives have been met?** At first glance, the answer might seem obvious. If turnover is bad, the objective will be met when turnover is reduced. If sales are not what they should be, the objective will be met when sales increase, and so forth. However, you can easily see that there is much room for a difference of opinion. Will your client be satisfied if turnover decreases 25, 10, 5, or 1 percent or if sales increase 5, 10, or 15 percent? You are looking for an exact figure so that both you and your client will know when the specified objectives have been met.

4. **Should you watch for particularly sensitive issues?** Any organization made up of human beings contains political situations of one sort or another. As an outsider attempting to insert yourself into and analyze a problem, you may stumble onto some complicated political situations in the organization. For some types of consulting and for some clients, this is not very important. For others, however, your client may not want you to disturb some very sensitive issues. Certain individuals or subjects may be off limits for interviews. If you are not sensitive to these political issues, you could end up leaving the company in a much worse situation than when you came, even though ostensibly you solved the client's problem. Take pains to ask about and to understand such issues. Pay attention to detail so that you don't stumble around like a bull in a china shop; instead, demonstrate the finesse of a real pro.

5. **Who will be your main point of contact?** Usually this is the individual who contacted you first, but not always. The only way to

find out is to ask. Be certain that you have the name, title, e-mail address, and telephone number of this key individual.

6. **Will there be a backup contact?** Even if your main contact plans to be available throughout the assignment, request a backup contact. Your primary contact may have to leave on an unforeseen trip or be absent from the company just when you need an important decision. So you lose time, and you may be forced into making a poor decision that could easily have been avoided. Always ask for the name of someone else in the company with the necessary authority on your project, and get his or her title and telephone number as well.

7. **What authority does each player have?** This is a key question. A player is anyone who has an impact on your engagement. If you do not take the time and trouble to identify the players, their responsibilities, and their authority, you could find yourself misdirected, either innocently by well-meaning individuals or deliberately by those within the company who have a different agenda. Some individuals may give you instructions or even verbal modifications of your contract even though they have no authority to do so. Then you may find yourself in the difficult situation of being unable to bill for the work, or the work may be something not desired by your client who has the authority to supervise your consulting. Of course, beyond the loss of time and money, misdirection of this type can cause you to lose an important client.

TAKING NOTES

The only way to remember all you learn during the initial interview is to take notes. For this purpose, I recommend a notebook. I carry mine in my briefcase, and as soon as we start our conversation, I take it out and begin to take notes. If I don't understand a point, I ask the client to repeat what was said.

Some consultant students have asked whether a tape recorder is a better way to record this information accurately, but I don't recommend it. A tape recorder can be intimidating. Information that you are given as a consultant is frequently confidential; somehow pencil and notebook seem less threatening to a client's confidentiality. I have found that clients are usually more forthcoming and open if you use a notebook and a pencil.

I want to emphasize that during the first interview, you must find out everything that you possibly can. Never hesitate to ask for such information as the company's annual report or product brochures if you believe it will be useful to you. In fact, even after you have returned to your office, do not be afraid to call and ask for additional information if it will help you consider different ways to attack the client's problem.

HOLDING OFF ON GIVING ADVICE

During the first interview, most consultants are eager to help the potential client and show that they both recognize the problem and have the solution. However, in their haste, they make a basic mistake: They immediately begin giving advice.

Do not do this for several reasons. One is that you usually do not yet really know enough about the situation to give advice. This is probably true in 95 percent of the cases. However, even in the 5 percent when the answer is obvious, do not volunteer anything unless you are already being paid for your time. After you have solved the problem, what reason does the client have to hire you?

I used to make this mistake myself, but not anymore. Once a client called me about an exploratory interview and then suggested that I join him and his wife for dinner at a nearby restaurant. The net result was that I spent an evening of my time during which he and his wife pumped me for information over a delicious steak followed by drinks. The meal and company were delightful, but, after all, I was in business. They received several hundred dollars' worth of free consulting. On top of that, because I solved all their problems during our meeting and the meal, they did not hire me. Why should they? Their problems appeared to be gone. Maybe the recommendations I made would have been different had I had time to think about them. Maybe I could have served my clients better. So both sides may have lost.

INTERPRETING BODY LANGUAGE

Psychologists have confirmed by research what salespeople have learned intuitively: What buyers say may be less important than the messages they transmit by how they hold their body when communicating. A potential client who speaks with arms folded across his chest, eyes avoiding yours, brow wrinkled, and fists clenched is probably feeling threatened by the situation and is not communicating openly with you. You are not getting all the information you could get, and the client may not be convinced by what you are saying.

When you observe these physical signs, back off and try a different approach. Try anything to break this attitude and get the client to relax. A sign that you have been successful at this is that the client begins making direct eye contact and leans toward you. If he looks relaxed, with hands no longer clenched but open or extended, you have gotten through, and he is probably comfortable with the overall situation and is now ready for more open communication. But if he begins to turn his body away from you, avoiding direct eye contact again, you know he either does not want to discuss the issue you brought up or is suspicious of the approach you have taken. Again you are not getting through. To be successful, you must try a different approach.

Also watch to see whether the client strokes her chin or neck, chews the end of a pencil, or leans back with hands clasped behind her head. These behaviors indicate that what you are saying is being evaluated; the client is listening, and you are getting through. Continue to observe, and you will know whether you should continue that approach or attempt a new one.

Finally, you may observe a ready, almost eager attitude on the part of the client; he sits on the edge of the chair, leans forward, and catches your every word. Clearly you are making a favorable impression, and the client is demonstrating a readiness to act on your suggestions.

Many complex issues are involved in observing body language, and you need to know much more if you want to become an expert. But if you simply observe your clients and think about what their bodies are telling you, you will learn quite a lot.

Three books in particular can help you understand body language.

Body Language by David Lambert (HarperCollins)

Body Language by Julius Fast (Pocket Books)

How to Read a Person Like a Book by Gerard I. Nierenberg and Henry H. Calero (Cornerstone Library)

MAKING USE OF LISTENING TECHNIQUES

Certain listening techniques encourage various responses. You should use such techniques to your advantage to draw the client out and to obtain all the information you possibly can. Many of these listening techniques you already know. You learned them naturally, from the time you were a toddler. However, few of us think about them. Consequently, we fail to use them in some situations when we are distracted by emotion. So reviewing them will help to ensure that you have them at your disposal and can use them consciously in your client meeting.

If you want to keep the other person talking, neither agree nor disagree with what is being said, but use neutral words in a positive way. Phrases like "I see" and "How interesting!" and even "No kidding!" indicate your interest and encourage your client to keep talking.

On the other hand, if you wish to let your potential client know that you understand the information she has been giving you and want her to move to the next point, restate what has been said to you. Say something like, "As I understand it ..." or "In other words ... ," and then summarize.

If you wish to probe for additional information at the same time, you must lead the individual toward that information tactfully. Ask questions such as, "Why do you think this is so?" or "Why do you think this happened?"

Finally, at some point summarize the conversation and the ideas you've had. This is extremely important because you will play back these ideas when you develop your proposal. You should do this recap when you control the interview. Take your time and use your notes to make certain you have it right. You can say, "Now, if I understand you correctly, these are the main objectives that you wish to cover ... for the following reasons."

IDENTIFYING EMOTIONS FROM FACIAL EXPRESSIONS

You do not need to be a social scientist to identify happiness or sadness from the expression on a person's face. But other emotions may be more difficult to spot. Scientists have done considerable research in this area. According to Dr. Ronald E. Riggio, a psychology professor and director of the Kraviss Institute of Leadership at Claremont McKenna College in California, your ability to do this even affects your charisma.

See whether you can identify the human emotions on the ten faces shown in Figure 5-1. You may find the exercise more difficult than you thought. The answers appear at the end of this chapter.

Like body language and listening techniques, your ability to instantly identify facial expressions can help considerably in working with your client and successfully completing the initial interview with a sale.

WHAT TO DO WHEN THE INTERVIEW IS OVER

For some short assignments and some special situations, the client may wish to hire you on the spot. When you sense this—and you will learn

Figure 5-1. Ten common human emotions.

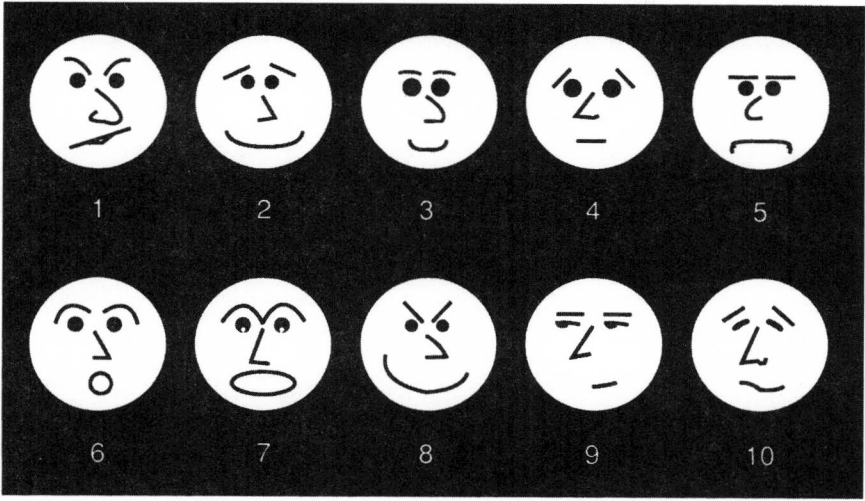

to recognize it with more experience—simply ask for the assignment. Tell your potential client how you bill and ask whether she would like you to help her with the problem. As I explain in Chapter 8, even though this type of assignment constitutes a verbal contract, it is very important that you follow up with a letter confirming exactly what you will do and the compensation you will receive.

However, many engagements, especially the larger ones, require a formal proposal and additional analysis on your part to determine the appropriate methodology, the time frame, and the price for your services. Therefore, at the end of the initial interview, you will not be in a position to offer a proposal, only to indicate when you will submit one. If a letter of proposal is satisfactory, always ask whether you can call should you have additional questions; if not, ask what form the proposal should take. You should also ascertain whether you are the only consultant being contacted or whether your proposal must compete with others. Most government proposals are competitive. Deciding whether you wish to bid on a competitive contract is up to you. Many consultants refuse to bid on any type of contract and will politely withdraw if there is competition. My own recommendation is to consider all aspects of the situation, including your probability of winning.

Once you have established that a proposal is requested and when it is due, thank your client, leave your business card, be certain to get his or her business card, and depart. If there is no specific deadline for your proposal, submit it as soon as possible. You never know what changes can take place in just a few days that would alter the demand for your services.

THE COMPANY AUDIT

To show you the scope of questions that might be useful in an initial interview, I have included as Appendix C a comprehensive checklist of questions, The Consultant's Questionnaire and Audit. Do not think that you must ask all these questions at every initial interview. Also do not feel that because a question is not included, you may not ask it. In every situation, you should modify this list for the specific client before the interview. During the interview, if additional questions seem appropriate, make sure that you ask them as well.

IDENTIFICATION OF FACIAL EXPRESSIONS IN FIGURE 5-1

1. Angry
2. Sheepish, Embarrassed
3. Happy, Contented
4. Puzzled, Uncertain
5. Upset, Disgusted
6. Surprised
7. Fearful
8. Sly, Devious
9. Bored, Disinterested
10. Tired, Relaxed, Relieved

If you identified eight out of the ten correctly, you're doing pretty well. Five to seven is fair. Fewer than five says this is something you might want to work on.

SUMMING UP

In the next chapter, we will look at what to do after the interview: how to write a proposal.

6

HOW TO WRITE A PROPOSAL

IF AN AGREEMENT to begin a consulting assignment is not reached during the initial interview—and this is often the case—the prospective client will expect a written proposal. In this chapter, we find out what a proposal must do and why it is necessary. All the essential elements of a proposal are listed and explained, and a proposal structure is provided.

WHY A WRITTEN PROPOSAL IS NECESSARY

A written proposal accomplishes five tasks that are critical to getting a contract and beginning work as a consultant.

1. **The proposal finalizes the agreement.** Sometimes, even after an excellent exploratory interview, you have not yet made the sale. It is not unusual for a potential client to ask for a written proposal even though he is 90 percent certain about hiring your services. The proposal, then, is a sales document that ties together all the loose ends and closes the deal.

2. **The proposal documents what you are going to do.** Both you and your client should clearly understand the services you are going to perform in this consulting engagement. A proposal does exactly that; it spells out in black and white exactly what you are going to do, providing a clear and documented basis for understanding.

3. **The proposal documents the time frame of your performance.** Just as what you are going to do is important, so is how long you will take to do it and the scheduling of each event. Sometimes the client will want to have partial information at certain points before the project is fully completed. If so, the client may not hire you if she is not certain she will get it. Documenting reporting due dates assures your potential client that she will get what she wants when she wants it.

4. **The proposal documents what you are going to receive for your services.** Unless you are independently wealthy, even though you probably enjoy consulting, you aren't in business as a consultant just for the fun of it. The proposal specifies the compensation that you are going to receive for your intended services. Documenting this compensation can save you much trouble in getting paid later on.

5. **The proposal forms the basis for a contract.** As I will show you later in the chapter, the proposal can be the basis for a contract. In fact, you can frequently turn a proposal into a contract just by adding a few sentences.

HOW TO WRITE A GOOD PROPOSAL

Remember four points in writing a good proposal.

1. **Keep the structure clear and logical.** I will cover the structure of the proposal later in this chapter.

2. **Use a professional but friendly style.** When you submit a proposal, just as in a face-to-face meeting, be professional but friendly. In fact, if you are writing a proposal letter, you can be downright folksy; as long as you avoid stepping over professional bounds, a down-to-earth style will only enhance your chances of being hired.

3. **Don't spring surprises in your proposal.** As explained in Chapter 4. Although avoiding surprises sounds very simple, it is one of the hardest things to do. After you return from your initial meeting, you will frequently get new ideas that are different from what you and your client originally visualized. These ideas may be so good that you find it very tempting to include them in the proposal. Resist the temptation, unless you can check with your client first. The client may not be able to accept your new ideas for reasons you don't know about. He may need time to sell ideas to others, even top management in the company. If you surprise your client in the proposal, he may not have sufficient time to do this. Therefore, unless you can discuss new suggestions with your client before submitting them in the proposal, don't include anything different yet. You can always propose a change or modification after you get the contract.

4. **Double-check before you send.** If at all possible, double-check the main points of the proposal with your client. If you are preparing a short letter proposal, call the client and read it to her over the phone. For government contracts and some industrial proposals made on a competitive basis, this may not be allowed, but always ask. The worst someone can say is no. It is in everyone's best interest that the proposal be exactly what everyone wants even before you send it. Don't assume that you can make changes to your proposal after your client receives it but before he accepts it and you are on contract.

THE STRUCTURE OF A LETTER PROPOSAL

Sometimes, especially with large or competitive contracts, the client will specify the structure of the proposal. (This is especially true of government and large industrial companies.) In this case, follow the specified structure. However, a letter proposal is quite sufficient for most of your consulting engagements. Let's see what one looks like.

OPENING

Simply state that you are writing to submit your ideas for the project discussed earlier. However, write out the ideas to give your prospective client the confidence that you understand exactly what is wanted.

BACKGROUND

Begin by *restating* the background of the consulting situation, that is, your client's assumptions and other general facts in the case. This reassures the client that she has made an astute analysis of the situation. If the client's assumptions are not correct, then you must convince her of this *before* submitting your proposal. If the customer is determined to use previous assumptions anyway, even if you have explained why they are incorrect, then you have a choice. You can use the client's assumptions or refuse the assignment. If you refuse, be as tactful as possible. The client will probably respect your stand and may contact you in the future for a different project.

OBJECTIVES

State the objectives of the engagement precisely. Describe exactly what your client will learn or receive as a result of your work. I like to present these objectives in a way that makes them stand out visually, by using bullet points, for example:

- Identify at least three secondary retail markets for a new product line.
- Develop sales projections for 6 months and for 12 months.
- Recommend staffing increases to achieve sales projections.

STUDY METHODS

Describe alternative methodologies for accomplishing the objectives. Discuss the advantages of each alternative and then indicate which method you propose to use and why. When you describe the methodology, consider your audience. If your client is technical, use technical language; if not, do not confuse them with technical formulas or terms. Stating all the alternatives, even those you do not intend to use, is extremely important, especially if you have competition. Competitors may propose alternative methods, and it is important to show why these methods will not work as well as why the method you have chosen will work. If you are convincing enough on this point, your potential client can use your proposal to help swing other decision makers in the organization to your way of thinking and to adopt your proposed methodology.

POTENTIAL PROBLEMS

Any project has inherent potential problems that could limit or even prevent success. Do not omit or gloss over potential problems; write them out clearly, but also state how you will handle them if they occur. Clients who are smart enough to hire a consultant are smart enough to realize that problems can come up. You cannot fool them into thinking that your approach is problem-free. In fact, they will respect you more for anticipating the problems, as long as you have thought through what corrective actions you will take.

DATA FLOW CHARTS AND PRODUCT DEVELOPMENT SCHEDULES

One type of a data flow chart is called a PERT chart. PERT (program evaluation and review technique) was developed for the management of complex multimillion-dollar projects for the government. This type of chart shows what tasks you will accomplish and in what order for the most efficient project management. It is more appropriate for very complex programs, but it can always be included in the proposal. If nothing else, it adds a bit of showmanship to your proposal and demonstrates the control you have over the project. A product development schedule will probably be sufficient for most projects. I discuss how to build both in Chapter 9.

THE FINISHED PRODUCT

Your client will want to know what to expect in way of a final report. Will you be furnishing a report? A staff study? Photographs? How many copies will you provide? This last point can be important, because frequently the client will need to distribute the information to others, perhaps the board of directors or other managers in the company. Specify exactly what you will furnish and what it will contain, the number of copies, drawings, photographs, and other details. Include the date on which you will complete your study and submit your final report.

COST AND PAYMENT INFORMATION

For most small contracts, it is not necessary to break down cost information unless the client requests such detail. However, the timing of payments is important. The client will want to know not only how much you want, but when you want it. For example, do you want 50 percent of your fee up front and 50 percent at completion? One-third upon signing the contract, one-third at some intermediate point, and one-third at completion? Work-in-progress billing with monthly invoices? Or everything in one lump sum when you submit your report? The last, by the way, is not recommended: It leaves your client with all the leverage and you with none.

CONVERTING A PROPOSAL INTO A CONTRACT

The last paragraph is a close. "Close" is a sales term meaning that you complete the deal with a prospect such that he agrees to what you propose under the terms you propose. This part of the proposal can and should be friendly, but it can also serve as a contract if you combine it with an authority to proceed. Here's how to do this in a friendly but professional way. Write something like:

> Please simply sign at the bottom where indicated, for authority to proceed under these conditions, and return the original to me. However, if you have any questions or suggestions pertaining to this proposal or the work you would like accomplished, please do not hesitate to call me at 555-1234.

If you decide to use the suggested last paragraph and allow the proposal to be converted into a contract, you may want your attorney to review this information.

An example of a letter proposal is shown in Figure 6-1.

Figure 6-1. A typical letter proposal.

April 24, 20XX

Mr. Joseph Black
Unique Sales Co., Inc.
4571 Plainview Avenue
Pasadena, CA 91107

Dear Mr. Black:

We enjoyed the pleasure of meeting with you on Wednesday, April 18. We were amazed to learn that you had been selling government surplus, mainly through the mail, and more recently over the Internet, for over 33 years.

The purpose of this letter is to present our proposal for a research study based on the objectives discussed in our meeting with you. Please keep in mind that this is a proposal and subject to your ideas and suggestions. However, it can be accepted exactly as stated within.

A RESEARCH PROPOSAL FOR:

An Investigation of the Seasonal Sales Trend of Unique Sales Co., Inc.

Background

Unique Sales Company sells government surplus to individual consumers as well as to governments of foreign countries. The company originally sold marine equipment but has now expanded its sales to other items, such as aircraft parts, auto parts, and hydraulics.

Unique Sales Company's main objective was to sell government surplus items; however, recently there has been a significant reduction in the availability of government surplus items.

The sales trend of this company has its peak months around the first five to six months of the year; the other months are slow. In the eastern part of the United States, weather very much affects sales. The more severe the winters are, the higher the sales are, because consumers tend to stay at home and read the sales catalog.

Objectives

The primary objective of this study is to gain an insight into the factors causing cyclical variations in sales for the mail-order industry and specifically for Unique Sales. Recommendations for Unique Sales' actions will be made upon evaluation of the data collected.

More specifically, the following areas will be investigated:

I. Sales trends (cross section)
   A. Industrial-oriented mail-order house
   B. Consumer goods–oriented mail-order house
   C. Industrial/consumer-oriented mail-order house

II. Factors affecting sales
   A. Weather
   B. Product line
   C. Target market
   D. Advertising effectiveness

Study Methods

Several market research methods will be incorporated into this study.

The first will be an exhaustive search for all readily available secondary market statistics and data, including statistical information already published or obtainable at a nominal cost. Possible valuable sources for this information are U.S. government agencies, trade associations, the National Weather Bureau, and trade periodical publishers, as well as the standard business bibliographies.

In addition, personal telephone calls will be made to selected individuals in this industry. These will be those recognized as the most knowledgeable in the industry. From these telephone calls, an attempt will be made to obtain data not uncovered during the search for secondary information.

Potential Problems

In most secondary research studies, the existence of relevant market statistics and data cannot be determined until the actual study is begun.

Market statistics do not exist for all industries and, in some cases, exist only in the files of private firms. In these cases, the information is considered proprietary and is generally not released to the business community.

In many instances, the use of personal interviews can compensate for the lack of published data and bring to the forefront valuable data otherwise not available.

Overall, even with possible information gaps, the research team is confident we can supply the Unique Sales Company with a viable, well-documented report.

The Report

Our report will consist of a description of the study objective, design, and the findings reported at three levels of detail. (1) First will be what we see as the major findings or highlights of the study, including our conclusion and recommendations. (2) This section will be followed by a more detailed and documented discussion and analysis of the findings. (3) An appendix will contain brochures and other supplementary materials.

Cost and Timing

The cost of this completed study will be $5,500, one-half payable on authorization to proceed and one-half payable on delivery of the final report, two copies of which will be delivered in its final form. The study will be compiled, and the reports delivered, four weeks after authorization to proceed.

We know that you are busy. Therefore, simply sign below to authorize us to proceed with this work as outlined. If you have any questions or suggestions to make regarding this proposal and the proposed study, please feel free to call us at once.

Sincerely yours,

_____

W. W. Smith
Director of Research

_____

Mark Tizon
Principal Consultant

Authorization to Proceed

I agree to the terms in the above proposal and grant authorization to proceed in accordance with these terms.

_____

Joseph Black
President
Unique Sales Company

SUMMING UP

Now you know how to write a proposal. But how much should you charge for your services? We'll discuss fees in the next chapter.

7

Pricing Your Services

PRICING IS another topic that requires some thinking. As well as determining the size of your billings and profits, it has an important effect on your image as a consultant. In this chapter, I will show you how to price your services. I will discuss the three basic price strategies available to you as a new consultant, explain the different methods of billing for your services, and present some tips on how to disclose your fees.

PRICE STRATEGIES AND SOME OTHER CONSIDERATIONS

THREE PRICE STRATEGIES

The three basic price strategies available to you are (1) a low-price strategy, (2) a high-price strategy, and (3) a meet-the-competition strategy. Let's look at each one in turn.

A Low-Price Strategy

A low-price strategy is basically penetration pricing. The purpose is to enter the marketplace with a price lower than those of your already established competitors; your bargain prices will attract clients. This strategy can work for new consultants, and with it you will be able to attract more business than you could otherwise.

However, the strategy has some serious shortcomings. First, because you are essentially selling your time, you have to work harder than those established in your profession to make the same amount of money. Your competitors will therefore have additional financial resources to fall back on if the resources are needed for an assignment or for marketing. Second, price has an image connotation. In the minds of many, low price means "cheap," and a low-priced consultant may be viewed as a low-quality consultant. You may be given only the less rewarding, grubbier types of assignments, not those that provide high exposure to top-level management. Finally, after choosing a low price, you may find it extremely difficult to raise your price later, as your practice grows.

As an example of what can go wrong with a low-price strategy, George W. is a CPA specializing in tax consulting. When George first started out as an independent consultant, he worked part time and after hours. To build his practice, he chose a low-price strategy; his billing rate was only 50 percent of the average rate for his type of services. Some years later, after his part-time practice had grown, George quit his full-time job and bought an established tax consulting practice whose clients were billed at more than twice the rate George had been charging. George now had two different rates for his clients. Because he was now full time, it seemed to make sense to raise his fees to the higher rate. However, as soon as he did so, every one of his former clients threatened to quit using his services. George needed these clients, so he reversed himself and maintained two different prices for his old clients and new ones.

However, he was hardly comfortable with this solution. He felt he was cheating his new clients by charging them so much more. But George also felt he was cheating himself, because he was clearly now worth the higher figure even if his older clients would not pay it. When George brought this problem to me for advice, my suggestion was to raise the lower rate slowly. George did so, raising his prices from 10 to 15 percent every year. In a couple of years, the amount he charged his lower-priced class of customers was close enough to that of the higher-priced class that he could finally accept the loss of the clients who refused to go along with the single, higher billing rate.

A High-Price Strategy

Another option that any consultant has, whether new or established, is to adopt a high-price strategy. This one is somewhat more risky. You are telling the world that you are worth more money; your image is that of a high-quality consultant. However, your potential clients may not believe you. It goes without saying that you had better be what you advertise.

Nevertheless, the high-price strategy is a viable one that many new consultants overlook for various reasons. They are afraid they are not worth the money, because they somehow have a nagging feeling they are ripping off their potential client, or they fear they will get no business if they charge higher prices. The truth is that in many cases, you are not only worth much more than you think, but may be worth more than established consultants who are already earning big fees. Before you reject a high-price strategy, consider the following stories; they are all true, but I've adjusted the dollar amounts to put them in today's dollars.

My former student, Harry S., graduated with an MBA and went to work for one of the large consulting firms. The day after he left the university, the firm that hired him billed Harry's time at $2,000 a day plus $600 overhead. His pre-MBA income had been less than $50,000 a year.

I got together with two old friends who had been classmates of mine when we went for our doctorate. One had been the city manager of a major U.S. city and had retired into consulting; the other was the general manager of a division of a major aerospace company. The former city manager said, "Boy, this consulting is great. Do you know that I'm getting $100 an hour?" This friend had more than 30 years' experience as the manager of various cities and a PhD. At the time, I was billing $200 an hour, and I said, "Bob, you are not charging nearly enough. I'm billing at twice what you're billing at. I'm billing at $200 an hour." The general manager of the aerospace company looked at both of us and smiled. "You're both undercharging," he said. "We pay our consultants $500 an hour, and to my knowledge none of them is as qualified or as smart or experienced as either one of you."

Once I received a telephone call from an individual who identified himself as Jerry S., a former undergraduate student at my university. Jerry said that he had been referred to me, even though he had not been my student, and that he had graduated eight years previously with a bachelor's degree. He explained that he and his partner gave seminars for companies on management styles and had put together a workbook for the seminars. Because I was known as an expert in direct response marketing, he wanted some advice on how they might self-publish this workbook and sell it through the mail. During our talk, I became intrigued with Jerry's frequent mention that his clients were top management, and I finally asked him who his clients were. "Oh," he said, "We give special seminars for small groups of top management of large companies. Usually there are no more than five to seven in each group." I asked about his pricing. "Oh, we go high, for image purposes," Jerry replied. "We charge $10,000 a day." I laughed and told him that he understood the marketing of his services very well. I knew many PhDs who weren't charging as much.

A friend of mine, Mary T., was going to start a part-time consulting business doing copyediting for writers. As an aside I happened to mention my concern that those in consulting of all types generally charge too little for their services, and I told her not to be afraid to charge what she was worth. I thought she knew the going rate for editorial services because her questions had to do with promotion. A week later, she told me she had her first client. I asked how much she had charged. I almost fell over when I learned that she had received three to four times the amount usually charged by experienced copyeditors. However, her client was well satisfied with her services and employed her again at this rate, which became her standard pricing.

In all these cases, the consultants had little difficulty getting the higher fees they charged. In fact, their clients were quite ready to pay them. Again, the reason was the image value of the consulting services offered. Therefore, if you are good at what you intend to do as a consultant, do not be afraid to use this pricing strategy. More consultants err by not choosing to use it than by choosing it. It is not a rip-off if you are good at what you do. In some cases, you may find that clients will *not* even want to engage your services if you charge too low a price. They will feel that either your work is not top quality or you are too inexperienced. Therefore, even from the standpoint of idealism and wanting to do the greatest amount of good, consider the high-price strategy.

A Meet-the-Competition Price Strategy

Employing this strategy, you choose a price that is approximately the same as what your competitors or potential competitors are charging. If you choose this strategy, you must offer something else in addition to your regular services. Otherwise, why should anyone deal with you? But if you do offer some differential advantage, and if you promote it to your potential clients, the meet-the-competition price can also be a successful strategy. Differential advantages may include quicker service, specialized additional services not offered by anyone else, around-the-clock availability to answer consulting needs, quicker results, or better results.

If you are going to choose this strategy, spend some time thinking through your differential advantage: What additional service can you offer above and beyond your competition? Or how can you make the consulting service you offer clearly better than anyone else?

OTHER CONSIDERATIONS

Take two other considerations into account when you are considering your pricing strategy: industry pricing and client price adjustment.

Industry Pricing

Certain industries have accepted prices for certain services. It is very difficult to violate this norm and build a viable practice. For example, employment agencies, on receipt of a job order, send the client several candidates to interview. If one of their candidates is hired, the agency may be paid from 10 to 15 percent of the individual's annual salary.

Executive search firms, which deal at a higher level of employment, supply three or more candidates for a particular job; if one of their candidates is hired, they get up to 30 percent or more of the executive's annual salary. Sometimes they get paid on an hourly or per-diem basis whether one of their candidates gets hired or not. They perform essentially the same service, but note the significant difference in pricing.

Therefore, when you are developing your fee schedule, consider the industry you are in. Employment agencies are simply not going to be paid the same as search firms, no matter how good a job they do. Of course, you can deviate from the normal range of pricing in your industry, but if you do, you may find it much more difficult to get and keep clients.

Client Price Adjustment

Some consultants charge different amounts to different clients, depending on who they are or how big they are. For example, sometimes the government (federal, state, or local), by policy or by law, has certain restrictions on the amount it can pay consultants. If you expect to do government work, this type of restriction will affect your pricing strategy.

Similarly, small companies generally cannot afford to pay as much as large companies. The examples I gave of the aerospace company that paid consultants $500 per hour and the consulting firm that billed the recent graduate's time at $2,000 a day both had clients that were large companies. Clearly, smaller companies cannot pay these kinds of fees.

You are therefore faced with a decision about billing if you deal with both large and small firms. You can base your billing on the size of the company, have one low price for all, or have one higher price for all. The higher price eliminates a certain segment of your potential market, but so may the lower price because of image. A two-price system may also lead to problems. You must make this decision yourself after considering all the relevant factors.

INVESTIGATE THE MARKETPLACE

At this point you probably have a rough idea of what you are going to charge for your services. Before you pick a strategy and finalize your price structure, investigate your market for a reality check. If you know other consultants in your field, ask them what they charge. (You should know them well enough to be comfortable asking and also to be relatively sure they are giving you accurate figures.) You don't have to copy them, but you should at least know how much they're getting—or say they're getting.

You can also contact potential clients. If you don't know them personally, attend professional meetings or trade shows, and you'll meet plenty, as well as other consultants you can ask. You can also contact professional associations and the editors of professional journals in your field of expertise. Both keep close tabs on what is going on in their fields, and if they don't know the going rates off the top of their heads, they can tell you where to get this important information. Conducting Internet research is another excellent way to investigate pricing in your field.

Your job now is to consolidate all this information: industry pricing, client price adjustment, the marketplace in your geographical area and area of expertise, and the pricing strategy you have decided on. Put it all together, and you have established your price structure.

Now let's look at different methods of billing.

METHODS OF BILLING

Basically there are four methods of billing: (1) daily or hourly, (2) retainer, (3) performance, and (4) fixed price. Let's look at each.

DAILY OR HOURLY BILLING

Billing on a time basis is fairly common among consultants, but deciding whether to bill on an hourly or a daily rate takes some consideration. As with so many other things, it's a trade-off. Some consultants feel that just getting started on any project will take the better part of a day, so they will not bill at less than a full day's rate. Even if a client wants just two hours of their time, they bill their daily rate as a minimum. Other consultants, especially those who work part time and those who want maximum flexibility in their scheduling, use the hourly rate. Billing hourly lets them work at home or at some other location; they can also work for a couple of hours on one project and a couple of hours on another, and in that way they work with several clients in a single day. Of course, you can also bill for fractional hours.

If you are considering a daily or hourly rate, be very certain you do not price your services so low that you can't make a decent living. Even if you elect to go with a penetration-price strategy, be very careful when you set your fee level. Sometimes new consultants get into the field simply because they do not want to work for someone else. They are perfectly willing to work for the same amount that they made at their previous job. At first glance, the logic seems perfect, but you should avoid the trap of using your previous salary to set your hourly rate. Let's try out some numbers. (Pay attention! This is important.)

Let's say you are currently making $62,000 a year as an employee, and your fringe benefits are worth another $5,000; that's a total of $67,000 in annual income. If you work 40 hours a week times 48 weeks (you will have two weeks vacation and two weeks for other holidays), that's 1,920 hours a year. But remember that you are going to spend at least one-third of that time marketing, and that time will not be available for billing. So that leaves about 1,280 hours available for billing.

If you divide $67,000 by 1,280 hours, you arrive at $52.34 per hour (rounded off to cents). So should your billing rate be $52.34 an hour? Absolutely not! This figure does not account for the fact that when you are working on your own, you will have overhead. Even though you will try to keep this overhead as low as possible, you will be surprised how fast it adds up. For example, let's make the following assumptions about your yearly overhead expenses.

Clerical support	$ 5,000
Office rent	8,000
Telephone	3,400
Automobile	8,000
Insurance, benefits, etc.	6,000
Advertising expenses	20,000
Entertainment	2,000
Professional dues and subscriptions	1,000
Accounting and legal fees	3,000
Miscellaneous	2,600
Total	**$59,000**

Therefore, to receive $67,000 income a year—what you earned working for someone else—you must charge $67,000 plus the $59,000 overhead, for a total of $126,000 a year. You've got to earn this in 1,280 billable hours. That works out to about $98.43 per hour. That's what you must charge just to earn the same compensation you were getting when you worked for someone else earning $62,000 plus $5,000 in fringe benefits.

WORKING ON RETAINER

In a retainer arrangement, you receive a constant monthly fee in return for a guarantee that a certain number of your hours will be available to your client. The retainer relationship has advantages for both sides. For you it gives a guaranteed income and cash flow, which can be very advantageous. Moreover, depending on the agreement with your client, if the hours are not used, you get paid anyhow. In fact, most consultants are willing to take a retainer at a reduced fee to ensure that money comes in every month. For your client, a retainer guarantees that you will work for him when needed and that he get first priority on your time.

PERFORMANCE BILLING

Basically, performance billing and a performance contract (discussed in Chapter 8) mean the same thing: compensation based on results. You decide on a percentage you will get based on the results you will achieve. For example, for every dollar saved through your recommendations, you might get 25 cents.

Performance-based fee structures, also called value-based and equity-based structures, are becoming more and more common, with some consulting firms reporting that 50 to 70 percent of their fees are based on performance. Surely a few may do all of their fee structuring this way.

Keep in mind that:

1. Performance billing is a good marketing tool.
2. Putting all terms in writing is critical.

3. Tying performance to profits is a mistake because profits can be manipulated for accounting or taxation purposes.

FIXED-PRICE BILLING

In a fixed-price contract (explained in Chapter 8), you agree to do a certain job and get paid a fixed amount for it. The number of hours you work on the project is entirely up to you, but you must put in however many it takes to get the job done. With a fixed-price contract, you can make more money, but at a greater risk because you guarantee accomplishment.

For a fixed-price contract to be profitable, you must be sure to follow these five guidelines:

1. Pad your estimations; overestimate a little to allow for miscalculations.
2. Use good estimating techniques, as discussed in Chapter 10.
3. Control your costs closely.
4. Carefully document exactly what you are required to do.
5. Be sure all changes to the contract are put in writing.

Among the various formulas for setting the fee in a fixed-price contract, a typical one consists of four computations for:

1. Direct Labor
2. Overhead
3. Direct Expense
4. Profit

A typical computation is shown in Figure 7-1. In this formula, overhead has been included as 65 percent of direct labor. Obviously you must cover your overhead some way, and applying a percentage to your estimate is an attempt to spread the annual overhead among your clients. To arrive at the overhead percentage:

✦ Estimate, in dollars, what you think your yearly overhead expenses will be.

✦ Convert that dollar amount into a percentage of your estimated annual income.

✦ Then add that percentage to the labor costs of each contract.

In this example, assume that a billing rate of $100 an hour would yield $100,000 annual income; if the estimated expenses are $65,000 a year, overhead works out to 65 percent ($65,000 ÷ $100,000 × 100%).

This formula incorporates a profit of 10 percent. The profit percentage is somewhat arbitrary, although it may be regulated in government contracts or contracts with companies that limit consultants' profits by policy.

Figure 7-1. Sample computation for a basic fixed-price contract formula.

1. *Direct labor:*

Consultant	12 days @ $800/day = $ 9,600.00	
Assistant	4 days @ $120/day = $ 480.00	
Secretary	5 days @ $100/day = $ 500.00	
Subtotal		$ 10,580.00

2. *Overhead* (65% of direct labor): $ 6,877.00

3. *Direct expense:*

Air travel	$ 1000.00
Rental car	$ 200.00
Special printing	$ 100.00
Travel expenses (hotel, etc.)	$ 500.00
Subtotal	$ 1,800.00
Subtotal for calculation of profit	$ 19,257.00

4. *Profit* (10% of subtotal): $ 1,925.70

   Total Fixed Price $ 21,182.70

DISCLOSING THE FEE

Some clients will not accept a daily or hourly rate; they prefer a fixed-price contract. In that case, calculate your fee using all three methods. If one method of billing is unacceptable to your client, try another. However, in disclosing the fee, provide the minimum amount of financial data required. For a fixed-price contract, if possible, indicate only the bottom-line price. In the example in Figure 7-1, indicate the fixed price as $21,182.70. If you are billing on a daily rate, give just the rate plus expenses.

Some clients, especially the government, require full disclosure. In such cases, you have to make a full presentation, like that in Figure 7-1, showing exactly how you arrived at your figures. Otherwise, the average client does not care about your overhead, and certainly there is no value to you in divulging it. Simply include it in your daily or hourly rate or in the fixed price if your fee is stated in this fashion.

SUMMING UP

Now you have your pricing structure and you know the various methods of billing. Let's see how we will use this information in the next chapter to develop consulting contracts.

8

WHAT YOU MUST KNOW ABOUT CONSULTING CONTRACTS

IN THIS CHAPTER, I show you why consulting contracts are necessary and how you can develop your own. I also discuss the different methods of incurring a contractual obligation, the different types of contracts, and the major elements of any contract. Finally, I include a sample contract to help you develop your own.

WHY A CONTRACT IS NECESSARY

You may think a handshake should do it among people of goodwill—and it might. In fact, a handshake may be contractually binding. But the kind of contract we are talking about does more because it is written.

A good written consulting contract:

✦ **Ensures that you and your client both fully understand the services you are to perform.** For your part, this will prevent wasted time, wasted resources, and wasted effort. It will also help ensure that you have a happy client at the end of the engagement. And a happy client will give you more work in the future and good referrals to others.

✦ **Helps you to get paid.** Even though you really enjoy your work, you must get paid to survive in business. Consulting may be a lot of fun, but without getting paid you will not be around to enjoy it. Having a written contract that documents your compensation will help you to gently remind your client of the financial obligations. If all goes sour and you must sue to get paid (this rarely happens, but it can), a signed contract is almost a necessity.

DEVELOPING YOUR OWN CONTRACT

You can certainly develop your own standard consulting contract and use it in every situation with only minor changes regarding the client specifics, services, compensation, time period of engagement, and other factors. (I talk more about this later in this chapter under the heading "A Sample Contract.") If you choose to do so, have your attorney assist you, but do not dump the whole project on her. If you do, it will cost you excessively. A better procedure is to develop each element yourself, using the information in this chapter, and rough out the contract the way you would like it. Use the sample contract shown in Figure 8-1 as a guide. Even though I've called it a consulting agreement because that is a little less intimidating for some clients, it is still a contract. Once your rough contract has been formulated, have your attorney review it and put it into final form.

IF YOUR CLIENT HAS A STANDARD CONTRACT

Sometimes your client will be a large corporation with a standard contract, and you may be asked to use this contract rather than yours. Naturally the final decision is always up to you. You should have your attorney review it, but usually these contracts are not unfair, and you may find them entirely acceptable.

(text continues on page 102)

Figure 8-1. Sample consulting contract.

_____, 20___

CONSULTANT AGREEMENT

AGREEMENT made _____, between _____,
                                 date   name of client
with principal offices at _____ hereinafter called
                                       client's address
"Client" and _____ of _____
                     name of consultant   consultant's address
hereinafter called "Consultant."

     1. Services. Consultant, as an independent contractor, agrees to perform, during the term of this Agreement, the following services: _____

_____
_____
_____

under the terms and conditions hereinafter set forth.
     2. Products. The term "Products" shall mean the client's line of _____

     3. Compensation.
        (a) Client shall pay Consultant at the rate of ____ per hour for each hour that Consultant shall perform services during the term of this Agreement, provided that the number of hours does not exceed _____ without the written consent of Client.
        (b) In addition to the hourly compensation provided herein, Client agrees to pay Consultant $_____ under the following conditions: _____

     4. Term. The initial term of this Agreement shall commence on the _____ day of _____, 20___, and end on the last day of _____, 20___, provided however that either party may terminate this Agreement at any time during the initial term of any extension term by giving the other party _____ days' notice in writing.
     This Agreement may be extended beyond the initial term or any extension term only by the written agreement of both parties prior to the expiration of the initial term or any extension.
     5. Designation of Duties. Consultant shall receive his requests for services to be performed from _____, _____,
                            client's name   title
_____.
                    company and address
     6. Restrictive Covenant. During the term of this Agreement, Consultant shall not make his services available to any competitor of Client in the specific field in which he is performing services for Client.
     7. Indemnity and Insurance. Consultant shall indemnify and hold harmless Client, its officers, and employees against all losses, claims, liabilities, damages, and expenses of any nature directly or indirectly arising out of or as a result of any act of omission by Consultant, its employees, agents, or subcontractors in the performance of this Agreement.
     If Consultant uses, or intends to use, a personal automobile in the perform-

(continues)

Figure 8-1. (continued).

ance of this Agreement, Consultant shall maintain throughout the term of this Agreement automobile liability insurance in accordance with the law of the State of _____ and not less than _____ .

8. Patent Rights. Consultant agrees during the term of this Agreement and for a period of 12 months after the termination of this Agreement, to assign to Client, its successors, assignees, or nominees all right, title, and interest in and to all inventions, improvements, copyrightable material, techniques, and designs made or conceived by him solely or jointly with others, relating to Products, in the performance of this Agreement, together with all United States and foreign patents and copyrights which may have been obtained thereon, and at Client's request and expense, will execute and deliver all proper assignments thereof.

9. Confidentiality. Consultant shall not disclose, publish, or authorize others to publish design data, drawings, specifications, reports, or other information pertaining to the work assigned to him by Client without the prior written approval of Client. Upon the expiration or sooner termination of this Agreement, Consultant agrees to return to Client all drawings, specifications, data, and other material obtained by Consultant from Client, or developed by Consultant, in connection with the performance of this Agreement.

10. Reimbursable Expenses. The following expenses will be billed in addition to compensation:

(a) Travel expenses necessary in order to perform services required by the Agreement. Use of personal automobile will be billed at ___¢ per mile.

(b) Telephone, telegraph, and telex charges

(c) Computer charges

(d) Printing and reproduction

(e) Other expenses resulting directly from performance of services in the Agreement.

11. Warranty. Consultant services will be performed in accordance with generally and currently accepted consulting principles and practices. This warranty is in lieu of all other warranties either expressed or implied.

12. Limitation of Consultant Liability. Client agrees to limit any and all liability or claim for damages, cost of defense, or expenses against Consultant to a sum not to exceed $_____, or the total amount of compensation, whichever is less, on account of any error, omission, or negligence.

13. Payment Terms. Terms of payment are as follows: $_____ due on the signing of Agreement and $_____ due _____ , 20_____ . $_____ due on delivery of _____ . A _____% per month charge will be added to all delinquent accounts. In the event Consultant shall be successful in any suit for nonpayment, Consultant shall be entitled to recover reasonable legal costs and expenses for bringing and maintaining this suit as a part of damages.

IN WITNESS WHEREOF, the parties have signed this Agreement.

_____
Consultant

_____
Client

METHODS OF INCURRING
A CONTRACTUAL OBLIGATION

A consultant can enter into a contractual obligation in five ways: (1) the formal contract, (2) the letter contract, (3) order agreements, (4) purchase orders, and (5) verbal contracts.

Let's look at each of these in turn.

FORMAL CONTRACTS

The formal contract is a written document describing the obligations of both parties. For most assignments, I would recommend that you formalize your engagement in this way because it will save you many problems, heartaches, lost fees, and misunderstandings. For example, I used the sample contract shown in Figure 8-1 as the basis of a contract with a major multibillion-dollar corporation.

LETTER CONTRACTS

A letter contract can be evolved from a proposal. It is in written form, but it is much simpler than a formal contract. However, it contains the basic elements of the contract, and though it may look like a letter, it qualifies as a contract.

ORDER AGREEMENTS

Order agreements have the force of contracts. They are typically used for the purchase of consulting services to be accomplished over a period of time. They commit both you and your client to contractual terms before the work is authorized. For example, an order agreement may commit you to so many hours of consulting over, say, a year's time and specify how much you will be paid. However, your client decides when to initiate the agreement. In other words, an order agreement ties both you and your client to terms, but not necessarily to a start date. In some cases, the order agreement will be combined with an option: The client retains flexibility on whether actually to use the services, but if the services are used, the terms are as set forth in the order agreement.

PURCHASE ORDERS

A purchase order is an internal form authorizing you to do work and to bill for it. It is generally used by larger companies to acquire relatively low-cost products or services. Consulting services may be ordered on a purchase order rather than negotiated in a formal contract because your client can do this quickly and simply, instead of going through the formal contractual process, which could involve your client's legal staff and some delay. Usually company management specifies a dollar limit on purchase orders, such as $25,000 or under.

VERBAL CONTRACTS

A verbal contract is still a contract. Verbal contracts are very common in consulting, but they are not always desirable. They are definitely not recommended in two situations: with new clients and for large projects. If the consulting circumstances with a new client are such that a formal written contract is not possible, try to get a significant part of the payment up front before you start work. Also be very clear with your client; spell out your objectives, what you are going to do, and how and when you are going to do it. It is an unfortunate fact of life that memory is imperfect, and once you have completed the work and expect your fee, memory is all you have to fall back on.

With larger contracts, the risk of not having the details in writing is simply too great. In a famous incident in history, Thomas Edison, the well-known inventor, offered Nicola Tesla, an immigrant physicist in his employ, a $50,000 bonus if he could fix Edison's error-prone design for DC generators. Tesla worked for over a year including weekends and evenings and succeeded. However, Edison refused to pay Tesla, saying that he had only been joking. Tesla quit Edison and partnered with Westinghouse as a consultant to develop usable AC. The system he developed was adopted worldwide, and his written royalty contracts with Westinghouse made him one of the wealthiest men in the world.

TYPES OF CONTRACTS

There are four basic types of contracts in consulting, each with variations: (1) fixed-price contracts, (2) cost contracts, (3) performance contracts, and (4) incentive contracts.

No one type of contract is best for all situations, but there is one best for a given situation. Therefore, you should know the advantages and disadvantages of each type.

THE FIXED-PRICE CONTRACT

In a fixed-price contract, you agree to do a certain job for a predetermined amount. With few exceptions, no price adjustment is made after the award of the contract, regardless of your actual cost in performing it. As the consultant, you assume all the cost risk. If your estimate is poor, you can actually lose money on a fixed-price contract. On the other hand, if you can reduce the cost below the original estimate, you have the potential for making increased profit. Therefore, the more certain you are of your cost and your potential for reducing it, the more willing you should be to enter into a fixed-price contract. Conversely, the more difficult it is to estimate a particular job, the more risk you assume and the less willing you should be to accept such a contract. With all types of contracts, accurate estimating is important, but with the fixed-price contract, it is crucial.

THE COST CONTRACT

In a cost contract, you are paid on your actual cost of performing the services; that is, your time plus related expenses such as the cost of reproducing your reports. As long as you put the time in, you are paid.

Obviously this type of contract involves a very low risk to the consultant. However, some clients will not accept cost contracts; they want to ensure that the project is actually completed within a certain budget. Thus, even when costs are difficult to estimate, you may have to choose between a fixed-price contract and no contract at all.

An alternative to no contract at all may be to break the overall task into subtasks. The subtasks that you can cost out with minimum risk can be taken on under a fixed-price contract; others you can accept under a cost or performance contract (performance contracts are described in the next section). Another solution may be to insert a not-to-exceed clause in the contract, so that you are paid for the work you actually do, but the client is guaranteed that your fee will not be higher than an agreed-upon amount.

The cost contract has several variations, two of which—cost plus fixed fee and cost plus incentive fee—are frequently used by the government for research and development projects. With the fixed-fee type of cost contract, the consultant is paid a total of the cost plus a fixed amount agreed to by both parties prior to performance. With the incentive-fee type, the consultant is paid the cost plus a variable incentive fee tied to different levels of performance agreed to in the contract. The incentive type of performance contract is discussed in more detail in a later section.

THE PERFORMANCE CONTRACT

In the past, pure performance contracts were rare, but now more firms are using them. In fact, in some firms up to 50 percent of fees are based on quantifiable results, which may include cycle time reductions, inventory reduction, margin enhancements, profit improvements, or revenue increases. More commonly, performance contracts may be made a part of a modified-cost or fixed-price contract, wherein increased performance may earn a higher fee or reduced performance a lower one.

With a performance contract, your payment is based solely on actual performance. Executive recruiters who work on contingency—that is, they receive a fee only if one of their candidates is hired by the client—are actually working on a performance contract. Performance contracts can also be based on an increase in sales, a decrease in turnover, or some other measurable factor.

A cautionary note: Do not accept a performance contract based on profits. Profits have too many definitions and are too easily adjusted upward or downward for accounting and taxation purposes. Although you may have done a great deal to increase performance, your success may not show up in accounting profits or on profit increases at the end of a year.

A performance contract, or at a least a proposal for one, is useful in closing a deal. Here's how to use a proposed performance contract to help you come to terms with a potential client. Let's say you have been negotiating with a prospective client, and while he seems satisfied about most aspects of the project, he is not quite ready to finalize and sign a contract with you. Perhaps you have been thinking along the lines of a fixed-price contract, which comes to $5,000. To close the deal, you could say something like this:

> Look, Mr. Smith, I am absolutely convinced that I can do this job for you and do it within the time period and at the price I indicated. However, I can see that you're hesitating, so let me make an offer that I don't think you can refuse. Let me design and implement this marketing campaign for you, and if it doesn't increase your sales by at least 25 percent, you pay me nothing. However, if your sales increase by 25 percent or more—and I have every confidence that it will be more—then you will pay me the $5,000 called for in my proposal.

You can see how the performance contract works. Your compensation is based solely on your performance. In the example, you have guaranteed your performance or you receive nothing. That's why it's such a great close during negotiations. Your prospective client thinks, "Well, now, if this individual is ready to take a performance contract, what have I got to lose?" Sometimes your client will agree to your original terms and will not even insist on the performance terms. However, if the performance terms are accepted, you must be ready to agree to the clause you proposed, and if you don't perform, that is the risk you are taking.

THE INCENTIVE CONTRACT

Incentive contracts are also tied to performance. A type of incentive may also be combined with a fixed-price or cost contract based on achieving certain preset objectives or goals. When setting these goals, you must help your client; be certain that the incentive-fee structure is not unrealistic for either side. You are trying to build a long-term relationship, and terms that are unreasonable to you or your client, even if agreed to at the time, could lose you business in the future.

A client once asked me to help him increase attendance at his seminars. In return I would receive, in addition to a fee, an additional $20 for every seminar attendee above an agreed minimum (which was his maximum the previous year). I was to receive this $20 bonus not for just this one seminar or even for all similar seminars in a single year, but for life. As long as attendance was higher than the previous year's high attendance, with no increase in costs, I was to receive $20 for each and every attendee above that number, whether I performed any additional services for his company. In my opinion, these terms were unreasonable and unfair to my client. We finally restructured the compensation, consisting of an incentive contract in which I was reimbursed with a fixed amount up front and then with an amount for each seminar attendee over the minimum; however, I was to get this for three years, not for the rest of my life. (On the other hand, there may be a situation in which receiving compensation for life for your services would be warranted.)

ELEMENTS OF A CONTRACT

A contract should have five basic elements:

1. **Who?** Who is the consultant, who is the client, and who are any other parties involved in any way in the project?
2. **What?** What services are to be provided to the client?
3. **Where?** Where are the services to be provided? What is the address of the client, what is the address of the consultant, and are special locations involved in the consulting?
4. **When?** When are the services to be performed? When is compensation to be paid?
5. **How much?** How much does the consultant receive for his services?

In addition to these five basic elements, other important conditions of the engagement are:

✦ Competitive Restrictions
✦ Patent Rights

✦ Insurance Coverages
✦ Confidentiality

A SAMPLE CONTRACT

Look again at the sample contract in Figure 8-1, noting how the contractual elements fit in. You can use this sample as a basis for developing your own contract. But don't forget to have your attorney go through it to ensure that everything applying to your situation has been taken care of and that your rights are fully protected.

SUMMING UP

In the next chapter, you will see how to plan and schedule the consulting project. Effective planning and scheduling affect your costing of a project and enables you to take on and complete several projects simultaneously. The information from your planning and scheduling will also go into your proposal, and it may well influence the type of contract you decide to accept.

9

PLANNING AND SCHEDULING THE CONSULTING PROJECT

PLANNING AND SCHEDULING all but the simplest of consulting engagements is absolutely essential. Not only are these steps necessary for preparing the proposal, but once you are on contract, having a firm and realistic schedule in hand will save you time and money and increase the quality of your performance. Every organization I ever worked with that had problems with project management had one thing clearly in common: a failure to plan and schedule their projects properly before they began work. Proper scheduling is not difficult. In this short chapter, I will give you a special form that will help you with this step.

THE PROJECT DEVELOPMENT SCHEDULE

Refer to the project development schedule in Figure 9-1. Start with the column headed "Task." Your first job is to list every task associated with the consulting project that you intend to undertake. Next, figure out how long each task will take to complete in days, weeks, or months (in Figure 9-1, the numbers at the tops of the columns represent whichever time period you choose). The hours each task takes will be put in later numerically. Measurements of task length (days, weeks, or months) and task time (hours) are not identical. A market research survey may require 80 hours of labor, which would be two weeks of eight-hour days, or four weeks if only four hours per day were spent on the project. An organizational audit that requires interviews with 20 different company executives may take four calendar weeks to complete (because of the difficulty of scheduling executive time), but only 40 hours of your time.

You also need to decide who will accomplish each task. If you are doing all the work yourself, this is easy. But in some cases, you will have other consultants or even other organizations working for you.

Figure 9-2 shows a project development schedule in which the tasks have been determined. After you write each task down on the schedule, draw a double horizontal line, starting at the place where the task will begin and continuing to the right until the task is complete. Consider each horizontal row as representing either days, weeks, or months after the authority to proceed. (Note that in the example in Figure 9-2, the time period being used is months.) Later, when you get the contract, you can write in the actual days, weeks, or months and use this schedule to manage the project. Convert the hours into dollar expenses for each period and total both hours and costs. Use a diamond figure (♦) to indicate critical date and times when something of great importance to the project must occur, such as the date a report is due. Later, when the critical task is complete, you can color the diamond to represent task completion.

Once you are on contract and have the authority to proceed, you can use the schedule as indicated in Figure 9-3. On a new form, substitute the actual dates for the estimated time periods.

On Figure 9-3, note that, for example, month 1 is replaced by June, month 2 by July. Copy onto your new form the double horizontal lines that show when each task will begin and end. As you proceed to perform the contract, shade in portions of the rectangular block formed by

(text continues on page 114)

Figure 9-1. Project development schedule form.

Task	1	2	3	4	5	6	7	8	9	10	11	12
Totals												

Figure 9-2. Proposed project development schedule, showing tasks and hour and cost estimates.

Task	$50/hr 1 Hrs/$	2 Hrs/$	3 Hrs/$	4 Hrs/$	5 Hrs/$	6 Hrs/$	7 Hrs/$	8 Hrs/$	9 Hrs/$	10 Hrs/$	11 Hrs/$	12 Hrs/$
Months After Award of Contract												
Development of Research Tool	20/1000											
Secondary Data Collection	10/500											
Interviewing			20/1000	20/1000	20/1000	20/1000	20/1000	20/1000				
Data Recording			2/100	5/250	5/250	5/250	5/250	5/250	3/150			
Data Analysis and Computations				5/250	5/250	5/250	5/250	5/250	10/500			
Follow-Up Interviews				2/100	3/150	2/100	1/50	1/50	5/250			
Final Report Preparation										40/2000	Report due end of ninth month after award of contract	
Totals 269/$13,450		30/1500	22/1100	32/1600	33/1650	32/1600	31/1550	31/1550	18/900	40/2000		

Figure 9-3. *Project development schedule after project initiation.*

Task	Hours F/A* June	Hours F/A* July	Hours F/A* Aug.	Hours F/A* Sept.	Hours F/A* Oct.	Hours F/A* Nov.	Hours F/A* Dec.	Hours F/A* Jan.	Hours F/A* Feb.	Hours F/A* Mar.	Hours F/A* Apr.	Hours F/A* May
Development of Research Tool	20/18											
Secondary Data Collection	10/13											
Interviewing		20/16	20/21	20/16	20/	20/	20/					
Data Recording		2/3	5/6	5/5	5/	5/	5/	3/				
Data Analysis and Computations			5/4	5/4	5/	5/	5/	10/				
Follow-Up Interviews			2/3	3/3	2/	1/	1/	5/				
Final Report Preparation										Report due March 1		
Totals	30/33	22/19	32/34	33/28	32/	31/	31/	18/	40/			

New estimated completion date

*Forecast/Actual

the double line to show the percentage of the task completed. At the end of each month, fill in actual hours worked on each task and compare with hours forecast. If you know that a task must be delayed for some reason, adjust your schedule by the use of a triangle and a series of dashed lines as shown in the horizontal area to the right of "Interviewing" in the figure.

DEVELOPING A PERT CHART

PERT (program evaluation and review technique) was developed by the U.S. Navy Special Projects Office working with the management consulting firm of Booz, Allen, and Hamilton. As you might suspect, the U.S. Navy designed PERT for use with big contracts and projects. But that should not stop you from using it with a small consulting proposal. Not only will it help you when you implement the project, it is quite impressive to your prospective client as a part of your proposal. It really shows that you have thought things through!

PERT offers a lot of benefits. Specifically, it helps you in minimizing delays, interruptions, and conflicts in developing, coordinating, and synchronizing the various parts of the overall project, as well as in expediting completion.

EVENTS AND ACTIVITIES

PERT depends on just two elements: events and activities. An event is a specific task accomplishment that occurs at a recognizable point in time. An activity is the work required to complete an event.

As an example, the publication of an advertisement is an event. Writing the copy, getting the artwork, preparing the layout, and submitting the advertisement for publication are all activities. The events themselves take no time. However, they do mark the beginnings and ends of the activities needed to complete the events.

Look at the depiction of a PERT network shown in Figure 9-4. Events are represented by circles, and activities by arrows joining the circles. Remember, every event represents a specific point in time, and the arrow or activity connecting events represents the actual work done and the time needed to plan and do the work.

Figure 9-4. Sample PERT network with four events and four activities.

Event	Activity
1	1–2
2	1–3
3	3—4
4	2–4

With PERT, time is usually calculated in calendar weeks. A *calendar week* is the number of working days required divided by the number of working days per week. The expected time for any activity, also known as the *expected lapse time*, is calculated by the following equation:

$$T = \frac{a + 4b + c}{6}$$

where
T = the expected lapse time
a = the most optimistic time
b = the most likely time
c = the most pessimistic time

If $a = 1$ week, $b = 2$ weeks, and $c = 3$ weeks, then

$$T = \frac{1 + (4)2 + 3}{6} = \frac{12}{6} = 2 \text{ weeks}$$

EARLIEST EXPECTED DATE

The earliest expected date is represented by the letters TE, and it is the earliest possible date that a task can be completed. In Figure 9-5, you can see that there are two paths through the network: One path is represented by the numbers 1, 2, 4; the second, by 1, 3, 4. Path 1-2-4 takes 8 weeks (2 + 6); path 1-3-4 requires 12 weeks. Because all events have to occur before the project is completed, you must wait four addition-

Figure 9-5. Simple PERT network showing significance of TE.

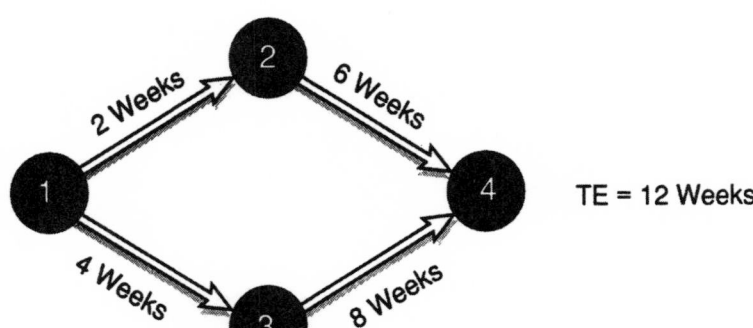

al weeks after completing path 1-2-4 before you can complete event 4. So the earliest expected date for the network shown in Figure 9-5 is 12 weeks.

LATEST ALLOWABLE DATE

The latest allowable date is represented by the letters *TL*, the latest allowable date that an event can take place and still not interfere with the scheduled date of the entire network.

Take a look at Figure 9-6. In this network, the *TE* of event 6 is 16 weeks. This is through path 1-3-5-6, the longest of the three paths through the network. Path 1-3-5-6 is therefore the critical path. So if any progress is to be made in reducing the time necessary to complete this project, you must reduce the activities on this path. It makes no difference whether you reduce the time of the activity on path 1-2; path 1-2 is not critical in this sense. Even if you reduce the activity on path 1-2 to zero, the *TE* remains 16 weeks. To reduce the *TE* of event 6, you must reduce the activities on path 1-3-5-6, which is said to be the *critical path*.

The earliest expected dates for six events are shown in Figure 9-6. You would expect to complete event 4 nine weeks after initiation due to the critical path 1-3-4. If activity begins immediately thereafter, you might expect to complete event 6 in a total of 14 after the project is initiated.

Figure 9-6. Simple PERT network showing earliest possible dates at each event.

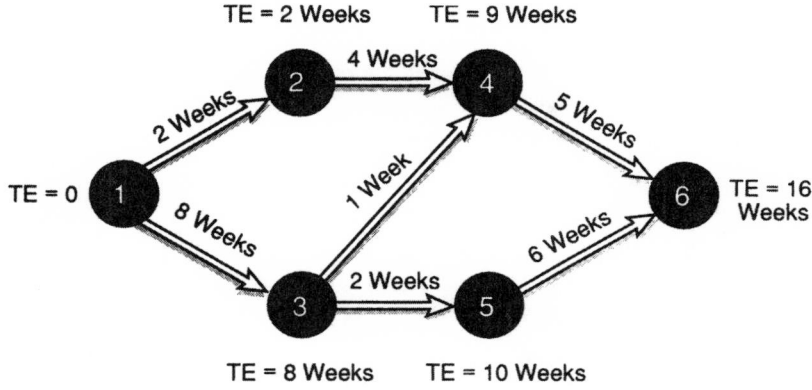

Adapted from Richard I. Levin and Charles A. Kirkpatrick, *Quantitative Approaches to Management,* 3rd ed. (New York: McGraw-Hill, 1975).

But a closer look tells you that the time is actually 16 weeks because of other required activities. This observation should also tell you that event 4 really does not need to be completed in nine weeks; it could actually be completed in 11 weeks (11 + 5 = 16) after the project is begun and still not interfere with the scheduled network time of 16 weeks at event 6.

That is the significance of the latest allowable date. For event 4, it is 11 weeks after the project begins because at that time you still have five weeks' work to complete activity 4-6 and exactly five weeks in which to do it.

SLACK

Slack (S) is the difference between the latest allowable date and the earliest expected date. At event 4 in Figure 9-7, slack time is two weeks (11 weeks − 9 weeks).

THE USEFULNESS OF PERT

You can see how you can control a complex consulting project fairly easily by using PERT. The technique shows you where you can save

Figure 9-7. Simple PERT network with latest allowable dates and slack time added.

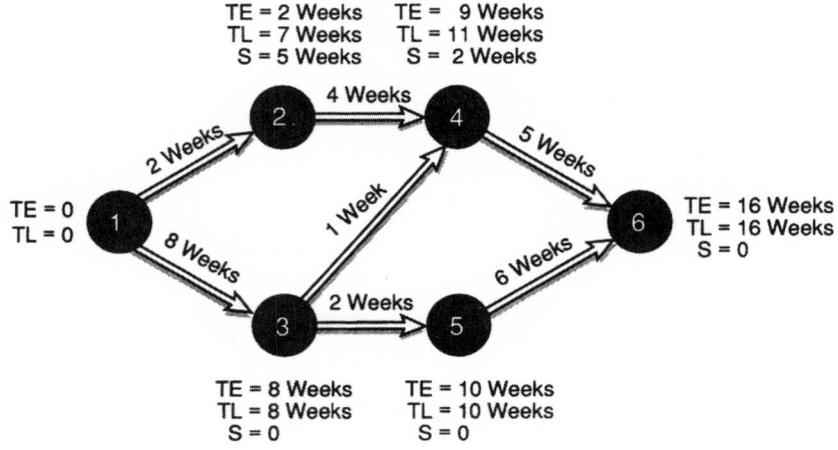

Adapted from Richard I. Levin and Charles Kirkpatrick, *Quantitative Approaches to Management*, 3rd ed. (New York: McGraw-Hill, 1975).

time and let the schedule slip and where it is critical to get an event done exactly on time. It shows you where to concentrate or where to switch resources from noncritical paths to critical paths to effect time savings. PERT also shows you how to save money by avoiding putting resources where they will be less effective in hitting critical dates.

PERT also demonstrates to your potential client that you know what you are doing and that you have carefully thought through the entire consulting project. It will give you a much better chance of having your proposal accepted. Once you are under contract, these management tools will assist you in controlling and avoiding slippages and cost overruns. You will have more happy customers and fewer worries and ulcers.

SUMMING UP

Now you are ready to go to work to negotiate everything you've prepared with your client. We'll learn how to do that in Chapter 10.

10

NEGOTIATING WITH YOUR CLIENT

WHETHER A CONSULTING ENGAGEMENT is profitable or unprofitable has much to do with your ability to negotiate with your client. Why? Even if you perform flawlessly, if you negotiate an unfavorable contract, you may ending up losing money, reputation, or both.

Robert Ringer describes an amazing negotiating incident in his best-selling book, *Winning Through Intimidation* (Funk & Wagnalls, 1973). Ringer had been observing a difficult negotiation in which a businessperson he knew had ruthlessly demanded and received outrageously advantageous terms. The other party had agreed to these terms because he was clearly desperate to get the contract. Further, there were heavy penalties for failure to comply with all the contractual terms. On the way out, Ringer commented to this businessperson that it would be very difficult for the other party to live up to the terms. The businessperson smiled and told Ringer something to the effect that, "If you look at the contract carefully, you will see that he is already technically in violation of the contract."

Unfortunately, many consultants become so desperate for a contract that they also negotiate extremely unfavorable terms for themselves. Don't let this happen to you. Plan the negotiation of the contract before you begin.

SIX STEPS IN CONTRACT NEGOTIATION, AS SEEN BY UNCLE SAM

The U.S. government negotiates billions of dollars in contracts every year. Sometimes we read about the screwups in the newspaper, such as the $650 toilet seats. But the truth is that, considering the fact that they negotiate more than a million contracts every year, government buyers do a pretty good job.

The government breaks down the process leading to final contract negotiation into six steps:

1. Evaluation and ranking of offers (if there are more than one), in light of the evaluation criteria in the request for proposal
2. Identification of the proposals that are within a competitive range
3. Identification and elimination of unacceptable proposals due to major problems with price or technical merit
4. Written or oral discussions with the remaining competitors, permitting the revision of proposals to correct isolated deficiencies
5. Notification of a cutoff date for receipt of a best and final offer
6. Selection for award or for final negotiations, if appropriate

If you are bidding a contract against competitors, whether dealing with the government or any client, you can assume that your prospective client will use a similar process. Note that the negotiating process may have several steps but that even in the last step, final negotiations may be necessary. In these final negotiations, some consultants "give away the store" and get into trouble.

APPRECIATING THE GOALS AND OBJECTIVES OF THE COUNTERPARTY

In a general way, your prospective client is simply trying to close the deal and make the final arrangements so that you can begin work. But you may never understand the full situation, including the limitations and pressures affecting the way the counterparty negotiates. You may be definitely interested in a win–win outcome, but there are very broad definitions of what a win–win negotiation is.

When I teach negotiation in my seminars and workshops, one of the simulations I use is negotiation for the purchase of a computer. The computer sellers are given the following or similar confidential instructions:

> You are the vice president of sales of a company that designs computer systems for business. Yesterday you received an emergency notice from top management. This message told you that you must immediately withdraw and junk one of your older models, the XC-1000 computer. The withdrawal is due to the implementation of a government regulation requiring additional features to prevent tampering, which this model does not have.
>
> Unfortunately you cannot modify the XC-1000, because it was built to "last forever." You can't even use it for parts. By law you must sell or get rid of all computer systems such as the XC-1000 by April 3. (This is April 2!) After that date, you cannot offer it to the market at any price. You can't even give it away.
>
> Fortunately, you have only one of the XC-1000s left in inventory. In fact, you haven't sold any of these models in several years. This morning your assistant contacted the Acme Junk Company, which agreed to pick up your XC-1000 and melt it down to sell for scrap, at no charge to you.
>
> Before you can make final arrangements, you receive a call from Consolidated Unlimited. Its director of MIS would like to meet with you tomorrow about the possible immediate purchase of an XC-1000. You tell him there is one left and that the price is negotiable. You delay your arrangements

with Acme and begin to prepare for your meeting with Consolidated.

Do not reveal any of this information to any person not on your team. You will have 30 minutes to complete the answers to the following questions:

1.   For what price do you expect to sell the XC-1000? Why?
2.   What is the lowest price you will accept? Why?
3.   What is your strategy for the meeting tomorrow?

Now, as the computer seller, you feel the pressure of having to sell to this potential buyer or getting nothing for the computer at all. Further, being in the business of manufacturing computers, you probably know all about the state-of-the-art of competitive systems. From your viewpoint, you are desperate to sell, yet you do not have much of a product. You are probably wondering why in the world Consolidated Unlimited wants such a system.

I designate another group as buyers. They also receive confidential instructions. If you knew the instructions, you would know that Consolidated Unlimited is desperate to buy your product and is probably willing to pay quite a bit more for it than you might expect. Here are the instructions to the buyers:

Several years ago, you became director of information management systems for Consolidated Unlimited, a small company manufacturing copper tubing. One of your first actions was to buy an XC-1000 computer. One of this computer's most attractive features was its negligible need for maintenance. In fact, when you bought the computer, it came with a three-year money back guarantee if the system didn't perform in any way. For three years and one month, the computer performed beautifully, but this morning your XC-1000 failed completely.

One of the first things you did was have your assistant look for a newer replacement model that would perform the same functions. Unfortunately, as your company grew, all functions were built around your XC-1000, so you have very limited options. As a matter of fact, the lowest-priced replacement computer other than an XC-1000 is $50,000.

You made some tentative calls around the country to other companies that you knew had bought XC-1000s.

You discovered that most companies had replaced them long ago. You were also a little concerned about buying a used model because none were less than three years old and the guarantee had expired.

You called the president to apprise her of the problem, but her response was, "Get another new XC-1000." You called the manufacturer of the XC-1000 and arranged a meeting with the vice president of sales tomorrow for an immediate purchase of an XC-1000. When you asked her the price, she told you there was one left and the price was negotiable. You began to prepare for your meeting.

Do not reveal this information to individuals not on your team. You have 30 minutes to complete the answers to the following questions:

1. What price do you expect to pay for the XC-1000? Why?
2. What is the highest price you will pay? Why?
3. What is your strategy for your meeting tomorrow?

Now you can see that both parties to this situation have a serious problem. If the sellers do not sell the computer, they get absolutely nothing. If the buyers do not buy the computer, they must pay $50,000 to get another system elsewhere. And of course, the president of the buyer's company has flat out ordered the IM director to purchase one of these computers. So you see, at any price other than zero or $50,000, both sellers and buyers gain. It is a win–win situation as long as they come to an agreement within this range.

However, if we were arbitrators calculating a fair price, we would probably select the midpoint between zero and $50,000, that is, $25,000.

However, neither side has the information that the other has. Both know only of its own problems, not about any problem that puts pressure on the other party.

What results do I get? Interestingly, the prices vary widely between zero and $50,000 among different groups of buyers and sellers negotiating on the same day. Yet the conditions are the same for all.

The last time I gave this exercise in the classroom and not in a workshop, it was to four groups of graduate students. The prices for which the computer was sold were $2,500, $12,500, $27,300, and $45,000, even though in every case the situation of every negotiating pair was exactly the same.

This should tell you something important about negotiating with a client: You do not know the client's side of the story, and the client does not know yours. Therefore, even if poor cash flow or some other situation causes you to be hungry for a job, you still want to negotiate for what you are worth. How can you best do this? The key is preparation.

PREPARATION: THE KEY TO
ALL CONTRACT NEGOTIATIONS

For all but the simplest of contracts, you can assume that your prospective client is going to be well prepared. He is going to do his homework, check the facts, prepare his case, anticipate your arguments, and develop responses to them. Most important, he will develop specific negotiation objectives related to your price, performance, or timing. To negotiate with him, you must be as well prepared as you can be:

+ Do more than review your facts. Know the areas in which you can afford to be flexible and where you must stand fast.

+ Know the price for your services below which you cannot go.

+ Know the areas in which you can speed things up and complete your tasks earlier and where you cannot.

+ Understand where you can increase or decrease the level of performance and what this will cost or save.

+ Write down your specific negotiating objectives. That way you won't forget them in the heat of negotiation.

If you prepare well and if your client fails to do his preparation or doesn't do it as well, you go in having a heavy advantage in the negotiation. You want to treat everyone fairly and do not want to take unfair advantage, but you should keep two things in mind. First, not everyone feels as you. Some potential clients operate like the businessman whom Robert Ringer described. These individuals will try to take every advantage they can—fair or not. Second, if you are in control of the situation, you will be better able to negotiate an engagement that works to your client's benefit as well as yours.

BE WARY OF TELEPHONE NEGOTIATIONS

Telephone negotiations may or may not be good for you depending on your preparation. But you should always be wary. If you are well prepared and ready to negotiate the deal, a telephone negotiation can be a quick way to close and get authority from your client to begin work. On the other hand, if you are not prepared, a telephone negotiation can be a disaster.

The problem is that, unless the telephone negotiation is set up ahead of time, you may have other things on your mind. You cannot think of two things at once—what you were working on and the negotiation—and trying to negotiate under such circumstances is impossible.

One day I was in the midst of handling an emergency. I received a call to finalize the price on an assignment I had been asked about several days earlier. I had not had an opportunity to work out the pricing. In those days, I used a formula to price this type of work. Still half-thinking about the emergency, I attempted to use the formula and negotiate the price, and I ended up negotiating a price 30 percent lower than what I usually charged. This happened not because of hard negotiating tactics by my prospective client, but rather entirely because of the distraction of the emergency and my own mistake. For various reasons the formula was inappropriate in this situation.

Do not make the same mistake. After submitting a proposal, be ready for a telephone call to finalize the contract. Keep your material close to the telephone. If you get an unexpected call, as I did, ask whether you can call back. Complete the project you are working on, clear your mind, review your material, and then call to negotiate the contract.

THE NEGOTIATION PLAN

To reach your objectives, prepare a negotiation plan, which should include an overall objective and a target price. Write down your limitations. As mentioned earlier, know your bottom-line price, below which you cannot go without losing money. Then work out a strategy to achieve your objectives.

Your strategy in reaching your planned price objective might be simply to restate the price in your proposal. If this is questioned, you might show how your pricing is similar to or lower than pricing on other jobs that you or others have done. You might compare this price against the benefits that will be achieved as a result of your work. Finally, if price is still an issue, you might have a few fallback positions to show what you can accomplish for lower prices.

At every step, you should anticipate questions or objections, work out answers to the other party's questions, and counter his tactics to overcome objections.

NEGOTIATION GAMESMANSHIP

Even when both parties try to look out for each other's interests, a great deal of gamesmanship goes on in any negotiation. Some tactics are no worse than beginning at a higher price than you actually want because you know that your client always tries to negotiate a lower price than the one you open with. However, some prospective clients, like the businessperson noted by Robert Ringer at the beginning of this chapter, see any negotiation as a competition that must be won at all costs. Such individuals may use a wide variety of tactics against you, some of which may be highly unethical.

Some people believe that lying in a negotiation is perfectly acceptable. A friend of mine who teaches negotiating says, "A lie is not a lie when the truth is not expected." He points out that when labor and management are negotiating, one or the other will say something like, "We will never, never agree to these terms. Never, never!" The next day, the contract is signed under the very terms they claimed they would never, never agree to. Was their statement a lie? You must make your own judgment, but in any case you should be ready when a prospective client uses this or any kind of negotiating tactic against you. Never believe a statement made by someone you are negotiating with unless you can confirm it or test it. Frequently false are such statements as "This is the absolutely most we can pay" or "We never pay more than this for consulting."

Here are some of the more common ploys.

MAKING THE OTHER PARTY APPEAR UNREASONABLE

A prospective client may point out that other consultants charge such and such or have agreed to certain terms that you will not agree to. The implication is that something is wrong with you and the way you do business—that you are being unreasonable.

One defense against this tactic is to point out how this situation is different from the others. Of course, you can always add what I consider the ultimate response: "I am a lot better consultant than those you have mentioned." Or, "I'm sure you can purchase these services elsewhere at a lower cost. However, you can't purchase my consulting services for a job like this anywhere else at any price."

English sales consultant Peter Thomson tells this anecdote:

Potential Buyer: That's an unreasonable price. Another seller asks only half that price.

Consultant: Why don't you use the other seller?

Potential Buyer: He's too busy to take the engagement right now.

Consultant: You know, it's the same with us. When we're too busy, that's the price we charge.

Of course, I would never actually say this to a prospect. It would be insulting, and I would lose the client. Just be aware that your pricing may be questioned and that you want to have an answer ready.

PLACING THE OTHER PARTY ON THE DEFENSIVE

A prospective client may ask a question for which you are unprepared—another good reason to make certain that you are as prepared as you can be.

Maybe the party you are negotiating with has a top dollar limit to her negotiating authority, which you both know is $100,000. During the negotiation, you agree not to go above this amount. Just as you think you have a deal, your prospective client asks a question like this: "You aren't going to embarrass me by making your price so close to $100,000 that my supervisors will suspect what we are doing?" Being on the defensive, you could end up dropping your price several thousand dollars to protect the other party's reputation. You may still be profitable at the lower level, but if that level is below your standard price, it is less than you are worth, and the difference comes out of your pocket. Chances are your negotiating partner gets her bonuses this way.

If you are prepared for this ploy, you can say something like, "I'm sorry. I've been negotiating in good faith. This is my best offer."

BLAMING A THIRD PARTY

Your prospective client attempts to shift the blame for his unwillingness to give in on a negotiating point to someone or something over which he has no control: "I agree with what you are saying, but it's the policy of the company. It won't allow me to do it."

This is a difficult problem to overcome. It may mean that your prospective client absolutely will not give in on this point. If you feel strongly enough about the issue, you can test it by refusing to give in and suggesting that the negotiations be suspended while the other party checks out the situation with a superior. Or you can explore how you might achieve the results you want while not violating company policy. For example, if you want money up front but company policy is not to pay until work is done, you can suggest an additional progress payment shortly after an early contract milestone.

THE GOOD-GUY, BAD-GUY TECHNIQUE

The good-guy, bad-guy technique began with the interrogation of prisoners. One interrogator, the bad guy, would yell and scream and even beat the prisoner. If he did not get the information he wanted, he would leave the room. Then the good guy would take over, offering the prisoner a cigarette and commiserating with him on what a monster the other interrogator was. He might even embellish his partner's performance by describing how another prisoner had died under the bad guy's interrogation. The good guy would suggest that the prisoner give part of the information or make a reduced confession just to appease the bad guy.

This approach works because of the contrast between the two interrogators. Someone under the extreme pressure applied by the bad guy is in need of support, which the good guy provides. The good guy's requests seem so slight in comparison with the bad guy's demands that the prisoner is more likely to go along with them.

The same technique is sometimes used when you are negotiating with more than one member of the prospective client company. The bad guy continually puts pressure on you and rudely presses home every point. Although you will not get slapped around, the bad guy may actually yell and scream. The good guy says something like, "Gee, I think it's terrible the way he's behaving. Maybe if you can give him just a little of what he wants, he'll be satisfied. If you can do that, I'll try to help."

When you see this kind of performance, just remember that it is probably exactly that: a performance. In fact, when they are negotiating with someone else in a different negotiating situation, the two may actually switch roles! Just remember that both are on the other side of the negotiation, and look out for your own interests.

GIVING UP ON STRAW ISSUES

Straw issues are nonissues. They really are not important at all to your prospective client. However, they may be aggressively introduced as a negotiating point so that they can be given up later in exchange for a real concession from you.

When the Soviet Union existed, the Soviets were quite good at negotiating, setting up straw issues all the time. They would sometimes introduce positions that were completely unreasonable. They would allow themselves to be negotiated out of these extreme positions in exchange for major concessions. As a result, some of the treaties negotiated with the Soviets were quite lopsided in their favor. Yet when our negotiating team members were asked how they could have possibly agreed to such terms, they would respond, "But you should have seen the position they started with!"

When your prospective client is unreasonable or introduces straw issues, offer little or nothing in exchange for dropping them. Just do not accept them.

THE WALKOUT

The walkout ploy is used infrequently because it may be difficult to get negotiations going again if the ploy fails. Your prospective clients say something like, "We can't pay any more and that's it." Then she prepares to leave. This is a supreme test, and you can either attempt to move toward her position or call her bluff and let her go. Many times, even if she leaves, you can call her later and reopen negotiations. Sometimes the client will even call you to reopen negotiations. Even though occasionally the counterparty is not bluffing, I am biased in favor of letting the client go, unless you really have been unreasonable. Otherwise the client is going to think you are desperate and take advantage of you even more.

THE RECESS

This is almost always a good tactic because it does not break off negotiations. It allows the air to cool and may offer an opportunity for either side to rethink its position. If your prospective client calls for a recess, or caucus, don't panic. The break may be called simply to put pressure on you while you ask yourself why it was called. Sometimes a prospective client calls a recess when you are in a hurry, perhaps to catch a flight. In that case, you can show your resolve by refusing to accept the pressure: Reschedule your flight. If necessary, stay an extra day, or reschedule the negotiations.

THE TIME SQUEEZE

You know time is money. So does your prospective client, who may try to put pressure on you to come to an agreement on his points by using delaying tactics. The recess is one way of doing this, but there are many others. For example, your prospective employer may say, "We can't continue to negotiate past three o'clock because we have some people flying in for an important meeting."

What can you do? Tell your prospective client, "I understand, but I want to be certain that the engagement gets started right. Then we won't have problems later. If you aren't available after three o'clock, let's reschedule for a time when we can complete our negotiations."

MORE NEGOTIATION TACTICS

My friend, Dr. Don Hendon, teaches negotiating. Here are a few of his favorites from more than 200 tactics he has documented:

- **Big Pot.** Make big demands at the beginning. This gives you more room to negotiate. Also, after making concessions, you still end up with more than if you started too low.
- **Whipsaw/Auction.** Let several competitors know you're negotiating with them at the same time.
- **Divide and Conquer.** Sell one member of the other side's negotiating team on your ideas. Get him on your side so that he can persuade the others.
- **Be Patient.** If you can afford to outwait your opponent because he needs something that only you have, you can win big.
- **Trial Balloon.** Leak your possible proposal to a third party before you make a proposal and test the reaction before you make the proposal officially.

SOME GENERAL NEGOTIATING HINTS

Here are some general hints for negotiating that will help you to negotiate fairly, yet competently:

1. When things get tense, try humor.
2. Don't ridicule or insult anyone. Don't be rude. Be courteous and considerate.
3. Don't try to make anyone look bad.

4. Be reasonable (unless you are being unreasonable as a tactic).

5. Try to find the best deal for both parties.

6. Negotiating means both talking and listening. Remember to do both.

7. Don't accept any statement made by the other party as 100 percent accurate. Remember that the person may be honest and trustworthy but that she may be "just negotiating."

8. You can give in on small points, but fight hard for the issues that are important to you.

9. Price may be only one aspect of the negotiation process. Remember that you can also adjust timing and performance. Sometimes your prospective client will give in on these to get a lower price.

10. Don't forget the computer negotiation example earlier in this chapter. You do not know your prospective client's situation. Chances are that you are in at least as good a position as your prospective client.

11. If you see a good offer, take it. Do not feel that you must always knock something off a deal that is offered you.

12. Don't discuss an issue you aren't prepared for. If something comes up for which you aren't prepared, defer talking about it until you are.

13. Don't assume that the other side completely understands all the advantages you are offering. Take the time to explain them and what they mean to her in the way of benefits.

14. Don't make big changes in your offer; give in very slowly and in very small increments.

15. Never tell anyone how you outsmarted anyone in negotiations. Boasting can come back to haunt you. Several years ago, Donald Trump sold Merv Griffin a casino for hundreds of millions of dollars. Trump even went on national television saying out loud how he had taken Griffin to the cleaners. Not too long afterward, Trump went bankrupt. Did the one event have anything to do with the other? I don't know, but if Merv Griffin had an opportunity to return the favor and renegotiate the deal

through his influence in another situation, you can bet he would have done so. No one wants to feel taken advantage of, certainly not publicly.

When you are eager to begin work, you may tend to rush into negotiations ill prepared and eager to get them over with. Negotiations are an important part of the overall consulting process. Take the time to do them right. Doing so will pay dividends during the engagement and will do much to enhance the profitability and reputation of your practice.

SUMMING UP

You've completed phase one and have one or more contracts. Now what? We will look at ways you can solve some of your client's problems next.

HOW TO EASILY SOLVE YOUR CLIENT'S PROBLEMS

IN THIS CHAPTER, I will show you a logical, step-by-step approach to problem solving, as well as some important psychological problem-solving techniques. The step-by-step methodology does more than help solve problems; it also organizes your thinking process and provides an outline for presenting your analysis, conclusions, and recommendations to your client, both as a written report and as a formal, in-person presentation. I cover every step in detail and then show you a sample problem that you can work out yourself, including forms to assist you. Then I go over the solution to this problem and analyze the results.

PETER DRUCKER'S METHOD OF SOLVING PROBLEMS WITH HIS IGNORANCE

When I was Peter Drucker's PhD student, a classmate once asked how he was so knowledgeable about so many different industries. Drucker said he did not bring his knowledge or experience to a new consulting assignment, but rather his ignorance. Sometime later, going over my class notes and other material, I realized that Drucker must have been, either consciously or unconsciously, using something called the Harvard Case Study Method, also known in the military as the Staff Study Method. The approach is also used by the legal profession to analyze cases and by the psychological profession in diagnosing and treating patients. It is a structured, step-by-step process of considering and analyzing the various alternatives available to solve a problem and honing in on the best solution.

Let's take a look at the six elements of this methodology:

1. Defining the Central Problem
2. Listing the Relevant Factors
3. Listing Alternative Courses of Action or Solutions, with Advantages and Disadvantages of Each
4. Discussing and Analyzing Alternatives
5. Listing Conclusions
6. Making Recommendations

DEFINING THE CENTRAL PROBLEM

Defining the single central problem in a situation is the single most difficult and important task in consulting problem solving. If you correctly identify the main problem in a situation, you can find many different approaches to solving it. But if the wrong problem is identified, even a brilliant solution will not correct the situation. You are well advised to take all the time necessary to be sure that you are indeed looking at the central problem.

One of the major errors that new consultants make in defining the central problem is confusing the symptoms with the problem. For example, low profits are not a central problem but a symptom of something else that is the central problem. Frequently a case has many different problems; in fact, there usually is more than one. The object then is to locate the *main* problem, the one that is more important than any other and is therefore central. If you find more than one major problem in a particular situation, you should handle each one separately.

Once you have identified the central problem, write an initial draft explaining it. Try to keep this statement as simple as possible by making it as short as you can; a one-sentence central problem statement is usually best. Be aware, however, that even if you have spent some time in both identifying the problem and wording it as concisely as possible, in many cases you still have to go back and modify it as you proceed through the analysis.

Keep your problem statement short by leaving out various additional factors. Even if the factors are relevant, they will only make the problem statement unwieldy, awkward, and difficult for any reader to understand.

Also be careful not to word the problem as if it were the solution, by assuming that one particular course of action is correct before you analyze it. In fact, your goal is to develop as many different courses of action as possible. Try not to word your statement so that only two alternatives are possible. For example, do not ask a question like, "Should a new product be introduced?" That kind of question allows for only two possible answers: yes or no. In some situations, only two alternatives need be analyzed. Usually, however, you can reword the problem statement so that it allows more than two courses of action.

In your statement, include important specifics about the problem. For example, "What should be done about the possibility of introducing a new product?" is not the best problem statement. It allows for more than two alternatives, but it omits specifics about the problem that may be important to readers of your report who are not as familiar with the problem as you or the individual who hired you.

With these cautionary notes in mind, begin formulating your problem statement. Phrase it as a question, beginning with who, what, when, where, how, or why. Or you may start with an infinitive, as in "To determine the best source for borrowing $10,000."

LISTING RELEVANT FACTORS

In the phrase "relevant factors," both words are important. "Relevant" is critical because, even though a situation has many factors, you are to determine and list only those that are relevant to the central problem you have identified.

In this task, you will be listing factors, not just facts. You may include estimates, computations, assumptions, and even educated guesses in addition to facts. Naturally, if one of your relevant factors is not a fact, label it accurately as an assumption, an estimate, or whatever it is, so that you do not mislead anyone.

LISTING ALTERNATIVE COURSES OF ACTION

In this section, you list every solution or course of action that could possibly solve the central problem, along with the advantages and the disadvantages of each. Frequently at this point, you must go back and modify your central problem statement. You may think of a solution that is excellent, but not a solution to the central problem as you originally wrote it. To include this course of action, you must restate your central problem so that it fits with the alternative. This is important: Each solution or course of action listed must potentially solve the central problem as you have stated it. For example, perhaps you have worded the problem as, "Shall we develop a new product or modify an existing one?" However, during your listing of alternatives, you realize that you could acquire the rights to make a new product developed by someone else. You would want to change the central problem statement to something like, "Shall we develop a new product, acquiring it under license from someone else, or modify an existing product?"

Although theoretically an alternative may have all advantages and no disadvantages, this is highly unlikely. If this were the case, the solution would be self-evident and this problem-solving procedure would be superfluous.

DISCUSSING AND ANALYZING THE ALTERNATIVES

In this fourth section, you analyze and discuss the alternatives thoroughly in light of the relevant factors you have listed. As you proceed, additional relevant factors may become apparent. If so, go back and add them to your list. However, the focus of this section should always be to compare and to discuss in detail the relative importance of the advantages and disadvantages of each course of action. For example, the disadvantages of one course of action may be unimportant when measured against the relevant factors, or an alternative could have advantages that are very important.

At the end of the discussion and analysis, and even as you are doing the analysis, certain conclusions will start to become obvious. Do not state these conclusions in the discussion and analysis section, however; save them for the next section. In fact, here is an accurate test of the clarity of your thinking so far: Show the entire analysis up to this point to someone who is not particularly familiar with the problem. Have the individual read your central problem, the relevant factors that you have identified, the alternative courses of action with the advantages and disadvantages, and finally your discussion and analysis. Then ask for his conclusions. If they are identical to yours, you have correctly worded your discussion and analysis. If the conclusions are different, you have made an error either in the wording of the discussion and analysis or in the logic of your conclusions.

LISTING YOUR CONCLUSIONS

In this section, you list the conclusions arrived at as a result of your discussion and analysis. Do not add any explanations; they belong in the previous section. Also do not list conclusions based on information that is extraneous to your analysis: Your conclusions are based solely on your discussion and analysis. Another common error in this section is to restate relevant factors as conclusions.

MAKING RECOMMENDATIONS

In this section, you explicitly state the results of your analysis and your recommendations for what your client should do to solve the central problem you have identified and defined. As in the conclusions section, do not include extraneous information or explanations; all such explanations go in the discussion and analysis section. If you are presenting this orally, your client can always ask additional questions; if this is a written report, your client can always contact you for additional information. However, if you have done the analysis correctly, there will be no need to explain your recommendations; your reasons will be obvious from the discussion and analysis.

Many consultants first learning this methodology ask about the difference between conclusions and recommendations. With a recommendation, you put your reputation on the line. You make it clear and unequivocal what you want your client to do. You are accepting full responsibility for the recommendations you make. A conclusion is written in the passive tense: "Marketing research should be done." Recommendations are written in the imperative: "Initiate marketing research." If a conclusion on your list reads, "A new accountant should be hired," the recommendation would be, "Hire a new accountant."

THE CHARLES BENSON PROBLEM: A CASE STUDY

Now we're going to work on a problem, using the methodology just discussed. Assume that the chief engineer of the Zeus Engineering Company has come to you for consulting advice. You are to analyze the chief engineer's problem, define it explicitly, and, using the six-step methodology, make recommendations to him. The problem situation, forms that will help you use the problem-solving structure to arrive at the solution, the solution, and a step-by-step critique follow. Do not read the critique until you work the problem in detail. Time spent now in learning to use and apply this problem-solving methodology will pay dividends later on.

THE CHARLES BENSON PROBLEM[1]

Charles Benson, 35, had been employed as a design engineer for the Zeus Engineering Company for seven years. He was a reliable employee as well as a skillful and inventive engineer. Seeking to earn additional money, he decided to pursue his own business evenings and weekends. His products were similar to those made and sold by Zeus Engineering. Benson's supervisor found out about Benson's business but took no action for several months, believing that the business probably would not amount to much and that eventually Benson would drop it. However, one afternoon Benson's supervisor found him using company time and a company telephone to order materials for his business. The supervisor reprimanded Benson on the spot and warned him that such practices would not be tolerated. He also said that the incident would be reported to the chief engineer. A few days later Benson received written notice from the chief engineer that he must divest himself of the business within the month or resign from the company.

A month later, Benson's supervisor asked him directly for his decision. Benson stated that he had thought it over and talked with friends as well as officers of his union, and he had decided that he would not give up the business, nor would he resign. He argued that he was a good employee and that his outside company did not interfere with his work for Zeus Engineering. The small amount of business that he did could not hurt the company, and he was neither using company resources nor soliciting its accounts. Therefore, what he did with his own time was of no concern to the company. Benson's supervisor reported the conversation to the chief engineer.

You are the chief engineer. What action should you take? Using the forms that follow, solve the Charles Benson Problem using the six-step method. Do not read on until your solution is completely written out.

Form to Use Solving the Charles Benson Problem

Central Problem

_____

_____

_____

_____

_____

Relevant Factors [*List*]

1. _____

2. _____

3. _____

4. _____
5. _____
6. _____
7. _____
8. _____
9. _____
10. _____
11. _____
12. _____
13. _____
14. _____
15. _____

Alternative Courses of Action

1. _____
   _____

Advantages

A. _____
B. _____
C. _____

Disadvantages

A. _____
B. _____
C. _____

2. _____
   _____

Advantages

A. _____
B. _____
C. _____

Disadvantages

A. _____
B. _____
C. _____

3. _____

Advantages

A. _____
B. _____
C. _____

Disadvantages

A. _____
B. _____
C. _____

4. _____
_____

Advantages

A. _____
B. _____
C. _____

Disadvantages

A. _____
B. _____
C. _____

5. _____
_____

Advantages

A. _____
B. _____
C. _____

Disadvantages

A. _____
B. _____
C. _____

Discussion/Analysis

_____
_____
_____
_____
_____
_____
_____
_____
_____
_____
_____
_____
_____

Conclusions [*List*]

1. _____
2. _____
3. _____
4. _____
5. _____
6. _____
7. _____
8. _____
9. _____
10. _____

Recommendations [*List*]

1. _____
2. _____
3. _____
4. _____
5. _____
6. _____
7. _____
8. _____
9. _____
10. _____

SOLUTION TO THE CHARLES BENSON PROBLEM

THE CENTRAL PROBLEM

Begin by zeroing in on the central problem; this may require several attempts. Here are some alternative central problems, along with criticisms of each.

1. **Should Charles Benson be retained as an employee of the Zeus Engineering Company or fired?** This way of stating the problem limits the solutions to two courses of action: retaining or firing.

2. **What should be done about Charles Benson?** This statement lacks specifics about the problem that are important if the analysis is to be presented to someone else.

3. **What policy should Zeus Engineering set regarding employees establishing outside businesses?** This may be a problem that needs to be worked on, but its solution disregards the specifics of Benson's case, including the earlier warning.

4. **What should be done about Charles Benson's outside business, considering the fact that he was warned, that the union may take action, and that he has been a good employee and a superior engineer?** This one tries to incorporate all the relevant factors, resulting in an unwieldy and awkward statement of the central problem.

5. **How to keep Charles Benson with Zeus Engineering?** This statement assumes one alternative course of action as the solution before the analysis is done.

6. **What action should be taken regarding Charles Benson's outside business activities?** This is a simple, concise statement of the central problem, and probably the best. In any case, we will use it to proceed with our analysis.

THE RELEVANT FACTORS

Facts

1. Charles Benson has been a superior engineer and a reliable employee prior to the problem.

2. Benson has been with the company seven years.

3. The products that Benson makes are similar to the products made by Zeus Engineering.

4. Benson's supervisor knew about the business but took no action for several months.

5. Benson's supervisor observed him doing business on company time and using a company telephone.

6. The chief engineer ordered Benson in writing to drop the business or resign from the company

7. Benson states that he will not give up the business or resign from the company.

Assumptions

1. Benson has stated that he has contacted union officers and that they support his position. This statement is presumed to be true.

2. Benson states that he is not soliciting company accounts. This statement is presumed to be true.

3. Benson's current level of business will probably not hurt the company in the sense of his being a competitor. Nor will his present product line directly compete with Zeus Engineering's product line.

4. It is assumed that Benson's business activities are no longer done on company time and that his outside work does not currently interfere with his work at Zeus.

5. Current company policies do not specifically forbid an outside business, although conflict-of-interest laws, secrecy clauses, and the company's ownership of ideas resulting from company work have an impact on the legal aspects of the problem.

6. Benson is not a key employee, in the sense that his leaving the company will not of itself have a major negative impact on the company.

ALTERNATIVE COURSES OF ACTION

Alternative 1: Discharge Benson

Advantages

1. Will enforce discipline because Benson was warned that he must give up the business or resign.

2. Will discourage employees in the future from starting outside businesses.
3. Will solve any problem with conflict of interest arising from the nature of Benson's business.

Disadvantages
1. May lead to union problems, considering their current support of his position.
2. May lead to a morale problem if other employees believe that the company has acted unfairly.
3. Will lose a superior engineer and an otherwise reliable employee.

Alternative 2: Retain Benson

Advantages
I. Will avoid any problem with the union.
2. Will retain a superior engineer and an otherwise reliable employee.
3. Will avoid any feeling among other employees that Benson is being treated unfairly.

Disadvantages
1. May result in a discipline problem because Benson was ordered to give up the business or resign.
2. May eventually result in a direct conflict of interest due to the nature of the products and the customers.
3. Will effectively establish a company policy on this matter that may not be desirable.
4. Will encourage other employees to start outside businesses.

Alternative 3: Discharge Benson as an employee, but retain him as a consultant, the mechanism for the discharge being Benson's resignation

Advantages
1. May avoid any problem with the union.

2. Will reward Benson for past performance as a superior engineer and otherwise reliable employee.

3. Will maintain discipline because Benson was warned that he must give up the business or resign.

4. Will solve any problem of conflict of interest arising from the nature of Benson's business.

5. Will avoid setting policy or precedent regarding employee businesses.

Disadvantages

1. May encourage other employees to become consultants rather than employees of the company.

2. May set a policy of a different kind: that employees who start their own businesses will be retained as consultants.

3. May not solve the problem if Benson refuses to resign to accept a consultancy.

DISCUSSION AND ANALYSIS

1. Several important issues bear on this problem:

   A. The disciplinary issue and the fact that Benson was told to resign or to divest himself of his business.

   B. The importance of fair treatment and its potential effect on other employees. Benson has been a "superior engineer and otherwise reliable employee." There is currently no conflict of interest, and no further misuse of company time is anticipated.

   C. The policy issue. Retaining Benson will tend to set policy and may encourage other employees to start businesses of their own.

   D. Potential union involvement and a legal suit.

2. All of these issues are important and must be considered in the decision. Therefore:

   A. Discharging Benson should be avoided because doing so has considerable potential for affecting the morale of other employees (who may consider it unfair treatment of a superior and otherwise reliable employee who made one "mistake") and because it could lead to problems with the union and a legal suit.

B. Retaining Benson should also be avoided because of its potential effect on discipline and its tendency to set policy and encourage other employees to start their own businesses.

C. Discharging Benson as an employee but retaining him as a consultant is the only solution that is not negatively affected by the main issues.

3. If Benson fails to accept the solution of resigning to become a consultant, then he should be discharged. Under these circumstances there is less chance of his treatment being perceived as unfair. Although the company still risks union problems and a lawsuit, discipline will be maintained, no policy on outside businesses will be set, and other employees will not be encouraged to follow in Benson's footsteps.

CONCLUSIONS

1. Discharging Benson as an employee but retaining him as a consultant is the best solution, considering the major issues involved.

2. If Benson fails to resign to accept a consultancy, he should be discharged.

3. The consultancy solution must be presented to Benson as the only all-around fair solution, not as punishment, in order to maximize his accepting it; however, it must be presented in such a fashion that other employees recognize that resigning or discharged employees are not automatically hired as consultants.

4. A policy on outside employee business should be established and publicized as soon as possible.

RECOMMENDATIONS

1. Discharge Benson as an employee and hire him as a consultant.

2. If Benson fails to accept this solution, discharge him immediately.

3. Establish and publicize a policy on outside employee businesses as soon as possible.

PSYCHOLOGICAL TECHNIQUES FOR PROBLEM SOLVING

The logical, step-by-step technique to problem solving is very effective, but it is based primarily on using only the left half of the brain. But the human brain has two halves, so it makes sense to use the right brain for problem solving as well, especially because the right side is the creative half. Also, the step-by-step approach uses only your conscious mind, but you can use your unconscious mind as well.

Some consultants avoid psychological techniques like the plague. They think psychological approaches are too uncertain and smack of a touchy-feely orientation. These same consultants would be surprised to learn that they have already used some of these techniques without realizing it. Have you ever awakened in the morning with the solution to a problem that had been bothering you? When your conscious mind was unsuccessful at arriving at a solution, your subconscious mind took over while you were asleep. When you woke up, it turned the solution over to your conscious mind.

Many famous and successful people use the subconscious mind to solve important problems and help in their decision making. When Thomas Edison had a problem that his conscious mind was unable to handle, he went into a darkened room and lay down. He refused to be disturbed until the solution came to him.

Builder and wheeler-dealer Donald Trump tells of an instance when his subconscious mind worked on a problem even after his conscious mind had come to what proved to be the wrong decision. "The papers were being drawn up, and then one morning I woke up and it didn't feel right." So, listening to the conclusions of his subconscious mind, Trump changed his mind. He didn't invest in a project that many experts—and his conscious mind—said was a sound investment. Several months later, the company engaged in the project went bankrupt, and the investors lost all of their money.[2]

WHY THE SUBCONSCIOUS MIND CAN HELP YOU

After your conscious mind has collected and analyzed all the relevant factors in a situation, your subconscious mind sometimes comes to a better decision than your conscious mind. Why is this so?

1. **No Pressure**. Your conscious mind may be under the pressures of time, a demanding client, or deadlines. Your subconscious mind does not acknowledge these pressures.
2. **Distractions.** Your conscious mind may be distracted by friends, family, or business problems, by noise, or even by a lack of sleep. Not so your subconscious mind.
3. **Limited Time.** Most consultants don't have the time to work on a single problem all day on a continual basis. But your subconscious mind has all night, and it will work effortlessly on a problem that needs solving.
4. **False Knowledge.** For a variety of reasons, your conscious mind may be influenced by false assumptions or inaccurate facts. Your subconscious mind may know better.

HOW TO HELP YOUR SUBCONSCIOUS SOLVE YOUR CONSULTING PROBLEMS

If you want to use your subconscious mind to help you solve a problem, first learn all you can about the problem. As when you use the Staff Study Method, gather all the relevant factors and spend a great deal of time arriving at the central issue. You can also mull over the alternatives, talk to other people and get their opinions, and do additional research. Do this until you feel slightly overloaded.

Before you go to sleep, set aside a half-hour to an hour to do nothing but think about the problem, analyze the data, and think about potential solutions.

Go to sleep in the normal way. Do not try to force a solution to your problem. Although the solution is usually ready for you sometime the next morning, it could come in the middle of the night. If it does, be ready for it by having pencil and paper nearby, and quickly scribble down the solution and any other insights.

Sometimes answers come in indirect and strange ways. In 1846, when Elias Howe was struggling to invent the sewing machine, he was stumped. Howe had invented a machine that could push and extract a needle into and out of cloth. The problem was the thread. Because the thread went through an eye in the needle at the end opposite the point, the entire needle had to go through the material and back again in order to make a stitch. That was impossible. Howe was at an impasse. Then, for several nights in a row, Howe had identical dreams; Howe's subconscious mind was trying to tell him something. In the dreams, Howe found himself on a South Pacific island where natives armed with spears danced around him. But the spears were very strange. Each spearhead had a conspicuous hole. Only after several days did Howe realize the solution to his problem: to construct sewing needles with eyes for the thread near the point rather than at the opposite end.

If you want outstanding solutions to your clients' problems, use both your right and left brains and your conscious and subconscious minds.

Here are some books that can help you:

> *The Confident Decision Maker: How to Make the Right Business and Personal Decisions Every Time* by Roger Dawson (Quill)

> *Decision Traps: Ten Barriers to Brilliant Decision-Making and How to Overcome Them* by J. Edward Russo and Paul J. H. Schoemaker (Fireside Press)

> *101 Creative Problem Solving Techniques: The Handbook of New Ideas for Business* by James M. Higgins (New Management Pub. Co.)

SUMMING UP

In the next chapter, we will see how to do the research that is necessary and that goes into any problem-solving activity.

NOTES

1. Adapted from George R. Terry, "Theodore Thorburn Turner," a case in *Principles of Management*, 4th ed. (Homewood, IL: Richard D. Irwin, 1964), p. 222.
2. Donald J. Trump and Tony Schwartz, *The Art of the Deal* (New York: Warner Books, 1987), pp. 27–28.

12

HOW TO RESEARCH

RESEARCH IS an important part of many types of consulting. Whether you are finding the demand for a product or service, discovering what the consumer wants or does not want, or looking for sources of raw materials, products, or capital—all such projects require some type of research. Peter Drucker said that two of the most important things any company must do is to find out who their customers are and what these customers value. This is true for business, including consulting, and it can be learned only through research.

In this chapter we will look at how you can do this research easily and for the most part at low cost. Knowing how to do research is like anything else. Until you know how, it is a mystery and seems to be not only complicated, but almost impossible to master, like flying a jet airliner or performing surgery. But to pilots or surgeons who have been properly trained, performing these complex tasks becomes almost routine. Research is much the same. If you haven't done it before, research may appear forbidding. But once you know how to do it, you will find that most of the research that you need for consulting is very simple. Usually, you have to learn something a little out of the ordinary only if you need to use some of the more sophisticated statistical techniques, and you can learn even these techniques in a night school course or from a book.

THE TWO BASIC KINDS OF RESEARCH

All research can be categorized into two basic types: primary and secondary. Primary research is research that you do yourself. Secondary research is information that someone else has researched and published, such as in a book, in an article, or on the Internet. All you need to do is find it.

For example, let's say you want to research a company. Always go to secondary sources first. If the company is public, check with *Standard and Poor's* and *Moodys* at your library. Get a copy of the company's annual stockholder report. If the company is fairly large, they may have a public relations department. Call and ask for information about the company, catalogues, product information, and the like. Check the company's Web site. This is all secondary research. Now, if you went beyond this secondary research and talked to the company's customers, suppliers, or employees, you would be conducting primary research.

Entrepreneur E. Joseph ("Joe") Cossman was my good friend, and we even wrote a book together. Joe was the man who sold over a million ant farms and various other products. After investing a great deal of time and money in his first deal in exporting laundry soap, he found that his supplier had disappeared. He went to the New York City Public Library and consulted a series of books that still exist called the *Thomas Register of Manufacturers*. In it he found more than 70 soap manufacturers throughout the United States. That's secondary research. Then he began calling each and every manufacturer on this list until he found one that manufactured, and had available, the laundry soap he sought. That's primary research.

This anecdote not only shows the difference between the two types, but it also demonstrates that you usually do secondary research before you do primary research. There are two reasons for doing research in this order:

1. **Secondary research is the far less expensive of the two.**
   Someone else has already done it. You might find your answer

during your secondary research and never need to do primary research at all. For example, if Joe had been able to identify which soap manufacturers made and had laundry soap available, he could have made only a single call to confirm that fact and place the order, not the more than 50 calls he actually made.

2. **In more complex primary research, you want to know all about the subject before you begin to invest your valuable time and resources.**

SOURCES OF SECONDARY RESEARCH

1. **Chambers of Commerce.** Chambers of commerce have all sorts of demographic information about geographical areas in which you may be interested, including income, education, businesses and their size, and sales volume. Check the phone book for your local chamber of commerce.

2. **Trade Associations.** Trade associations also have information regarding the background of their members and their industries. The easy way to locate them is on the Internet. (More on this in Chapter 16.)

3. **Trade Magazines and Journals.** Trade journals and magazines frequently survey their readership. They also contain articles of interest to you that describe competitive companies, products, strategies, and markets.

4. **Small Business Administration.** The U.S. Small Business Administration (SBA) was set up to help small business. Whether you own a small business or are a marketing planner in a large company, the studies sponsored can be extremely valuable to anyone doing research in the situational analysis of a marketing plan. The many printed aids supplied include statistics, maps, national market analyses, national directories for use in marketing, basic library reference sources, information on various types of business (including industry average investments and cost), and factors to consider in locating a shopping center. The SBA's Web site is at http://www.sba.gov.

5. **Databases.** Databases are electronic collections of relevant data collected by trade journals, newspapers, and many other public or

private sources of information. You can access them by computer, and companies sell the computer time to search their databases. Some databases can be searched free.

6. **Earlier Studies**. Earlier marketing studies are sometimes made available to interested companies or individuals. These studies may cost $40,000 or more if they have been done as primary research, and several thousand dollars for a short report is not atypical. The results are not sold cheaply, although in effect you are sharing the cost with other companies that purchase the results. Nevertheless, if the alternative is to do the entire primary research project yourself, it may be far cheaper to pay the price.

7. **U.S. Industrial Outlook.** Every year until 2000, the U.S. government published a document known as the *U.S. Industrial Outlook*, which contained detailed information on the prospects on more than 300 manufacturing and service industries. Because of its popularity and usefulness, the International Trade Administration is now working on an online version, *The U.S. Industry and Trade Outlook*. As of this writing, this new version is under development. You can check the latest status at http://www.ita.doc.gov/td /industry/otea/outlooknews.htm.

8. **The Statistical Abstract of the United States.** This abstract is also an annual publication of the U.S. government. It contains a wealth of detailed statistical data having to do with everything from health to food consumption, population, public school finances, individual income tax returns, mortgage debt, science and engineering, student numbers, and motor vehicle travel. It is published by the U.S. Department of Commerce, Bureau of the Census. It is now available online at http://www.census.gov /compendia/statab/.

9. **U.S. Department of Commerce.** If you are interested in export, the U.S. Department of Commerce has numerous sources of information, including amounts exported to foreign countries in the preceding year, major consumers of certain items, and detailed information on doing business in countries around the world. You can find the office of your local U.S. Department of Commerce in the U.S. government listings in your telephone book. The department's home page is at http://www.commerce.gov, with links to many other important subdivisions.

10. **U.S. Government.** The U.S. government itself has so many sources of information that it is impossible to list them all here. But so much information is available, and so much of it is free, that you would be well advised to see what can be obtained from federal government sources. The master site is at http://www.usa.gov.

11. **Internet.** This relatively new source of secondary research will be covered more completely in Chapter 16. Meanwhile, here are some additional sources pertaining to marketing research that you may find useful:

> *Free Marketing Research Sources.* ResearchInfo.com provides numerous links to marketing research resources at http://www.researchinfo.com.

> *PJ Marketing Research* provides links to worldwide marketing research experience, including how to write a market research report, at http://www.pj-marketing.com.

> *Market research and Internet marketing research,* KnowThis.com provides links to articles at http://www.knowthis .com/research.

> Marketing Research *Home Page.* This is an on-line supplement that accompanies a textbook, *Marketing Research,* by Donald R. Lehmann, Sunil Gupta, and Joel H. Steckel. This site provides you with access to a multitude of marketing research information sources and links, arranged by topic at http://www.prenhall.com/lehmanngupta/.

> *Quirk's Marketing Research Review.* Quirk has a great deal of information, articles, and other sources at http://www.quirks.com.

THE LIBRARY: STILL A GOOD BET AS A STARTING POINT

Your local library may still be your best starting point for many types of secondary research. First, tell your librarian what you need. Frequently, librarians can assist you, either sending you directly to the documents you need or giving you likely sources to check.

Next check some general sources at the library, such as an encyclopedia. These can give you general information about your topic and will also list additional sources, such as other books. Each source will provide not only additional information, but more sources. So the pyramid effect builds as you progress, and you can connect with almost unlimited sources of information about your subject matter.

EXAMPLES OF SIMPLE PRIMARY RESEARCH

The kind of research you do is limited only by your imagination. Some research can be done, even the primary type, at very little cost except for your time. Here are some examples of simple marketing research done by, or for, small businesses.[1]

1. **License Plate Analysis.** In many states, license plate numbers can lead you to information about where car owners live. Therefore, simply by taking down the numbers of cars parked in your location and contacting the appropriate state agency, you can estimate the area from which you draw business. Knowing where your customers live can help you in your advertising or in targeting your approach to promotion. By the same method you can find who your competitors' customers are.

2. **Telephone Number Analysis.** Telephone numbers can also tell you the areas in which people live. You can obtain customers' telephone numbers from sales slips, credit card slips, or checks. Again, knowing where they live will give you excellent information about their lifestyles.

3. **Coded Coupons**. The effectiveness of your advertising vehicle can easily be checked by coding coupons used for discounts or inquiries made about products. You can find out the areas that your customers come from, as well as which vehicle brought them your message.

4. **People Watching.** Simply looking at your customers can tell you a great deal about them. How are they dressed? How old are they? Are they married or single? Do they have children? Many owners use this method intuitively to get a feel about their customers. However, a little sophistication with a tally sheet for a week can provide much more accurate information simply, easily,

and without cost. It may confirm what you've known all along, or it may completely change your opinion of your typical customer.

MORE COMPLEX RESEARCH PROJECTS, AND HOW TO DO THEM

Some of the primary research you may need can be done only in a complex project. The four basic methods of doing this are by means of (1) personal surveys, (2) the mail, (3) the telephone, and (4) electronic surveys. Usually, these have to do with marketing research, though the methodologies work with all types of research. Each method has its advantages and disadvantages.

PERSONAL INTERVIEW SURVEYS

The personal interview survey is one of the most frequently used methods in marketing and in other types of primary research, primarily because of its flexibility. Of the three most popular methods—mail surveys, telephone surveys, and personal interview surveys—personal interview surveys collect the best feedback from voice, facial expressions, and body language. Many aids can be used in the survey, including pictures, problems, diagrams, and advertising copy. In addition, the selection of respondents can be very precise. For example, a marketing research study of brand preference for beer eliminated individuals who were intoxicated at the time of the testing. Accurate elimination due to intoxication would have been more difficult to determine without personal, face-to-face contact.

Furthermore, because of the rapport that can be obtained face to face and the reluctance of many potential respondents to reject a face-to-face request, the number of refused responses is much less when compared to other survey methods.

However, face-to-face interviews have their drawbacks. The primary disadvantage is their cost. The personal interview survey is the most expensive method. Even though cost can be minimized by keeping the researcher at one location or by using a limited number of respondents for exploratory research, you can expect to pay more for research done by this method than by any other.

MAIL SURVEYS

With the mail survey method, a single questionnaire is prepared, duplicated, and sent to a list of potential respondents. The method requires minimal time for gathering the research, and for this reason it is potentially very economical. In exchange for the costs of printing the questionnaire, mailing it, and providing return postage, a completed interview is accomplished.

Despite this major advantage, there are drawbacks for mail surveys. First and primary is probably the response rate. The response rate from the general public is generally very low, sometimes less than 15 percent. To get the maximum response rate, you have to make it as easy as possible for the respondent to send back a completed survey. This means keeping the questionnaire relatively short and easy to answer, as well as providing a self-addressed, postage-paid envelope so that the respondent needs only to put the answered questionnaire in the envelope and put it in the mailbox. It was once thought that personalization, such as hand-addressed envelopes, would add to the response rate. However, it has been found that computer labels can be used without a significant loss. Other factors that increase the response to mail surveys are the length of the interview, subject matter, use of mail and/or phone reminders, and the use of incentives. Reminders can have a tremendous effect, in some cases doubling or tripling mail survey response rates. Incentives can be given after you receive the completed questionnaire, or they can be included right in the envelope along with it.

A typical incentive is money. A very successful survey from one researcher included a questionnaire that was accompanied by a brand-new one-dollar bill. In the cover letter, the dollar bill was described as a small gift in appreciation for the time spent in filling out the survey. The bill was extremely effective in increasing respondents' results because of its psychological impact. On the one hand, it is very difficult, if not impossible, to throw the "gift" away. On the other, it is equally difficult to pocket the money without feeling guilty if the survey is not completed.

However, if you are going to include something of value to increase response, you may need to advertise this fact on the outside envelope. A textbook publisher wanted to use this technique to increase the response rate in a survey of professors. A one-dollar bill was included in every envelope, which was also marked with the publisher's logo. Unfortunately, the publisher had been using a similar envelope for its advertising literature. The marketing researcher won no kudos when it was discovered that most of the recipients, who thought that this was more advertising literature, had thrown away the envelopes unopened with their dollar bills still inside. (The results may also say something about the company's advertising material.)

Mail surveys can be highly successful, however, for special populations for whom good lists are available, and high cooperation is possible because of the population's intrinsic interest in a given topic.

TELEPHONE SURVEYS

Telephone surveys combine some of the advantages and disadvantages of both mail and personal interview surveys. Like mail surveys, telephone surveys avoid interview travel expenses, and they are useful for research over wide geographical areas. They are more flexible than mail surveys because, based on verbal feedback, interviewers can ask more detailed questions or encourage respondents to answer questions when respondents hesitate. However, it is more difficult to obtain the same rapport than is possible through face-to-face personal interview surveys, because researchers lose the advantage of what they can see. Additional problems with telephone interviews are that respondents must be limited to those with telephones and with listed numbers and that there is a nonresponse bias due to busy signals, no answers, and refusals, which are more common than with personal interview surveys.

For more than 50 years, the most widely used method for obtaining market research and other survey data has been by telephone. There are two major reasons for the switch to telephone surveys:

1. Telephone sampling became a much more attractive alternative as the percentage of households with telephones increased from less than half before World War II to more than 90 percent by the 1960s and to a current level of about 95 percent.

2. The costs of door-to-door surveys has increased steeply due to the reduced availability of respondents. The rapid rise in the percentage of working women means that it is time-consuming

and costly to find people at home, even if interviewing is done on evenings or weekends. For door-to-door interviews, this translates into large interviewer travel expenditures and cuts interviewing costs roughly in half.

However, because of increased use of the telephone for sales as well as for research, potential survey subjects have become increasingly less cooperative, and the telephone has become correspondingly less useful.

ELECTRONIC SURVEYS

Widespread computer ownership created a new way to reach the general population and administer surveys, just as rising telephone ownership once did. Given the potentially favorable costs of electronic surveys, the interesting capabilities of computer-based data collection, and the declining effectiveness of telephone surveys, it seems likely that electronic surveys will heavily displace telephone surveys as the method of choice within the next quarter century.

Every new technology brings sampling challenges, but regardless of the technology, some sampling basics remain. Samples that depend solely on voluntary response will almost always be subject to significant biases. Samples gained by first attempting to gather information in a survey aimed at the target market from which you want the information will always yield more reliable results. It is tempting simply to put a questionnaire on a Web site and to collect information from whoever happens to respond, but this approach is simply a more technologically sophisticated version of a volunteer survey with potentially large biases. Unless the site attracts the population you want to survey, this is not a good way to proceed.

You can capture reasonably good samples for electronic surveys in two ways:

1. Many companies that sell to businesses have e-mail directories of their customers. This allows them either to e-mail questionnaires to a particular sample or to post the questionnaire on a Web site and use e-mail to ask customers to visit the site and complete the questionnaire. As with mail surveys, multiple follow-ups will increase response. You can also rent e-mail lists of this type from e-mail list brokers.

2. You can sample visitors to a Web site after you have prequalified them as part of a target market. Visitors can be asked to register when they come to the site, and the information in these registrations can be used to qualify and generate a list for later sampling purposes. Visitors who can be qualified immediately due to a purchase or with an expression of interest for information can also be taken immediately to a questionnaire.

YOU CAN RESEARCH ANYTHING

Research is a very broad topic. There are consultants whose entire practices consist of nothing but research. These include marketing research firms, political pollsters, television (the Nielsen rating folks), and even so-called finders. The latter make their money from finding everything from venture capital to a buyer for several tons of scrap plastic or for reclaimed railroad track. All this tells us that we can research anything and find the answer somewhere, if we ask enough people or look in enough places.

Here are some books that will help you:

The 10 Minute Guide to Business Research by Thomas Pack (Que)

Find It Fast: How to Uncover Expert Information on Any Subject by Robert I. Berkman (HarperCollins)

Successful Business Research by Rhonda Abrams (The Planning Shop)

SUMMING UP

Now we are ready to look at a very important but frequently ignored topic that can affect your consulting practice throughout its existence: ethics. You will find this discussion in the next chapter.

NOTE

1. Many of these ideas were suggested by J. Ford Laumer Jr., James R. Hams, and Hugh J. Guffey Jr., all professors of marketing at Auburn University of Auburn, Alabama, at the time, in their booklet *Learning about Your Market,* published by the U.S. Small Business Administration.

13

THE IMPORTANCE OF ETHICS IN CONSULTING

SOME TIME AGO I completed an in-depth study of leadership and later published the results in a book. After surveying more than 200 combat leaders, including 60 generals and admirals, eight principles showed up time after time. The principles did not appear, even by frequency, in any particular order—except one. This principle was clearly so important that many of the individuals I surveyed wrote me notes or letters to explain their feelings. This first principle, or what I call the universal law of leadership, was to maintain absolute integrity.

The complete list of principles is:

1. Maintain absolute integrity.
2. Know your stuff.
3. Declare your expectations.
4. Show uncommon commitment.
5. Expect positive results.
6. Take care of your people.

7. Put duty before self.
8. Get out in front.

When you are practicing as a consultant, you are in a leadership role. You are helping, coaching, and influencing someone else to reach a better state. You are a leader. Therefore ethics, closely aligned with integrity, must be a primary consideration.

Ethics has a strong impact on everything we do as consultants. This chapter explains why the application of ethics to a consulting practice is so important, along with some thoughts on how we consultants must practice ethically. As we will see, ethics is not simply a matter of obeying the law; nor are ethical problems always so simple.

BUSINESS ETHICS: SOMETIMES NOT CLEAR-CUT

If ethical questions could be expressed in clear, black-or-white terms, decisions regarding corporate conduct would be easy. But black-or-white decisions are seldom the case. Let me tell you about a few situations where decisions of business ethics were not all that straightforward.

ETHICS VERSUS JOBS: THE LOCKHEED CASE

Thirty years ago, senior Lockheed executives paid bribes to members of the Japanese government in exchange for subsidizing the purchase of the L-1011 passenger jet for All Nippon Airways. As a result, Lockheed Chairman Daniel Haughton and Vice Chairman and President Carl Kotchian were forced to resign from their posts in disgrace early in 1976. They gained nothing from the sales of the L-1011 in any way. Why did these two Lockheed executives commit such a stupid act?

In 1972–1973, 25,000 Lockheed employees faced a significant threat of unemployment after cutbacks in the U.S. government order of military aircraft and missiles. Because of delays due to difficulty with the foreign supplier of the L-1011's engines, All Nippon Airways was the only major airline that had not already made a commitment to purchase a wide-body jet from a competitor. If a major contract could not be secured for the L-1011, many jobs at Lockheed would be lost.

The two executives gained not a cent in monetary or any other advantage from their act, which was committed solely to help their employees. Had Lockheed simply abandoned the L-1011, instead of paying the bribe, stock price analysts determined that company earnings, stock price, and bonuses and stock options for the two Lockheed executives involved would have substantially increased. Everyone knew that because of the delays the L-1011 was a loser and could no longer make money. In fact, the project never made any money despite these and other sales. The bribe was clearly against U.S. law and a very poor management decision.

But was it a violation of ethics?[1]

THE ETHICS OF MARKETING RESEARCH

Marketing research can be completely honest and aboveboard. However, marketing research is frequently competitive research, and the presence of competitiveness presents an opportunity for questionable practices. Let me tell you about my own introduction into this field.

As a newly promoted manager of research and development, I studied the possible solution to a problem my company faced. Because the business was heavily government oriented, our production was a continual series of peaks and valleys. The government orders all came during one part of the year, when we would become extremely busy, producing like mad to fulfill our contracts. Other parts of the year, we had practically no business at all, and our workers were idle. The choices in such circumstances are usually pretty limited. We could either try to manufacture our products for someone else, retain our workers and pay them for essentially doing nothing for part of the year, or fire our workforce every year. None of these solutions was very attractive.

Obviously, making a product to fill the valleys when no government work was under contract would solve the problem. Our company was very much involved in fiberglass protective products, such as pilot helmets. An additional fiberglass product that we considered was personal protective body armor for the military and police, but we knew very little about this market. To learn more, we decided to hire a marketing research firm as an independent consultant. Bids were requested from several of the leading firms in our area. The firm that won the opportunity to undertake this task had a fine proposal and a good reputation for performance and ethics.

One aspect of the research bothered me. Because the information we required involved the total size of the market along with competing products, sales, and other proprietary information, I wondered how such information could be obtained. As I recall, I even commented to one of the executives of the research firm that I didn't know how they were going to get this information because obviously they couldn't just call up a competitive company and ask for it.

Two months after the contract began, I was given a final report of several hundred pages, along with a personal presentation by a representative from the marketing research firm. The information was exact, precise, and explicit. It had all the information about our potential competitors, the size of the market, the sales, and even in some cases strategies that the competition intended to follow in the coming years. I was amazed at the detail. Innocently I asked how such information could be obtained. I was told that the gathering had been done in a very straightforward fashion. The researcher had simply called the president of every company in the business and misidentified himself as a student doing a report on the unusual product of body armor. In almost every case, this researcher had gotten complete information that was highly competitive and proprietary.

WHAT WASHINGTON RESEARCHERS DISCOVERED BY SURVEYING THEIR SEMINAR ATTENDEES

Washington Researchers was a well-known consulting firm that conducted competitive research on companies, products, and strategies. It also conducted seminars around the country on how to accomplish various types of competitive research. It is still in existence.

Almost thirty years ago I had the good fortune to attend one of these seminars. As a part of the seminar, all attendees participated in a survey of company research techniques. This survey was developed originally because participants had asked the company for judgments about the ethics of various companies' means of information gathering. Washington Researchers decided that the issues were too complex to allow for easy answers. So they decided to conduct this survey as a simple measurement of individual and company practices. Most had to do with the technique of pretending to be someone you were not.

On a confidential survey form, they asked participants to assume that each was asked to find out everything they could about the finances, products, marketing strategies, and other aspects of their company's closest competitor. Several research techniques were suggested, all of questionable ethics. The participants were to respond either yes or no to each. In all cases, most attendees stated that competitors used these questionable techniques, their companies used them, and they used them themselves.

AN EXECUTIVE RECRUITING STORY

Along the same lines, I would like to tell you this story about executive recruiting. The neophyte executive recruiter (a headhunter) has two tasks. One is to cold call companies, as described in Chapter 2, to obtain what are known as job orders—the authority to do a search. The other task is to identify candidates with the qualities specified by companies and to recruit for the position. Both components of this task are challenging.

This neophyte headhunter was told to cold call a list of potential clients and get as many job orders as he could and then to start recruiting candidates for these jobs. Naturally, not all the companies called were in need of a headhunter's services, and some of the contacts were not particularly polite. One of the companies this neophyte called was the Dynamic Petroleum Company, whose vice president of engineering gave a most memorable response. He began to yell, shout, and curse at the headhunter. He said that he never dealt with headhunters, that no one in his company was permitted to talk to headhunters, that he fired any of his engineers or even his secretary for talking to headhunters, and that furthermore if he was ever called again, he would institute legal action. With that he hung up. This unnerved the neophyte, who was observed by the president of the search firm. The president of the search firm said, "Let me show you how to handle this. A guy like this isn't a client; he is the source of our product. These are the people whom we recruit from."

The president immediately phoned that same vice president at Dynamic Petroleum. He said that he was a college student whose professor had told him to contact one of the petroleum engineers at Dynamic, that he had forgotten this engineer's name, and that he was afraid to call his professor back. Over the next half hour, this vice president of engineering proceeded to read off the names of over 150 different petroleum engineers in his organization, describing them by specialty, background, years of experience, and personal appearance. He gave away an immense amount of intelligence, which was ultimately used by the headhunter who was calling for recruiting purposes.

I once told this story to a group of approximately 50 managers. Several commented on the lack of ethics of the search firm president. But one individual present was himself the president of a search firm. He protested, "But that's the business. That's how it's done. You can't be a headhunter if you don't operate this way."

Again, do not draw any conclusions about my personal feelings regarding these matters. I want you merely to consider that at least some headhunters consider this practice common, if not ethical.

Now before you adopt a situational ethical view, consider the following: These techniques, sometimes called pretexting, were all considered legal at the time. However, then came, in 2006, the Hewlett-Packard case. Chairwoman Patricia Dunn was accused of spying on some of her employees, leading to a number of other actions. The FTC and several state attorneys general eventually got involved and brought enforcement actions against pretexters for allegedly violating federal and state laws on fraud, misrepresentation, and unfair competition.[2] So, if now you use pretexting, you can go to jail.

A JAPANESE VIEW OF DUTY

When I was his student, Peter Drucker told me the story of a large Japanese company that wanted to open an American plant. After an investigation of many locations in several different states, a suitable site was located. So important was this operation that a special ceremony was scheduled that included the governor, many senior state officials, and the CEO from Japan.

The Japanese CEO spoke fairly good English; however, to ensure that everything he said would be understood despite his accent, the company hired an American of Japanese descent to translate the speech into English.

With dignity and measured tones, the Japanese CEO began to speak, noting the great honor it was for his company to be able to locate in this particular state in the United States with mutual benefits to his company and the states' citizens. He also discussed the benefits to the local economy and to Japanese–American friendship. Then, nodding in the direction of the governor and other state officials, he said: "Furthermore, Mr. Governor and senior officials, please understand that we know our duty. When the time comes that you retire from your honored positions, my corporation will not forget and will repay you for the efforts which you have expended in our behalf in giving us this opportunity."

The Japanese–American translator was horrified. Instantly she made a decision to omit these remarks in her English translation. The Japanese CEO, who understood enough English to realize what she had done but not why, continued his speech as if nothing had happened. Later, when the two were alone, the executive asked the translator, "How could you exclude my reassurances to the governor and officials? Why did you leave this important part out of my speech?" Only then could it be explained to his amazement that what is ethical, even a duty, in Japan is considered unethical and corrupt in the United States.

ETHICS AND THE LAW ARE NOT THE SAME THING

Some years ago, when jet turbine engines were first being developed, General Electric, Westinghouse, and Allis-Chalmers formed what would technically be considered a cartel. Cartels, of course, are illegal under the antitrust laws of this country, and this one was declared illegal and abandoned. But the net result was that when the cartel broke up, prices went up, with a resulting drop in demand, bringing a considerable loss of jobs and the eventual bankruptcy of Allis-Chalmers. Again, the question is, although I don't recommend either breaking the law or establishing cartels, was it ethical to cause a bankruptcy with the related loss of many jobs?

An even more glaring example of the distinction between law and ethics occurred in Nazi Germany. Under Nazi law, Jews were persecuted: They could not practice in the professions, they could not own land, they could not be employed by non-Jews, and they could not attend universities. Later, they were rounded up, sent to concentration camps, forced to work as slave laborers, starved, and killed. It was against German law to help Jews. To help them, you had to disobey the law. You risked going to jail or worse. Were those who disobeyed the law and sent to jail unethical? Obviously not.

TYPICAL PROBLEMS PERTAINING TO ETHICS IN CONSULTING

In the practice of consulting, you will eventually be involved in numerous ethical questions. Fortunately, some of them can be anticipated. Consider the following example from my own seminars and courses on consulting. Usually there is no simple solution, although some issues are easier to resolve than others.

1. **The client already knows the solution that she wants to a problem.** This situation typically occurs when a client requires an outsider to confirm information that he already knows. Suppose a division of a company has already done a very thorough internal study suggesting that it should get into the such and such business. However, because the study was done by the division itself, it is suspect. Top management may wish to have an independent study conducted by a consultant. You may be engaged by that division of the company, and yet the client makes it very clear to you what answer is expected. Do you accept such a consulting engagement?

Some consultants say that a foregone conclusion does not make any difference. You are getting paid to do the study even if the answer is known. If the client makes it very clear at the beginning that she expects a yes answer, that's what she is paying for and that is what she will get. Other consultants take the position that they will do the job and provide whatever answer results from their analysis. If the client insists on having a yes answer and nothing else (usually this insistence is not stated explicitly but is very subtle), they will refuse to undertake the study.

In such instances, you have to consider many different issues. It will be difficult to escape your need for cash and possible additional business from this client later. But there is no right answer. You have to consider it yourself, and my only advice is to think about the alternatives now because you will almost certainly encounter this situation sooner or later.

2. **The client wants you to omit information from your written report.** This request generally occurs when you have included information in your report that your client feels will hurt him with others, either inside or outside his company. After reviewing your report in draft form, he may ask you to delete certain information. Some consultants take the position that they will decide how to handle such a request based on the information's relevance to the central issue. If it is not relevant, they will exclude it. Otherwise they will refuse. However, other consultants feel that because the client is paying and because "the customer is always right," if the customer wants information left out, it will be left out. Still others stand on their professionalism and refuse to change so much as a comma. You pay your money and you take your choice.

3. **The client wants proprietary information that you learned while employed with someone else.** This situation usually arises when you first become a consultant. A former competitor immediately contacts you about a potential engagement. It soon becomes clear, however, that he is hiring you not for what you can do but rather for what you know about your former employer. This situation can also come up when a potential client realizes that you have completed a consulting job for a competitor.

If clearly all the potential client wants is proprietary information, most consultants will refuse to get involved. Unless you do professional industrial spying—which, by the way, is illegal aside from being uneth-ical—a client who hires you for information you learned working for a competitor will suspect you of betraying his proprietary information to some future client. As a result, he will probably not hire you for any other purpose.

On the other hand, if a competitor wants to hire you for a job sim-ilar to one you did as a consultant in another company, it may be com-pletely acceptable. "I heard about the great job that you did with the ABC Company; we'd like you to do the same thing for us," he may say. One fully ethical approach is to tell your potential client something like this: "I'd be happy to do this for you if I can get permission from the ABC Company. I don't think that I would be giving away any of their secrets if I did the same job for you. However, since you two are com-petitors, I would rather have their concurrence. Is that okay with you?"

A question that sometimes comes up is who owns proprietary data or information that you develop as a consultant? Usually this is more of a legal question than an ethical one. Many companies, as well as the U.S. government, are well aware of this issue. Your contract may specify that your client owns all data developed unless you negotiate the contract otherwise. Anything that you develop as part of a consulting engage-ment but consider your own might possibly be challenged in a court of law in the future. Therefore, if you think something that comes out of an engagement may be useful to you in the future, it is better to agree what will belong to whom up front.

For some types of information, claiming rights may not be a prob-lem. It's just too difficult to prove that techniques or methodologies that you developed came out of one specific assignment, not out of many. However, some marketing research done for a company or information about a company clearly belongs to the organization for which you developed it. So in all cases, it is better to make ownership clear con-tractually. Then you know where you stand from the start. Most com-panies could care less about who owns consulting methods or tech-niques. But they rightfully feel that the information developed from these techniques, which they pay for, belongs to them.

4. **The client wants you to lie to the boss.** This request usual-

ly comes from a lower-level manager who wants you to lie to a manager at a higher level or from the president of a company who wants you to lie to the board of directors or someone else outside the company. Some consultants have stated that it depends on the lie. They might go along with a harmless, so-called white lie to protect someone's feelings. Others would not.

Let's say that you are on assignment for the vice president of a company that is owned by the president, and as a part of this job you have to analyze the efficiency and effectiveness of all managers working for the vice president, one of whom happens to be the president's son. You rate the son as a very poor executive. When the vice president sees the report, she says something like this: "Look, the president of our company has a heart condition. If you report that his son is a very poor executive, it could easily upset him and may actually bring on a heart attack. How about toning this down a bit and saying that this executive is unsuited to his present position?" Many consultants would consider this a white lie and would go along with the request. Other consultants might take the position that this executive was very poor and that this is what they intended to put in their report, heart attack or no.

Other lies are far more questionable in both their motives and the net result on the company officials, the company's well-being, or even the general public. Some would say that agreeing to lie would depend on the effect that the lie would cause. Others say simply that they would refuse to lie under any circumstances.

5. **You are a headhunter, and a member of a client's company wants you to recruit him for a job elsewhere.** This situation again demonstrates that what might be ethical under some circumstances is totally unethical under others. To honor this request is unethical for any headhunter. Under no conditions can a headhunter recruit from his client's company, and no ethical headhunter would even consider doing so. If a member of a client's organization wants you to recruit him, you should first seek approval from the individual's boss. Alternatively, you can refer the individual to another headhunter.

A question that comes up, however, is for how long a period after you complete a search for a company is the firm still considered a client? Few would regard a company as a client after five years with no new assignments. For a shorter period, you have to make your own decisions. Many headhunters indicate that clientage lasts something less than three years after a search is completed.

6. **The client wants you to bill for more or for less than the actual amount of billable time.** Inappropriate billing can be unlawful as well as unethical. And you can be certain that the IRS would take a very dim view of this suggestion. But, aside from its possible legal connotations, it is also a lie. Would you do it or not?

All these are typical problems, and you might see other forms of them in your practice. In all cases, only you can decide on the action to take. Some otherwise unethical practices are often considered ethical because of the nature of the work accomplished. These would probably include the marketing research and headhunting situations noted earlier, which are acceptable in their professions but certainly considered unethical for anyone else. By analogy consider wartime spying. The professional soldier is prohibited from spying. Spying is illegal, and a soldier caught spying may be hanged. Yet for a spy, spying is considered ethical behavior.

Years ago, a young Air Force lieutenant was ordered by a superior officer to falsify a report to make a score from a simulated aircraft attack appear better than it actually was. This lieutenant faced a serious moral and ethical dilemma; his future career in the Air Force seemed to hinge on an outright lie. Despite considerable pressure, the lieutenant resisted the pressure and refused to lie. The threat of punitive action was never carried out, and he had an outstanding career right up until the time he left the Air Force. Today this lieutenant has major responsibilities outside the government that have little to do with flying. He rates his success in entirely different activities in no small part to this instance when he decided who he was and how he would live his life.

Most ethical questions are not as simple to sort out or as easy to resolve. Frequently the decision is not whether to lie, cheat, or steal but of doing either the greater good or the lesser evil. Whatever you do, you must be able to respect yourself in the future. Otherwise you will be useless to your clients and to yourself.

Entire books have been written on this complex subject. In the space of this chapter, I can offer only three final thoughts:

1. Before doing something questionable, remember that you have to see yourself in the mirror every morning. You'll be a lot happier with what you see if you don't lie, cheat, or steal.
2. Peter Drucker pointed out that ethical questions are frequently complex, so he recommended that we measure ethics and integrity primarily by the oath of the Greek physician Hippocrates: *Primum non nocere* (First, do no harm).
3. The consulting profession has a code of ethics.

THE INSTITUTE OF MANAGEMENT CONSULTANTS (IMC) CODE OF ETHICS

The IMC is a not-for-profit, national professional association founded in 1968 to set standards of professionalism for the management consulting profession. You can find IMC's address in Appendix D. IMC members pledge *in writing* to abide by the Institute's Code of Ethics. Their adherence to the Code signifies the voluntary assumption of self-discipline above and beyond the requirements of the law. Key provisions of the Code require that IMC members and their Certified Management Consultants (CMCs):[3]

✦ Safeguard confidential information.

✦ Render impartial, independent advice.

✦ Accept only client engagements they are qualified to perform.

✦ Agree with the client in advance on the basis for professional charges.

✦ Develop realistic and practical solutions to client problems.

My Commitment to My Clients

- 1.0 I will serve my clients with integrity, competence, independence, objectivity, and professionalism.
- 2.0 I will mutually establish with my clients realistic expectations of the benefits and results of my services.

- 3.0 I will only accept assignments for which I possess the requisite experience and competence to perform and will only assign staff or engage colleagues with the knowledge and expertise needed to serve my clients effectively.
- 4.0 Before accepting any engagement, I will ensure that I have worked with my clients to establish a mutual understanding of the objectives, scope, work plan, and fee arrangements.
- 5.0 I will treat appropriately all confidential client information that is not public knowledge, take reasonable steps to prevent it from access by unauthorized people, and will not take advantage of proprietary or privileged information, either for use by myself, the client's firm, or another client, without the client's permission.
- 6.0 I will avoid conflicts of interest or the appearance of such and will immediately disclose to the client circumstances or interests that I believe may influence my judgment or objectivity.
- 7.0 I will offer to withdraw from a consulting assignment when I believe my objectivity or integrity may be impaired.
- 8.0 I will refrain from inviting an employee of an active or inactive client to consider alternative employment without prior discussion with the client.

My Commitment to Fiscal Integrity

- 9.0 I will agree in advance with a client on the basis for fees and expenses and will charge fees that are reasonable and commensurate with the services delivered and the responsibility accepted.
- 10.0 I will not accept commissions, remuneration, or other benefits from a third party in connection with the recommendations to a client without that client's prior knowledge and consent, and I will disclose in advance any financial interests in goods or services that form part of such recommendations.

My Commitment to the Public and the Profession

- 11.0 If within the scope of my engagement, I will report

to appropriate authorities within or external to the client organization any occurrences of malfeasance, dangerous behavior, or illegal activities.

- 12.0 I will respect the rights of consulting colleagues and consulting firms and will not use their proprietary information or methodologies without permission.

- 13.0 I will represent the profession with integrity and professionalism in my relations with my clients, colleagues, and the general public.

- 14.0 I will not advertise my services in a deceptive manner nor misrepresent or denigrate individual consulting practitioners, consulting firms, or the consulting profession.

- 15.0 If I perceive a violation of the Code, I will report it to the Institute of Management Consultants USA and will promote adherence to the Code by other member consultants working on my behalf.

SUMMING UP

Performing your work in accordance with high ethical standards is tough. But it is worth it. When you respect yourself, others will respect you as well. Not only are high ethical standards and integrity the right principles to maintain, you will find that their maintenance is good business.

NOTES

1. Peter F. Drucker, *The Changing World of the Executive* (New York: Truman Talley Books, 1982), p. 242.
2. David A. Kaplan, "Intrigue in High Places," *Newsweek Business* (September 5, 2006), p. 3, accessed at http://www.newsweek.com/id/37886, December 3, 2008.
3. From the Institute of Management Consultants Web site, accessed at http://www.imcusa.org/ethics/imc_usa_code_of_ethics /imc_usa_code_of_ethics/, July 3, 2008.

14

MAKING PROFESSIONAL PRESENTATIONS

THE SUCCESS OF A CONSULTING ENGAGEMENT is based not only on actually doing the assignment professionally, but on your ability to present the results of your work to your client. Presentation is crucial. Yet one survey of company presidents showed that more were afraid of public speaking and presenting than of dying. In this chapter I will discuss the important skills and techniques of presentations and show you the five keys to presentation success.

OBJECTIVES OF PRESENTATIONS

With a presentation, you want to inform your client of the results of the assignment, make recommendations that will benefit the client, and confirm that you have done a good job so that you will be retained in the future. Each of these objectives is, in its own way, important.

If you don't take the time to build a case for your recommendations, explaining the measures taken during the engagement, your client is less likely to accept your recommendations. Your client wants to know how you arrived at the conclusions that led to the recommendations, as well as why you used one methodology rather than others. If you ran into problems during the performance of your consulting, your client also wants to know about them and how you handled them. If you had to make assumptions because you could not obtain certain information, telling your client about them is important. If there were changes to the original contract, even though prior approval was already given, you should restate them, both to remind your client of the changes and to inform others.

The quality of your work, the information you provide, and the usefulness of recommendations you make for action are the bottom line of the consulting engagement. You get paid for results. Without them, the engagement, although it might make an interesting case study, is of no benefit to your client.

Confirming that you have done a good job so that you will be retained in the future is also important. If you have done well, you deserve recognition for a job well done. You can get this recognition only by convincing your client, through your presentation, of your effectiveness. If you do the presentation properly, your client will come away from the consulting engagement looking good, and you will be retained again. Furthermore, you will get referrals to additional clients who would like you to duplicate your success for them.

FIVE KEYS TO A SUCCESSFUL PRESENTATION

Every successful presentation has five essential requirements: (1) professionalism, (2) enthusiasm, (3) organization, (4) practice, and (5) visual aids.

Let's look at each in turn.

PROFESSIONALISM

The quality of professionalism must be evident throughout your presentation and demonstrated by your dress and personal appearance, by the quality of the visual aids you use, by your demeanor, by your preparation, and by your delivery.

+ If you show up for a presentation wearing a suit that needs pressing or clothes that are not appropriate for the occasion, you will not be perceived as a professional.

+ If your visual aids contain typographical or grammatical mistakes or if the lettering is sloppy, you will not be perceived as a professional.

+ If how you handle yourself during the presentation indicates that you are unsure of yourself or defensive or that you do not know what you are talking about, you will not be perceived as a professional.

+ If things go wrong during your presentation because of an obvious lack of preparation, you will not be perceived as a professional.

But if your presentation is clear and well organized, if it goes off like clockwork and you are prepared to answer all questions, if your appearance matches your performance, *then* your professionalism will be obvious.

ENTHUSIASM

Enthusiasm is crucial. If you do nothing else, be enthusiastic! If you are not enthusiastic about what you did, I guarantee you that your client will not be either. In my opinion, enthusiasm is the most important secret of making a good presentation.

What should you do if you really are enthusiastic? First of all, it is very difficult for me to believe that you could ever become a good consultant and *not* be enthusiastic about what you are doing. But if, for whatever reason, you really are not enthusiastic about a particular assignment but you still want or need the job, you can do only one thing: *Pretend.* Whenever I speak about the absolute necessity of enthusiasm in presenting, I always tell the story of General George S. Patton Jr., one of the most successful generals of World War II. He won battles *and* saved the lives of his men by motivating them to do their very best. And he sometimes did so by pretending.

I have read Patton's published diaries, which go back as far as the turn of the century, when Patton was a cadet at West Point. During World War I, when he was still in his twenties, he was a colonel in command of the U.S. Army's first tank corps. Patton wrote his wife, Bea, regularly, and these letters were published with the diaries. In one letter, Patton says, "Every day I practice in front of a mirror looking mean." Patton called that his war face. Can you imagine, a hard-boiled colonel of the U.S. Army practicing in front of a mirror looking mean? But Patton did this for a reason. He knew that his ability to motivate his men—sometimes by joking, sometimes by intimidation—could win battles and save lives. So he created his war face—and sometimes pretended.

If Patton could act and pretend to save lives and win battles, then you and I can pretend if we need to do so, and we can act enthusiastically to make a successful consultant presentation. Remember, *you must do this.* A lack of enthusiasm is not an option. Enthusiasm is the most important secret of success in presenting. You must be enthusiastic, and you must show your enthusiasm to your client audience. I promise you that the enthusiasm, even if self-generated, will come through, and it will help make your presentation successful.

ORGANIZATION

You can't just stand up and speak without having thought ahead of time about what you are going to say. Even an accomplished off-the-cuff speaker would get into trouble making consultant presentations that way. If you try it, invariably certain facts will be left out, and then your presentation will not be as clear, as logical, and as complete as it must be. If you are questioned because of this lack of clarity, the pressure on you will increase, and your difficulties will mount.

Proper organization of your presentation ahead of time will prevent many problems once you are face to face in a formal presentation setting with your client. Fortunately, you already have the ingredients of your presentation from the work you did in earlier chapters, including material from the contract, the proposal, and even your initial interview. So you can organize the facts of the engagement and present them to the client in a clear and logical manner using this generic outline:

1. Background of the Consulting Assignment and the Problem to Be Solved

2. Statement of the Project Objectives

3. Methodologies Used to Do the Assignment, Along with Alternative Methodologies and Reasons They Were Rejected

4. Problems Encountered During the Engagement and How Each Was Handled

5. The Results or Conclusions Stemming from the Engagement

6. Specific Recommendations to the Client on What He or She Should Do as a Result of the Work You Have Done, Not Excluding Additional Work That You or Someone Else Must Do in the Future

Frequently you can incorporate the problem-solving methodology explained in Chapter 11. This is especially useful in presenting your analysis of alternative solutions to a problem, which will lead logically to your recommendations.

PRACTICE

Practice does not mean that you must memorize anything. In fact, the contrary is true. Memorization will make your presentation boring and stilted. It is not natural. Even if you have the ability to memorize quickly, I do not recommend doing so in a consulting presentation. First, the time spent in memorization can be better used in getting your presentation together. Second, there is always a chance that, under the pressure of the presentation, your timing and memory may be thrown off by a question asked out of turn or a discussion initiated by your client. Of course, if you memorize you may end up doing something worse: reading your presentation word for word. Now *that* is really boring.

I learned this lesson the hard way. As a young Air Force officer flying B-52s out of Altus, Oklahoma, I was extremely interested in navigation. On one occasion, the Association of Texas Math and Science Teachers contacted my wing commander to ask for someone who could travel to its annual meeting in Wichita Falls, Texas, and speak for about an hour on a subject of interest to the members. The wing commander asked me, and, because I had waited for a chance to do research on space navigation, I jumped at the chance. Using notes collected over several months, I wrote a superlative one-hour presentation (at least I thought it was superlative, and it must have been reasonably good, because a national magazine later published it). I was also given the opportunity to have excellent artwork prepared as 35-mm slides. I felt that I had the very best support possible. Unfortunately, I made one mistake: I memorized every single word in that one-hour presentation. I even knew where to pause for the commas!

When the time came, I drove to Wichita Falls, Texas, about two hours away and, in full uniform, looked out at nearly 300 math and science teachers. I had been a junior high school student in that very same city, and seeing so many teachers looking at me immediately had its effect. I forgot parts of my presentation, became flustered, and eventually had to read it word for word. What should have been a very exciting and informative presentation was more boring than informative. Though space was on everyone's lips in the early 1960s when this event took place, I think most of the audience slept through this presentation. However, the experience taught me a valuable lesson, and I haven't memorized anything since then, even though I am frequently a guest speaker for many different organizations. Do not repeat my mistake. Do not memorize, and do not read anything.

If you don't read and you don't memorize, how are you supposed to make your presentation? That's easy. Once you have your material organized, you can use either 3×5-inch file cards or visual aids to help you discuss each point. You might have one card that says "Background of the consulting assignment and the problem." You would then simply look up at your audience and talk to them about this background. If you do not wish to leave out any important statistics, put them on other cards. Reading off numbers is OK to make sure you get them right. Other main ideas can also be put on sequential cards. But you should write no more than one sentence on each card. The idea is not to read what is written on each card but rather to talk about that one sentence. If you are using visual aids, they could display the key sentence or statistics to remind you of what you are going to talk about at that particular time.

Controlling Time

When you practice, it is extremely important to stay in control of the time available for your presentation. If your client wants a one-hour presentation, make it a one-hour presentation. If your client wants 30 minutes, make it that. Do not extend your presentation unless requested to do so under any circumstances. To do so is disaster. Let me tell you two stories to prove my point.

I was once associated with a major aerospace company that was bidding on a multibillion-dollar contract for the government. On one of the final reviews, representatives of the government visited our organization for a four-hour briefing by our engineers. These engineers lost control of the time and went well over the limit requested by the customer. Despite frantic signals from company employees, they completed their presentation more than an hour and a half late. The customers remained the extra hour and a half without complaint, but many missed their return flights. Although this was probably not the only reason that the large contract was lost, there is no doubt that irritating the customer at this critical time did not help.

My second story concerns a hiring at a university. Some years ago, I was on a search committee to find a new professor for our department at the university. The procedure in academia is somewhat different than that in industry, and in many cases the professor must be voted on and accepted by the department before the university can make an offer. Usually a candidate for faculty membership must not only interview with many department members but make a formal presentation to the department sitting as a group.

On this occasion, the candidate, who had only recently obtained his PhD, was asked to make a 20-minute presentation on the research for his dissertation. The time limit was necessary because many faculty members had other meetings to attend. The candidate had graduated from an excellent university, and prior to his visit most of the department members had made their minds up to vote for his hiring based solely on his university education and a reading of his research.

During the visit, the individual interviews seemed to be going fairly well. The presentation was the final obstacle before the department voted on his hiring. He began his presentation. Five minutes passed. Ten minutes passed. Fifteen minutes passed. Twenty minutes came and went. The presentation continued on and on. The entire department became restless; all of us were late for other meetings. Individuals slipped out, one after the other. Finally, after 45 minutes, the candidate concluded. By then the once receptive faculty was no longer so receptive. The faculty did eventually vote to hire, but only for a one-year appointment. In fact it was two years before this individual was finally granted the permanent position that he all but had even before his visit. It is no exaggeration to say that his failure to control time for 25 additional minutes cost two years of promotion, pay, and other benefits.

Never think that time control is a small item: It is very important.

The Practice Sequence

I use the following practice sequence: First, I note the time available and outline the presentation using the organization structure indicated earlier in this chapter. I write this information on 3×5-inch file cards. I then go through the presentation once, using the cards. In this run-through, I change the cards, add facts if required, and delete or change others if they don't seem to fit. I watch my time closely as I make this presentation to myself, and I make adjustments, by inserting or deleting material, so that my presentation is several minutes less than the time I have been allotted. This is important because frequently your presentation will not go exactly as planned. So a little bit of pad never hurts.

If there are several presenters, I insist that we practice together. Some consultants simply divide the available time and develop separate presentations, but I have found that such a presentation does not quite fit together when done before the client. Further, frequently one or more of the presenters will exceed the amount of time allotted, and the total presentation runs much longer than anticipated.

I practice at first very informally, perhaps in a room by myself, perhaps sitting around a table with the other presenters. I do this several times until I am confident of the overall structure and the time. Now I also know what visual aids I will need, and I can have them made.

The Formal Practice Presentation

The formal practice presentation is done as if it were real. In fact, I insist on doing it in front of someone who can give me constructive feedback. Usually this is my wife, but it has also been a colleague or someone else who was not involved in the presentation itself. You must present it to an outsider who is not part of the consultant presentation team.

The Live Demonstration

If you have to do a demonstration as a part of the presentation, practice that too. This is essential to make sure that it fits into the allotted time and that the results of the demonstration are as anticipated. You will find that in actual presentations everything that can go wrong will go wrong. Therefore, you must anticipate and eliminate potential problems before they actually happen.

Let me give you an example of how important practicing demonstrations can be. Once I attended an annual meeting of the Survival and Flight Equipment Association, an organization of industry, military, and civilian airline personnel who develop and manufacture life support equipment for people who fly. A project manager from the Navy made a very interesting presentation on a very important piece of equipment he had developed.

A Navy flyer has special problems because he flies over the sea. If he or she must eject from the aircraft, he eventually enters the water. He must climb into a small life raft while weighted down with equipment, such as survival gear, boots, and helmet. Doing all this is difficult enough on a calm sea, but it is almost impossible if the parachute is still attached to the pilot's body because even the slightest wind can cause problems. If the open chute fills with water, it can drag the aviator straight to the bottom. So the approved procedure is to use a quick release, attached to the harness, to get rid of the parachute just as the aviator's boots touch the water. The problem with this procedure is that judging height over a flat surface like the ocean is very difficult, and even more difficult is making the judgment call in the dark and under the pressure of emergency conditions. As a result, some aviators who think they are just about to touch the water are actually 100 feet or higher in the air. Jettisoning the chute at that height is clearly not recommended.

The Navy's solution was highly innovative as well as effective. A small explosive charge, called a squib, in the parachute harness separates the chute from the harness on contact with water; the water completes an electrical contact. Thus, when the aviator enters the water, the parachute is blown away from him automatically.

Now you may be thinking, "That's just fine for an ocean landing, but what if a pilot must eject from the aircraft and parachute through a rain shower? Will the apparatus become wet and release the parachute from the aviator thousands of feet in the air?" The Navy anticipated this problem. The device worked only in seawater, which has a high salt content.

The Navy project manager explained all this in a most interesting fashion and finally came to the most dramatic point of the presentation. He donned a parachute. Although he could not submerge his whole body, he had two live wires leading to the squib and had a glass of seawater on a table before him. He then described in vivid terms exactly what would happen. He would take the two wires and thrust them into the seawater. We would see a flash and hear a loud bang, he said, and the parachute would be separated from the harness instantly.

The entire audience waited in great anticipation; several people stuck their fingers in their ears. Knowing that he had everyone's attention, the presenter, with the parachute strapped tightly to his body, took the two wires and dramatically thrust them into the seawater. Nothing happened! He repeated the process with the same results: nothing. At first there were smirks; then scattered laughter spread throughout the room. This presenter—who had otherwise made an impressive presentation—took the harness off and discovered that someone had failed to replace the electrical batteries in the harness.

Of course, under flight conditions, maintenance personnel would have checked this detail several times, and the pilot would also have done so during preflight. But the drama of the presenter's conclusion was ruined by the mishap.

Let these stories teach you the lesson that it taught me: Always prepare for any live demonstrations by actually doing them ahead of time. Do not assume that something will work as planned. Actually do the demonstration as a part of your practice.

VISUAL AIDS

Visual aids are also essential to a good presentation. In general you have several options for good visual aids: flip charts, overhead transparencies, 35-mm slides, PowerPoint, videos, handouts, and blackboards or whiteboards.

Flip Charts

Flip charts are charts on large sheets that are connected at the top and that are flipped over as each one is used. The main advantage of flip charts is that they do not require any type of projector. However, because they are large, they are sometimes difficult to transport. And depending on the size of your audience, you may not be able to make the lettering large enough to be seen by everyone in the room.

Overhead Transparencies

Overhead transparencies require the use of an overhead projector. Transparencies themselves usually have a viewing area of approximately $8\frac{1}{2} \times 11$ inches. Today you can make transparencies instantly on your computer's printer or a copier. Even if you own neither, many office supply stores, printers, and even hotels have facilities where you can make them yourself. This capability is extremely helpful because in the old pre-high-technology age a graphic artist made your transparencies, and you always had to allow sufficient time to correct typographical errors, which invariably occurred. Moreover, these overhead transparencies were very expensive. Nowadays, making these are a piece of cake, and they are much less expensive.

Transparencies themselves are fairly easy to carry around. They are not as small as 35-mm slides, but they are easier to use than slides and much easier to transport than flip charts. I put each of mine in a clear transparent plastic covering. The covers have holes for a loose-leaf binder. This protects your transparency during both transportation and use. This is important because transparencies can still cost you a couple dollars each.

35-mm Slides

Slides are very easy to transport, but they require the use of a slide projector, and they can be expensive. As is sometimes the case with transparencies, slides require additional lead time, usually a week or so. For some types of presentations and multimedia presentations where high-quality photographs are to be used, this method is the only one that makes any sense. I try to avoid them, however. Somehow gremlins always manage to turn at least a couple of your slides the wrong way in the tray, and getting them put back in right side up and right side out while your audience is waiting is always a pain. Nowadays, most images can be imported into a PowerPoint presentation, so you generally do not have to use slides.

PowerPoint

PowerPoint is a Microsoft software program that allows you to create color presentations, notes, handouts, and more. Other similar programs are on the market, but PowerPoint is the most popular. I now use PowerPoint to construct all my presentations. To transport a PowerPoint presentation, you can burn it onto a CD-ROM, load it onto a USB drive (also known as a stick or bullet), or just have it on a computer (most presenters use a laptop for this purpose). You also need a projector that interfaces with your computer. Most corporations, hotels, universities, and business centers have a projector set up already. In most cases all you need to do is connect your computer or, if you bring only a disc or USB drive, to put it in your client's computer.

Videos

You have a number of suboptions with videos. You can use a VHS, Beta, or DVD. I guess somewhere someone is still using 16mm film! All work, but DVD is the current state of the art and also the most convenient because you can put it on your computer and use the same projector as you would with PowerPoint. My main concern with the use of any type of video is whether it really adds to your presentation. In fact, some consultants attempt to make their whole presentation a video, and in my opinion this is a mistake. Clients want to see a real person talk about the consulting engagement—not a talking head.

Handouts

Handouts can consist of text and/or graphics, perhaps in color. You can print out multiple copies from your office printer, make photocopies on the copier, or have the local printer make copies—all at a few cents per page. Handouts can be used for either small or large groups, and the expense depends on the number that must be reproduced. You can make the handouts yourself, and they can be prepared at the last minute without a long lead time, both of which are important.

For smaller groups, carrying around the handouts is fairly easy. However, for a large group and a lengthy handout, this type of visual aid becomes cumbersome and expensive. Fortunately, if the group you are presenting to is fairly large, they will frequently offer to reproduce the handout for you. Alternatively, many clients like you to put the handout on a CD-ROM or bullet, especially if there are several presentations by others and the intent is to reproduce all of the handouts on a disk that will be given to participants.

Another disadvantage of a printed handout is that your audience may tend to read ahead of you. If you have some dramatic point to make, it could be spoiled by your audience's getting there first.

You can develop a handout by printing one or more of your over-head projections on each page. Bound together, they make an excellent report to supplement your oral presentation. If you use PowerPoint, this is especially easy.

Blackboards or Whiteboards

Today, the so-called blackboards may be green or some other color. Also, there are smooth whiteboards on which you can write in wash-able pastel colors. I like the latter: no more scratching sound as you write and no more chalk dust on your hands and clothes.

Still, the advantages and disadvantages of all types of boards on which you write for group consulting presentations are the same. One advantage is flexibility. Until you actually touch chalk to board, you are not committed to revealing anything. Even after you use the board, changes are easy to make on the spot. Along with flexibility is the tim-ing of what you display. You do not write anything down until you need it. Cost is another advantage. There is no cost in preparing for a chalk presentation as long as you do not have to buy a board. Also, as long as you have something to write with and some means of erasure, there isn't much that can go wrong, as there is with electronic gadgetry.

As for disadvantages, you cannot reproduce a chalk presentation as you can with overhead transparencies. However, with some high-tech boards, such as SmartBoard (see http://www2.smarttech.com/st /en-US/Products/SMART+Boards/), you can. Also, if you have a lot to write down, what is your audience doing while you are writing?

I once started a presentation while my partner tried to write extensive material on a blackboard. Talk about distractions! Also, if you cannot print clearly, the professionalism of your presentation will suffer.

OVERCOMING STAGE FRIGHT

Every great presenter is a little apprehensive about making a presenta-tion. If you were not apprehensive, you would be indifferent, and the presentation would be boring. So a little bit of stage fright is fine. On the other hand, you do not want to be so apprehensive that you cannot make a smooth, forceful, and motivating presentation.

To overcome stage fright, I do two things. First, I conduct at least two live rehearsals before other people. These are formal demonstrations to people not familiar with the presentation so that I can receive feedback and criticism on what I say. This criticism allows me to polish my presentation and often uncovers rough points I never thought about.

The second thing I do is something called creative visualization. Somehow I stumbled onto this technique, and, because it is a little strange, for a long time I did not tell many people that I used it. But in an old issue of the *Wall Street Journal,* I read an article about it. A performance psychologist, Charles Garfield, had found one reason why some people were superior performers. It was the trick of mental rehearsal, something top athletes had done for a long time. Top chief executives would visualize every aspect of what it would be like to have a successful presentation—a sort of deliberate daydreaming. In contrast, Garfield said run-of-the-mill executives would organize their facts but not their psyches. Thus, my creative visualization got official blessing from a performance psychologist and the *Wall Street Journal.*

Believe me when I tell you that the technique is simple. I like to do it the night before I make the presentation, just before I go to sleep. While I am lying in bed with nothing else to do, I go through my entire presentation, not memorizing it but going through it in my mind from start to finish, from the time I first enter the room until my conclusion. I visualize everything that happens, including standing up and shaking hands and describing the background of the assignment, the objectives of the project, the methods I used and why I chose them, the problems and how they were handled, the resulting conclusions, and the recommendations to my client. I even visualize questions and my answering them forcefully and correctly. I visualize smiles all the way around, knowing that I have made an excellent presentation and that everyone, including and especially the client who hired me, is happy with the excellent job I have done. I do this more than once, repeating the visualization episode over and over again. This does not take a lot of effort because you can visualize an entire hour presentation in a few seconds.

To my way of thinking, this creative visualization technique offers several outstanding features. First, when you actually make the presentation, it does not feel new. You have done it dozens of times before. The technique takes the sting out of stage fright. Second, I believe that visualizing my presentation in a positive fashion—as a success—makes me feel that I am going to be successful. I believe that my presentation will be successful, and therefore it is. I sense that my audience will be friendly to me, and therefore they are. I have confidence in my ability to answer questions because I have already seen myself doing these things.

In my years of using this creative visualization technique, it has never failed me. I strongly recommend that you try it. The results will amaze you.

A variation of this technique is called the split focus technique. If bedtime is not a good time to be "working," you can visualize the presentation while you do something else, such as working in the garden or taking a shower.

ANSWERING QUESTIONS

Many presenters fear answering questions during a Q&A more than anything else; yet research has shown that 85 percent of the questions asked during a presentation can actually be anticipated. Therefore, when I prepare for a presentation, I sit down and try to anticipate questions that members of my client's company are likely to ask me, and I write them down. Some of the questions require answers that I feel should be included in my presentation, so I modify the presentation accordingly. Others I just think I should be ready for, so I simply think them through and write out the answers. If additional data or information is necessary to give a complete answer, I make sure I have the information available. In some cases, I even go as far as to make up a special visual aid with the information, which I hold in readiness to use only if I am asked this question.

During the Q&A session, when I am asked a question, I always repeat it. Repeating the question serves a couple of purposes: It gives me additional time to think about the answer and ensures that other members of the audience hear the question. After repeating the question, I first state my answer, and then why my answer is what it is, giving supporting facts. I try never to be defensive about a question, even if it is asked in a belligerent tone of voice. In fact, remembering that the customer is always right, I try never to get into an argument with a client. This does not mean I agree with the client if that's not the case. It simply means that I state the facts as I know them, and if the client insists on arguing, I explain my position as tactfully as possible and move on to something else.

One important key to answering questions and to the success of your whole presentation is to view members of the audience as friends, not adversaries, even if the climate is political and some members of the audience can be expected to snipe at you. You can at least treat them as friendly snipers, not as enemies out to demolish you. Also, do not give long-winded answers. Try to make your answers short and to the point. Long-winded answers only fuzz up the issue and may lead to more probing than you want to get into in a public format.

SUMMING UP

If you follow this advice, you cannot fail to have an outstanding presentation. Not only will you receive accolades for it, but your advice will be respected and followed, and will lead to further consulting assignments. In the next chapter we will take a closer look at some things we have hinted at previously: how the computer has changed consulting.

15

How the Computer Has Changed Consulting

COMPUTERS SUITABLE FOR CONSULTANTS did not exist when I first hung out my shingle. Today a computer can do more to raise your consulting productivity than any other single tool I can think of. Computers have become so valuable as tools that it is hard for me to imagine a consultant doing business without one, even though it is possible to do so. Although I know of a few who still have consulting practices without one, in this day and age, I find this almost unbelievable.

The computer can not only double or triple your productivity, but also help you create presentation and other types of material, market your services, and communicate with clients and others instantaneously. Word processing software alone has allowed me to double the work I turned out in a given amount of time, and the quality of the work is better too. But I soon discovered that my computer could do other things that saved me time and money and made my consulting operations more efficient.

PROPOSALS AND DESKTOP PUBLISHING

In the bad old days, I used to pay a graphic artist to do my layout and typesetting for proposals, brochures, fliers, or other print products. The artist typically cost a minimum of $100 or more per job and took at least a week before I even had the material to proofread. Now, using a software program costing less than a hundred dollars, I do everything myself. I have a wide choice of hundreds of different typefaces, styles, and sizes. As a bonus, I do not have to wait a week for the first draft. Except for my own time constraints, or those of people I hire to help me out from time to time, I get the work done exactly when I want it.

I still use a graphic artist, but much of the routine work I can do myself because I can buy thousands of copyright-free images, photographs, and other types of illustrations on a CD-ROM. Or I can sometimes find copyright-free images on the Internet. As a result, I can do the work better and faster than ever before. Moreover, inexpensive programs are available to help me design my own stationery, business cards, and brochures. I can design them and, using my own printer, print only what I need in a few minutes. Compare that to having to print a minimum of 300 brochures in the bad old days. Fewer than that made the printing uneconomical, but I would typically use fewer than half before something would change and I would need to update the material. Then, I'd just have to throw out the old brochures and start over. Now I never print more than 10 at a time, and I update my brochures every time I print them.

In addition to cost savings, speed is another benefit of using computers. A few years ago, I received 24 hours' warning that a delegation from a foreign country would unexpectedly visit an institute that I ran. I needed a special brochure for these visitors describing the capabilities of my institute. Graphic designers with a rush priority could do the job in a week. I had one day. I bought a brochure design program and a package of blank brochures, all for less than $20 at my local office supplies store. By electronically cutting and pasting institute information that I had on file, I produced professional-looking brochures in a couple of hours with my computer.

"The Stuff of Heroes" brochure in Appendix B, which I use to promote my seminars, workshops, and consulting, was done easily on my computer with the help of a word processing program. The only artwork is the Greek figure holding the torch with the shield bearing the words, "The Stuff of Heroes." This figure was drawn by nationally acclaimed and award-winning artist Cynthia Ing, who took a university course from me not in art, but in salesmanship.

NEED OVERHEAD TRANSPARENCIES?
NO PROBLEM!

You can generate overhead transparencies, which I still sometimes use for consulting presentations or seminars, with the same speed and at the same low expense. It once took at least a week to have these done. Moreover, there were always typographical errors, some of which I caught too late to have corrected. With my word processing and graphics programs, all that is past. I now prepare everything myself, with considerable savings in time and cost.

Another bonus is that l am able to save all of my material so that if I ever want it again, or want it with minor changes, it is easy to make the changes and print out the new material. All this material is filed on the hard drive of my computer, and backed up on a separate USB drive (or stick), about 2 inches long! The material is together where I want it, takes up little space, and is easily retrieved.

MANAGING YOUR PRACTICE

If you are concerned with managing the financial side of your practice, or if finances have been a drag in the past, worry no more. There are hundreds of programs available to help you with your financial decision making and record keeping. Some programs can track your income, accounts receivable, payroll, and inventory. Other programs can help you make loan decisions and decide whether to make or buy equipment. There are complex accounting programs, and there are very simple ones.

There are even programs that help you prepare your own state and federal income taxes. They will cut the time for tax preparation (if you do your own) by 50 percent or more, and they save you time even if you use an accountant.

DIRECT MARKETING

Certain programs allow you to merge a list of current or potential clients with one of your sales letters, creating a personalized letter for each individual customer. What once had to be done by someone else can now be done by you at home. This capability is especially valuable for relatively small mailings that would not be cost-effective if you had someone else do them. You can do these mailings almost on a moment's notice. If the list is already available, it is actually possible to mail an advertisement or announcement to thousands of people the same day you make the decision to do it.

CORRECTING YOUR WRITING

In addition to programs that correct your spelling, other programs correct your grammar, give you choices of the words you may want to use (a thesaurus program), help you make your writing more readable and interesting, and improve your writing in other ways. A computer software program probably cannot turn you instantaneously into a professional writer, but it certainly can make you a more competent one.

If you want help with copy writing for your ads, there are programs for this also. Some even automatically create headlines, theme lines, slogans, and jingles.

NAMING PRODUCTS AND SERVICES

Other programs can help you select names for products or services. Many consultants work with their clients on the crucial naming of new products or product lines. Naming programs analyze the statistical properties of letter combinations while using special filters for rejecting poor name formations. They even check names for hidden or embedded profanities in several different languages, and they have the "smarts" to review a trillion permutations of a 15-letter word. Try doing that for a client over the weekend without a computer.

MAKING FORECASTS AND PLANS

One of the most common computer uses for business is that of the spreadsheet. A spreadsheet program, such as Excel, can be used to do sophisticated calculations, provide data for graphs, make forecasts, view results by changing various what-if variables, estimate costs, and so forth. Basically, a spreadsheet is simply a chart with rows and columns, forming individual cells. But the beauty of this type of program is that you can embed a formula in each cell. Then, as you enter data, the formula performs the calculation for you, providing you with hundreds of accurate numerical results almost instantly. You just plug in the basic numbers that the formula calls for.

Other software programs assist you in developing all types of plans by incorporating the spreadsheet concept. Let's say you are developing a marketing plan for a client. Can you imagine the time you will save when all you have to do is plug in numbers? From those numbers, the program develops charts, alternative strategies, financial ratios, balance sheets, cash flow analyses, income statements, sales projections, and a lot more simply by pressing a few keys.

EVALUATING POTENTIAL EMPLOYEES

Big companies pay big fees to consultants to obtain complete psychological evaluations of potential key employees. Even this service has been computerized: You can obtain programs in which you input data based on a candidate's answers to a series of questions, and the output can tell you how the individual is likely to behave in different situations. Or the information can be used for vocational counseling. In Europe especially, handwriting analysis is popular for the prehiring evaluation of executives. Handwriting analysis computer programs are also available.

MARKETING RESEARCH

There are probably hundreds of marketing research programs. They not only help you to design your research tool but analyze data and interpret the results. Much of the time-consuming drudgery of manipulating the results from research is thus eliminated. The computer prints all the backup analysis for you, as well as the bottom-line results you need for your client.

VOICE-ACTIVATED WORD PROCESSING IS HERE!

Voice recognition programs have been around for several years. I have one, but to tell the truth, I do not use (I guess I am too accustomed to typing things out). However, a friend of mine is very pleased with such a program. He says he saves the time and expense of having a living, breathing secretary by simply dictating to his computer reports, e-mail, presentations, spreadsheets, and other programs.

SCANNING DOCUMENTS AND PHOTOGRAPHS INTO YOUR PRESENTATIONS

With a scanner you can scan documents or pictures right into your proposals or presentation overheads. No wonder it takes me only a couple hours to put a presentation together that once took me days. Did I say that the computer has doubled my productivity? It has increased it by several magnitudes.

INSTANT COMMUNICATION

You can use your computer for communication and for connection to the Internet (a discussion of which follows in the next chapter). As for communication, I cannot imagine anyone doing business without an e-mail program today. Few businesses limit themselves to what is now known as snail mail—delivery by the U.S. Postal Service. Communication is therefore another reason that having a computer is a must. With a computer you can communicate with anyone in the world instantly. Moreover, you can attach complete proposals, artwork, or photographs and get them to a client thousands of miles away in seconds. It is even possible for your computer to communicate with a fax machine and to send or receive a fax as well. Again, Microsoft has a popular e-mail program called Outlook on which you can communicate with e-mails, do scheduling, and even be reminded of appointments.

If that were not enough, with programs like Skype you can actually communicate around the world through your computer's audio system without the use of a telephone if your client has a similar setup. With a small camera attached to your computer, you can even have two-way visual as well as audio contact. For full details, see http://www.skype.com. For these calls, the cost is zero. Can you imagine what you can save on your telephone bill?

SOME READING SUGGESTIONS

Here are some books that can help you get started using a computer in your consulting practice:

Absolute Beginner's Guide to Computer Basics by Michael Miller (Que)

PCs All-in-One Desk Reference for Dummies by Mark L. Chambers (For Dummies)

PCs for Dummies by Dan Gookin (For Dummies)

Be sure to get the latest editions because this field is constantly changing.

SUMMING UP

Well, I could go on. And, in fact, I will do just that in the next chapter, where I will discuss the Internet. However, even leaving out the Internet, the list of benefits in this chapter is just a taste of what you will be able to do.

16

The Internet and Consulting

THE INTERNET HAS REVOLUTIONIZED how consultants of all types do business. Company research that once required multiple telephone calls and interviews, plus trips to the library and the purchase of various directories, now takes only a few minutes. Product information that took hours of expensive research time to uncover is now at your fingertips. Brochures, pictures, and other material, once so expensive, can now be made available instantaneously to potential clients at no additional cost to you. A direct mail campaign to potential clients once took weeks of preparation, hours of envelope stuffing, and several days or more in the mail, plus money for printing, envelopes, and postage. Now the same campaign can cost almost nothing and be available to hundreds, or even thousands or millions of prospects, in a few seconds. How can this not be revolutionary? In this chapter, we are going to focus on two major ways of taking advantage of this technology: research and marketing.

WHAT IS THE INTERNET?

The Internet is very much like a telephone line linking you with all other parties simultaneously. (I don't mean to imply that your telephone line and a modem are the only means of connection; I say more about connections shortly.) In this telephone metaphor, the number and locations of parties that are connected to your telephone line are virtually limitless, and the parties on the line are located all over the world. As I write this, the estimates of the numbers of individuals on this party line are more than 500 million, and the number is growing by millions every month. One source says a billion people will soon be connected. With a billion people seeking products and information, having needs and wants in their business lives, and making information, news, and advertising available, that is a lot of potential for a consultant for getting information and for reaching any target audience, including those interested in your services.

WHAT DO YOU NEED TO GET ONLINE?

To get on line, you need:

✦ A computer
✦ A modem, DSL, broadband cable, or wireless (wi-fi) connection
✦ A Web browser program, such as Microsoft Internet Explorer, Netscape Navigator, Safari, Firefox, or any one of numerous others
✦ A portal service, or Internet service provider (ISP), such as AOL (America Online), among many others

PRELOADED CONNECTION, BROWSER, AND PORTAL SERVICES

The connection, browser, and portal folks are constantly competing for your business, and that is why you may have received your personalized introductory offer code or a CD-ROM in your mailbox offering you free hours and an automatic connection. Or, when you buy a new computer with a connection capability, you will probably have both a browser and a connection company all loaded up and ready to go. All you have to do is agree to their terms (you pay extra for the service, of course, so have your credit card ready) and follow the directions provided, and you are online. If you use the preloaded system, you will probably also want a separate phone line, cable access, or wireless access; otherwise your time online will interfere with your phone calls and vice versa.

INTERNET CONNECTIONS

There are a number of types of Internet connections:

+ The modem is pretty much dated today, being the slowest means of connection.
+ DSL (digital subscriber lines) is called an always-on connection because it is, well, always on. It uses existing two-wire copper telephone line connected to your office and will not tie up your phone as a dial-up connection does if you do not have a separate line. It can be several times faster than the faster modems.
+ Cable uses a special cable modem and operates through cable TV lines. It is blazingly fast. Once you use it, I doubt whether you will want any other connector.
+ A wireless connection operates through radio frequency bands, and it usually takes only another box added to the cable modem. Like cable and DSL, it is always on, and it is as fast as cable. It can be accessed from anywhere within its range, which is determined by the power of the wireless box.

RESEARCHING ON THE INTERNET

In the chapter on research, I mentioned starting at the library. In a library, we use the library's catalog index, which may be on index cards or on a computer terminal. We search catalog indexes on the Internet as well, but the catalog indexes are called search engines. Further, whereas your library's catalog index may list, say, 40,000 entries, a search engine may have 100 million—and probably more!

Of the many search engines, some are specialized for certain areas of interest, and some search the whole Web. Even with a 100 million or more entries, I have found that what one search engine cannot locate for you, another can.

Here are some of the major search engines:

- AltaVista: http://www.altavista.com
- Galaxy: http://wwwgalaxy.com
- Go: http://www.go.com
- Google: http://www.google.com
- HotBot: http://www.hotbot.com
- Internet Sleuth: http://www.isleuth.com
- Lycos: http://www.lycos.com
- MetaCrawler: http://www.metacrawler.com
- WebCrawler: http://www.webcrawler.com
- Yahoo: http://www.yahoo.com

HOW TO USE SEARCH ENGINES

The best way to find out about these search engines is to do a search, so let's try one. There are four easy steps:

1. Type the Internet address into your Web browser software.
2. Enter a word or word group having to do with your research topic into the entry box on the engine.
3. Click the button on the engine to begin your search.
4. Review your results and further investigate the matching documents (listed as electronic links, which you can inspect by clicking on them with your mouse) that look good. If you received no hits, repeat step 2 through 3 with new words.

To refine your searches, you can use a handful of Boolean search techniques, which help you narrow your search requests. A good tutorial can be found at Internet Tutorials (http://www.internettutorials .net/boolean.html).

EVALUATING AND USING YOUR RESULTS

That's all there is to it. You can either print out the information you find or copy it electronically and paste it into other documents. Of course, you should be careful to credit anything you use by footnoting and also be careful not to run afoul of copyright laws protecting others' intellectual property. Material on the Internet is just like printed material in this respect.

Sometimes you have to use different related words to find what you want. Sometimes you need to try different search engines. But there is so much information out there that I have come to believe that you can get just about anything. It is just a matter of being perseverant. No wonder government security agencies were concerned a few years ago when they located accurate instructions on how to build an atomic bomb!

For an in-depth look at researching on the Internet, try the following:

> *The Extreme Searcher's Internet Handbook: A Guide for the Serious Searcher* by Randolph Hock (Information Today)
>
> *Find It Online* by Alan Schlein (Facts on Demand Press)
>
> *Researching Online for Dummies* by Reva Basch and Mary Ellen Bates (For Dummies)

MARKETING ON THE INTERNET

In the summer of 1999 a movie that cost $50,000 to make beat out *Star Wars Episode I* in per-screen average sales, taking in an average of $26,500 at every screening. The movie was *The Blair Witch Project*. Made by Hollywood nobodies with no-name actors and actresses, the movie became a blockbuster and grossed millions of dollars. What was the secret? Try http://www.blairwitch.com. It is still running and shows you what can be done using this medium.

If the Internet can do this for a film, what can it do for a consultant? Plenty, but you have got to be smart and know what you are doing.

Presently, there are three main Internet freeways that are useful in marketing for the consultant:

1. The World Wide Web
2. Usenet and Blogs
3. E-Mail

Let's look at each in turn.

THE WORLD WIDE WEB

As you probably already know, the World Wide Web consists of a giant freeway of homepages, catalogues, electronic stores, and other types of sites. It is in color, and it has graphics, sound, and even video.

To place a color advertisement of multiple pages in a magazine and run it continuously, month after month, would cost you a fortune. Never mind that a magazine does not have the flexibility of sound or video. Only the largest of corporations can afford such advertising, and even they are very selective. But on the World Wide Web, anybody—even you and I—can afford to do it, and we can compete with even the giants of our industry. In fact, I'm going to show you how you can do this for only a couple of hundred dollars a year.

How to Establish Your Own Web Site

There are alternatives to paying someone several thousand dollars or more to develop your Web site. One way is to do it yourself. No, you don't need to be a computer programmer with years of technical know-how or a room full of experts. Computer programs are available that will walk you through the steps. Several years ago, I bought the CD-ROMs Instant Web Pages and Web Ware for only $14.97 each![1] I am sure many other similar programs are around today. Some programs for helping you to build a Web site are free; I put the words "free Web sites" in a search engine and got 956,000,000 hits.

Also, many universities conduct courses in this subject. Some years ago I attended a four-hour course during which the instructor walked us through a step-by-step process, and we actually built our own site during the course. You may also find a university student or professor willing to build a Web site for you at a cut-rate price.

My Web site (http://www.stuffofheroes.com) was originally developed to help promote one of my books. A student, who was also an instructor in the subject at a community college, developed the original site. However, when I decided to convert it to promote my training and consulting, I rebuilt it completely and started from scratch. Originally I was going to have someone else construct the site for me. Another consultant had hired my services for the first leadership seminar in Perth, Australia. He suggested I hire someone in Australia to put a new Web site together because the cost would be much lower. I asked him who built his site, and he told me he built it himself using Microsoft's (again Microsoft!) FrontPage software program. I had this program on my computer, so I decided to play around with it, and I built the current web site myself.

ONCE YOU HAVE YOUR SITE DEVELOPED, THEN WHAT?

With your site in place, your next step is to get an Internet service provider (ISP) to put your site up on the World Wide Web and to pick a name for your site. A lot of mystery is built into these two choices—probably more than need be. A number of folks are advertising that they know the secret of getting your web site to be one of those first hits that come up on the search engines out of the thousands who are also offering similar products or services. I think that is all a lot of hooey. For these self-declared experts to be correct, there would have to be fewer than 10–20 clients in any field anyway, even if the experts had the secret. (If enough of these experts all promise to get their 10–20 clients in the top search result spots, how can that be possible?) Beyond the list of the first 20 sites listed, the chances of your site being viewed by a prospect as a result of a search drops dramatically.

You can certainly improve the position of your site on search engines—I don't doubt that. However, I would not make that my primary means of promoting a web site. The truth is that there are so many competitors doing business on the Internet in every field that if you're going to depend on the search engines as your primary marketing tool to get you business, you are going to miss out on quite a bit. If you want to improve your position on the search engines, I recommend http://selfpromotion.com. This web site will tell you how to do it. You'll learn what to do on your own, and you will save a lot of money too.

SELECTING AN ISP

There are hundreds of ISPs, and you can locate them through a search. My ISP is Solo Web Hosting services at http://www.websolo.com. You can register on the Internet, and they advertise they can activate you in 10 minutes. They offer a free domain name check at their site and will register your name for you with InterNIC (a registration agency discussed in the next section).

SELECTING A NAME

Pick a name that is short, easy to remember, and easy to reach. That way, whenever you give it out, whether face to face in casual conversation or more formally in a speech, people will remember it, whether they write it down or not.

Registering Your Domain Name

Once you have a name, you must register it with what is called InterNIC. They will also give you your domain address called a URL(universal resource locator). Among other things, registration prevents duplication in domain names. I registered with Network Solutions, Inc.[2] You can also register electronically at http://about .networksolutions.com. Yahoo! and others also provide this service nowadays.

Other Services

Other services may be of interest to you. For example, if you sell a product, you will want your customer to be able to order using a credit card. If you sell written information, giving your customer the opportunity to download the information on the spot saves you postage and printing costs and lets your customer get the material instantly. These and other services are all available at a nominal additional cost to you. You just have to check with the potential ISP and see what it provides, or you can do an Internet search using the words "credit cards merchant services."

WHY NOT A CYBERMALL?

Cybermalls, or virtual malls, have been heavily promoted with full-page newspaper advertisements on weekends, free seminars, videotapes, and you name it. At first blush, the idea sounds good. Just like regular shopping malls, you open a store or office on a cybermall. The cybermall develops your site and you pay yearly rent for it. Most offer some sort of training, which is really consulting to help you with marketing questions. And most cybermalls bundle services: e-mail boxes, free virtual banners advertising your service, and the like. Costs are high in comparison with an ISP, as much as $1,000 or more a year, compared with $100 to $200 or less for an ISP.

Is a cybermall worth the additional costs? For most consultants, I would say no. The mall theory assumes that (1) people come to visit the mall and stop in and buy your services just like a regular shopping mall and (2) clients come to a mall for one thing and see your listing and go to visit your site, too. The latter assumption is called spillover.

I do not go along with this theory. First, I believe the psychology of people visiting the regular shopping mall is not the same as those visiting the virtual mall. People go to a regular mall partly for a good time. They go to see what's new, they socialize, they have lunch, and they may even go to a movie. For many it is a day at the mall, and they shop till they drop. Those who visit a cybermall are usually looking for something specific. Few have the time to spend all day at a cybermall, which does not have the socialization with friends, spouse, or girlfriend/boyfriend that goes along with it. So even though the cybermall may be well promoted—and most are not—you are not going to get much walk-in business just because you are in a virtual mall. Besides, how many consultants do you see with storefronts or offices in real malls?

Second, spillover is not a cybermall phenomenon. Unlike the thrill of the chase in a day of buying, cybermall buyers will probably get what they want and get out. You would have to be pretty lucky for someone to see the business listing on their way out and start looking for a consultant on the spot. Contracting for most types of consulting services simply is not an impulse purchase.

HOW SHOULD YOU MARKET ON THE WORLD WIDE WEB?

The key to World Wide Web marketing is promotion, both online and offline. You have got to get people to your web site. You cannot rely on the search engine to do that for you. There is so much competition on the Web for any business or service that trying to build a business based on a search engine is ludicrous. Try this little exercise yourself. Type in "consulting services" in a search engine and see how many hits you come up with. "Consulting services" is a pretty general phrase, but when I did this on Yahoo!, I came up with 210 *million* hits.

PUBLICITY: THE NUMBER ONE SECRET FOR MARKETING ON THE WEB

Hot!Hot!Hot! was a web site that sold salsa hot sauce over the Internet. The owners sold out some time ago. They began in 1994, so Hot!Hot!Hot! was one of the first businesses to attempt to sell anything online. It became hugely successful and is one of the folk heroes of the Internet. As it happens, the salsa business was located in Old Town, Pasadena, near my home, and I participated in some consulting for the owners of Hot!Hot!Hot! in their new business. They told me that half of their salsa business came from their web site, the other half from their storefront.

Even in those days, the key was not a search engine. It was publicity. One of the owners had majored in public relations in college. She tirelessly promoted the business and the web site through articles she wrote and interviews she gave to newspapers and magazines about the uniqueness of the business and what was then the uniqueness of web site marketing.

As a consultant, you have got to do the same thing. Synergize your web site marketing with your other marketing efforts. Put your web site address on your business cards, stationery, brochure, and anything else printed having to do with your business. Whenever you talk to anyone, mention your web site address.

USING BANNERS

Banners, sometimes referred to as pop-ups, are the color advertisements you see floating around or popping up as you surf the Internet. You click on them, and they send you to the associated web site. The key is to spend your advertising dollar for banners only where prospective clients hang out. Amazon.com, the online bookseller, puts banners all over the Web, but each banner is specific to the topic of the web site in which it appears. Even so, much of Amazon's advertising dollar is probably wasted because frequenters of some web sites are probably not readers or buyers of books or other products being sold at the banner site. On the other hand, if you did consulting for a certain industry and could place a banner at that industry's trade association's web site, you would probably get some business.

You can get banner advertising free by putting someone else's banner on your site. One way is to find noncompetitive but compatible sites and offer a one-for-one exchange. There are also banner exchange services. If you use them, however, the exchange may not be one for one; that is, you may need to carry two ads for every one of yours. The reason is that exchange companies make their money by selling those extra ad impressions to companies willing to pay for more exposure. Here are some sources of banner exchange services:

✦ Index of banners: http://exchanges.nu/banners/

✦ Click4Click: http://www.click4click.com

✦ CoPromote: http://www.eliteweb.com/copromote/banners.htm

You can have banners created at http://www.bannermode.com or using programs at the preceding sites.

CYBERLINKS

Cyberlinks are electronic links connecting one web site to another.

Point your mouse at a link and click the button. Presto, you are taken to the web site.

Like much of marketing on the World Wide Web, cyberlinks are an example of using proven concepts in another environment. Find non-competing consultants and offer to exchange links. In other words, in your web site will be a cyberlink describing their consulting service and linking your site with theirs. On their site, you will describe your serv-ice, and there will be a similar link.

Again, it is a win-win for everyone. The other consultancy gets clients it would not normally get, and so do you. Moreover, the clients win too because you can build a directory of links at your site that can attract people who are looking for a unique type of consulting, which you may not offer.

Here are a few link exchanges to try:

✦ LinkAdage: http://www.linkadage.com
✦ GotLinks?.com: http://www.gotlinks.com
✦ LinkMarket: http://www.linkmarket.net

GIVING INFORMATION AWAY

The concept of giving information away seems to confirm the law that whatever you give away comes back to you many times over. That is the concept behind sending out a newsletter (described in Chapter 3). As a matter of fact, you can put your newsletter on your web site. If you come out with a new edition every month or so, you will get some people returning every month to read it. You can also promote your free newsletter to bring in traffic to your consulting web site, put articles you have published on your web site, and, of course, place all your brochure information on the site. But the reality is that your site is one big brochure with unlimited space and no printing or mailing costs.

However, do not put the article or newsletter on your web site directly; instead, connect them to a link whereby your clients or prospects can download the information to their computers. That way, you also can build a list of prospects by their e-mail addresses. This list is extremely valuable for Internet marketing, as we will see.

Usenet and Blog Marketing

The Usenet is a worldwide bulletin board system that can be accessed through the Internet or through many online services. The Usenet contains more than 14,000 forums, called newsgroups, that cover every imaginable interest group. It is used daily by millions of people around the world. People participate by reading the postings of others and maybe by adding their own in response. Some newsgroups are screened for what is allowed to be posted and what is not. Others are complete free-for-alls. Newsgroups have their own protocol and etiquette that you need to master before you market on them. A mass marketing of your services through postings—called spamming—would be ill-advised. It can get you banned by some ISPs, and many will not do business with you once you do it. It is important to know the culture of the newsgroup you are dealing with before you begin to market.

The Usenet is different from a blog, which is a special web site or a portion of a site that you start and run, in which you and maybe others can write or comment on whatever you want in chronological, journal-type entries. Blogging allows you to promote pretty much what you want. Of course, if this is pure promotion, you are going to get some negative comments from others for the world to see. For marketing either way, be subtle. Demonstrate your expertise; do not sell directly.

You can reach the newsgroup through your browser. Here are a few directories to begin with:

- Newsgroups: http://www.newsgroups.com
- Google and Yahoo Newsgroups: http://www.newsgroups-1.com
- Cyberfiber Newsgroups: http://www.cyberfiber.com

E-Mail Marketing

E-mail is electronic mail (as mentioned in Chapter 15). You type in a letter, press a button, and the message is instantly sent anywhere in the world. If you have the e-mail addresses of 1,000 or 10,000 potential clients, you hit one button, and—zap—you send your message to those 1,000 or 10,000 potential clients instantly, and sending them does not cost you a cent. Pretty good, right? There must me a catch. Well, there is, but it is a small one. If your message is unwelcome, then you are spamming, just as with the newsgroups. Trust me, you are going to regret spamming.

So it looks like catch-22. We have this wonderful method of direct marketing that is instantaneous and costs nothing, but if we use it, we can kill our business. What can we do? There are three solutions, and they all depend on sending our advertisement only to those we are certain want it. To do this, here are the three methods:

1. Do your research, offer something free, and make certain it is something the recipient is going to be interested in.

2. Ask visitors to your web site whether they would like to receive additional updates about your consulting activities periodically. Those who answer yes get on your e-mail mailing list.

3. Buy or rent e-mail lists of people who have specifically requested information about the kinds of products or services you are offering. It is extremely important to ensure that the names you use are permission based and that the lists contain opt-in e-mail addresses (that is, the individuals have asked to be on the list). Otherwise you will be spamming.

Here are some sources and descriptions of e-mail lists you can take a look at. They will also help you to select the specific search criteria and demographics for the businesses (sales volume, employee size, etc.) or individuals (age, income, etc.) to whom you want to send your promotion.

✦ infoUSA: http://www.infousa.com

✦ EmailResults.com: http://www.copywriter.com/lists/

✦ EMG Marketing Solutions:
   http://www.emgmarketingsolutions.com

WHY NOT AN E-MAIL NEWSLETTER?

You can easily develop your newsletter and distribute it by e-mail, saving all sorts of printing and mailing costs. Or you can use both forms for increased effectiveness.

E-Zinez.com publishes an entire free handbook on how to publish an e-mail newsletter at http://www.e-zinez.com.

BOOKS ON INTERNET MARKETING

For additional reference, here are three books on Internet marketing:

Business-to-Business Internet Marketing by Barry Silverstein (Maximum Press)

How to Use the Internet to Advertise, Promote and Market Your Business or Web Site with Little or No Money by Bruce C. Brown (Atlantic Publishing Company)

Internet Marketing for Less Than $500/Year: How to Attract Customers and Clients Online Without Spending a Fortune by Marcia Yudkin (Maximum Press)

SUMMING UP

The potential for doing research and promoting your practice on the Internet is incredible. Yet many consultants do not take advantage of the opportunity that the Internet presents. Integrate online marketing and research with traditional methods, and you will find your productivity much increased and you will get far more bang for each marketing dollar you spend on your practice.

Now we are ready to start up. Let's take a look at how to run your consulting business in Chapter 17.

NOTES

1. MEI/Micro Center, 119 Leap Road, Hilliard, OH 43026; 1-800-634-3478.
2. 13861 Sunrise Valley Drive, Suite 300, Herndon, VA 20171.

17

How to Run Your Consulting Business

NO MATTER HOW EXCELLENT YOU ARE technically as a consultant, unless you are a good business manager you will not realize your full business potential. Your business can even go bankrupt because of your failure to sustain a profit. Therefore, do not skip this chapter. I will explain the various forms of business organization, including proprietorships, partnerships, and corporations. I will include information on business licenses, resale permits, fictitious name registration, the use of credit cards, stationery, and business cards, insurance, and personal liability. I will also tell you about other important topics, such as how to keep your overhead low, what expenses to anticipate, and what records you should maintain.

SELECTING THE LEGAL STRUCTURE FOR YOUR CONSULTING FIRM

The law recognizes several structures from which you can choose for your consulting practice: the sole proprietorship, the partnership, and the corporation. Each structure has its own advantages and disadvantages, and you should select the one that is most suitable for you.

THE SOLE PROPRIETORSHIP

The sole proprietorship is a business structure for a company that is owned by only one person. All you need to do to establish a sole proprietorship is obtain whatever business licenses are required in your local area. This makes the proprietorship the easiest of legal structures to set up. It is also the most frequently used for many types of small businesses and certainly one that you should consider for your practice.

Advantages

1. **Ease and Speed of Formation.** With the sole proprietorship, there are fewer formalities and legal requirements. Sometimes you need only visit your county clerk, fill out a simple form, and pay the license fee, which is generally $200 or less. In most cases, there is no waiting period; you can satisfy all legal requirements the same day you make your visit.

2. **Reduced Expense.** Because of the minimal legal requirements, the sole proprietorship can be set up without an attorney, so it is much less expensive than either a partnership or a corporation.

3. **Total Control.** Since you have no partners and your business is not a corporation, you have complete control over its management; as long as you fulfill the legal requirements, you run your business as you see fit. Except for your clients, you have no boss. You and the marketplace make all the decisions. This feature has the additional advantage of responsiveness: You can usually respond much more quickly to changes in the marketplace.

4. **Sole Claim to Profits.** Because you are the sole owner, you are not required to share your profits with anyone. The profits are yours, as are all the assets of the business.

Disadvantages

1. **Unlimited Liability.** Although you own all the assets and can make all decisions in a sole proprietorship, you are also held to

unlimited personal liability. In other words, you are responsible for the full amount of business debts and judgments against your business. This could amount to more money than you have invested in the business. If your business fails with you owing money to various creditors, the debts could be collected from your personal assets. Of course, there are various methods of reducing this risk, such as with proper insurance coverage (discussed later in this chapter).

2. **No One to Talk To.** Because in a sole proprietorship you are a one-person show, your own skills, education, background, and capabilities limit you. You may be able to get advice and counsel from friends, relatives, or business acquaintances, but no one is motivated by personal investment to give you this advice, nor will the giver suffer the consequences if the advice proves to be poor.

3. **Difficulty in Absences.** Again, because you are the sole owner, you will have to find someone to cover for you when you are sick or on vacation. Of course, there are ways around this limitation. You could agree to watch over the practice of some other consultant who works in the same area with the understanding that he or she will do the same for you. You could also pay someone to cover for you during your periods of absence. But no matter what solution you select, until you have employees working for you who can perform certain services for clients, it is a limitation that must be considered.

4. **Difficulties in Raising Capital.** Potential lenders see the sole proprietorship as represented essentially by one person. As a result, they feel the risk is greater than if more people were involved, as in a partnership, or if you had a permanent legal identity, as in a corporation.

THE PARTNERSHIP

Legally, a partnership can be entered into simply by acquiring a business license from your county clerk. However, unlike the sole proprietorship, I do not recommend that you attempt to do this by yourself; get the help of an attorney. Partnership definitions may vary from state to state, and it is extremely important to document the obligations, as well as the investments and profits, of each partner with a partnership agreement. Such an agreement should typically cover the following aspects of the practice:

- Absence and Disability
- Arbitration
- Authority of Individual Partners in the Conduct of the Business
- Character of Partners, Including Whether General or Limited, Active or Silent
- Contributions by Partners, Both Now and at a Later Time
- Dissolution of the Practice if Necessary
- Division of Profits and Losses
- Salary, Including Draws from the Business During Its Growth State or at Any Period Thereafter
- Duration of the Agreement
- Managerial Assignment Within the Firm
- Expenses and How They Will Be Handled by Each Partner
- Name, Purpose, and Domicile of the Partnership
- Performance by Partners
- Records and Methods of Accounting
- Release of Debts
- Required and Prohibited Acts
- Rights of Continuing Partner
- Sale of Partnership Interest
- Separate Debts
- Settlement of Disputes

How a Partnership Differs from a Sole Proprietorship

It is important to understand what differentiates a partnership from a sole proprietorship. A partnership features:

1. Co-Ownership of the Assets
2. Limited Life of the Partnership
3. Mutual Agency
4. Share in Management

5. Share in Partnership Profits
6. Unlimited Liability of at Least One Partner

Advantages

1. **Ease and Speed of Formation.** Like the sole proprietorship, establishing a consulting business using the partnership structure is fairly quick and easy.

2. **Access to Additional Capital.** In a sole proprietorship, the initial capital must come from your personal funds or loans from other sources. In the case of a partnership, you have at least one other source of additional capital (i.e., at least one partner) for your consulting practice.

3. **Assistance in Decision Making.** Two heads are better than one. With a partnership, you have at least one other person to help you analyze the situations that you may come across in the management of the business and to conduct the consulting work itself.

4. **Vacation and Sickness Stability.** Having a partner makes it much easier to take a vacation or to have someone else handle clients when you are ill. Partners can cover for each other.

Like all other structures of business, partnerships have disadvantages too, and some of them are severe. In fact, many attorneys recommend against a partnership because of potential problems later on in the life of the business (even though many law firms themselves are organized as partnerships).

Disadvantages

1. **Liability for the Actions of Partners.** All partners are bound by the actions of any one partner, and under normal circumstances you are liable for the actions and commitments of any partner. Thus, a single partner can expend resources or make business commitments, and all partners are liable whether or not they agree.

2. **Potential Organizational Disputes.** Because organizations are made up of human beings, partners, especially equal partners,

may disagree. Even friends may find themselves at loggerheads if it is not clearly decided ahead of time, and in writing, who is the president, who is the chief executive officer, who is the vice president, and so on. It has been said that for this reason, partnerships have all the disadvantages of a marriage with none of the advantages.

3. **Difficulty in Obtaining Capital.** Like a sole proprietorship, a partnership may be viewed as less stable than a corporation. As a result, in comparison to corporations, partnerships find it relatively more difficult to raise capital when and if needed.

THE CORPORATION

Unlike a sole proprietorship or a partnership, a corporation is a legal entity separate and distinct from its owner. Also unlike the other two, a corporation cannot be viewed as a simple organizational structure. It is possible to set up a corporation without the aid of an attorney, but I do not recommend it. The reason is that state laws on corporations differ, and you need an attorney to explain the many consequences of the laws of the state you operate in. Also, corporations that do business in more than one state must comply with the federal laws on interstate commerce and with the laws of the various states, which vary considerably. Further, you can limit yourself severely and may actually be in violation of the law if you deviate from the purpose of the corporation as set forth when you incorporate. Again, attorneys can be of great help in all these areas; in my experience, the do-it-yourself forms found in books telling you how to create your own corporation often lead to problems down the road.

Advantages

1. **Limited Liability.** In a corporation, your liability is limited to the amount of your investment in the business. This protects you from creditors or judgments against you because you can lose only what you have invested, not your personal holdings outside the business. However, the limited liability concept does not apply to corporations that offer professional services, and it is entirely possible that some consultancies may fall into that category.

2. **Relative Ease in Obtaining Capital.** Many consulting firms need capital at one time or another for expansion or for other purposes. Lenders of all types are usually more willing to make loans to an organization with a permanent legal structure, such as a corporation, than to either of the other two basic types of structures. However, many banks may require the officer or officers of a small corporation to personally cosign loans.

3. **Additional Human Resources.** A board of directors is required for a corporation. As long as qualified board members are appointed, more help is available to you as an integral part of the business than is the case with either a partnership or a sole proprietorship. However, a one-person corporation is in the same boat as a sole proprietorship should the owner be absent; no one will be there to cover.

4. **Credibility with Clients and the Industry.** A corporation, because of its permanent legal status, generally has more credibility with potential clients. Admittedly, at some point in the lifetime of your firm this becomes a very minor advantage when your firm's reputation, whether incorporated or not, will be the primary factor. But at the start, incorporation can be of some importance.

Disadvantages

1. **Additional Paperwork and Government Regulations.** More paperwork and regulations are associated with the corporation than with either of the other two structures.

2. **Reduced Control.** A corporation must have a board of directors, and you must contend with additional local, state, and federal government regulations. Business activities thus tend to be much more restricted than in the simpler types of business structures. Also, the corporation cannot diverge from its mission statement without an amendment to its corporate charter.

3. **Expense Information.** The corporate structure is the most expensive to form because of the need to use an attorney. It is also slower to set up.

4. **Inability to Take Losses as Deductions.** If you lose money in either a partnership or a sole proprietorship, you can take these

losses as deductions for personal income tax purposes. With a corporation, losses sustained in the current year cannot be used to reduce other personal income. However, a corporation's loss may be carried forward or back to reduce another year's income. An exception in dealing with corporation losses involves setting up a special type of corporation, a possibility you should discuss with your accountant or attorney.

5. **Income Taxes.** A few years ago, favorable income tax treatment would have been considered an advantage of incorporating. But that was when the maximum rate of federal income tax on corporations was 46 percent of net profits, whereas maximum personal income tax was 50 percent. (At one time, personal income tax was as high as 90 percent!) Because tax laws change frequently, always check with an accountant.

Currently, income taxes are usually a disadvantage of the corporate form because of double taxation. Corporate profits are taxed once through the corporation itself as a legal entity. Then Uncle Sam takes a second bite through your salary or when profits are distributed to you as a shareholder. If profits are high enough, double taxation may not be a concern for you. You could be building your practice and then taking your money out when you sell the practice. However, if profits are not that high, you will be losing money through taxation instead of saving it. You should check the latest tax laws to judge the trade-offs.

The S Corporation

The S corporation is a type of corporation created especially by Congress to benefit small companies. At the option of the corporation, it can have its income taxed to the shareholders as if it were a partnership. This is a good deal for a couple of reasons. First, you avoid the double taxation disadvantage. Second, you can offset business losses incurred by the corporation against your personal income. The net result is that you have the advantages of incorporating without the taxation disadvantages.

To qualify as an S corporation, you must meet certain requirements. These are:

1. There may be no more than ten shareholders, all of whom are individuals or estates.

2. You cannot have any nonresident alien shareholders.

3. You must have only one class of outstanding stock.

4. All shareholders must consent to the election of S corporation treatment.

5. A specified portion of the corporation's receipts must be derived from actual business activity rather than passive investments.

Because of higher corporate taxes under changing tax laws, it may be better not to incorporate at all if your practice is enjoying high profits. So be sure to consult with your accountant before making the decision to be treated as an S corporation.

OTHER LEGAL NECESSITIES

Once you decide on a form of business structure, you still have a few other legal details to take care of.

OBTAINING A BUSINESS LICENSE

As already noted, unless you incorporate, you generally need only local business licenses, either municipal or county or both. The licenses may require that you conform to certain zoning laws, building codes, and other regulations set forth by local health, fire, or police departments. However, usually these restrictions are minimal and fairly easily met in the case of a consulting practice. Certain permits may be required for certain types of consultancies or activities that are considered hazardous or in some other way detrimental to the community. But if you are required to obtain such a permit, you will be so informed when you purchase the business license. Again, for a consulting practice, usually this type of permit is not required.

Some states require licensing for certain occupations, possibly affecting certain types of consulting practices. If so, you will be so informed when you get your local business license. For example, most states require personnel recruiters who place job applicants to be licensed. For complete information, contact your state department of commerce.

Also, federal licensing requirements for some businesses could affect certain types of consulting, such as an investment advisory service. Again, you will usually be informed if you need an additional license when you get your local business license. But to be absolutely certain, contact the U.S. Department of Commerce, which can be found under the "U.S. Government" listing in your local telephone directory.

THE RESALE PERMIT

If your state has a sales tax, it also has a state board to control and collect the tax. Usually this board will allow you to secure a resale permit.

The resale permit has two purposes. First, it assigns you duties as an agent of the state to collect sales tax. Second, it allows you to purchase items you intend to resell to someone else without paying the tax yourself. If there is sales tax in your state, you must either give your resale permit number to a vendor or you must pay the tax. If a fee is required to obtain a resale permit, the agency involved will inform you at the time you apply for it. Frequently, this agency requires security from you in the form of a cash deposit against the payment of future state tax on the products that you will sell. This amount can be sizable, as much as several thousand dollars in some states. If you fail to pay any sales tax due, the state can deduct this amount from your deposit, thus protecting itself even if you go bankrupt. In most states, there is no sales tax on professional services, only on the sale, rental, and repair of tangible personal property. You need to check your state's regulations.

It is definitely not to your advantage to tie up several thousand dollars of your hard-earned cash merely to satisfy a security deposit for a resale permit. In some cases, when the deposit is high, you can arrange for installment payments. However, the amount of money required—if any—depends on the information you provide at the time you obtain the resale permit, and minimum requirements are usually determined when certain conditions are met. These situations include if:

✦ You own your home and have substantial equity in it.

✦ The estimated monthly expenses of your consulting practice are low.

✦ Your estimated monthly sales are low.

✦ You are presently employed and your business activities are part time.

✦ You have no employees other than yourself.

✦ You have only one place of business.

Remember that services are usually not taxed, only products. But if products are part of your business or an adjunct to your consulting practice, you should obtain a resale permit if there is a state tax in your state.

FICTITIOUS NAME REGISTRATION

Fictitious name registration is required if you use any name in your practice other than your own. If you use a business name that includes names other than yours or your partners', that implies the existence of additional partners, or indeed that implies anything that your practice is not, you will need to register a fictitious name. For example, James A. Smith is a perfectly acceptable business name that does not require fictitious name registration as long as your name is actually James A. Smith. However, James A. Smith and Associates requires fictitious name registration.

Some fictitious names you usually cannot use at all. You cannot, for example, call yourself a university or research center or go by any other description that implies a nonprofit corporation unless you are one. Most states will prohibit you from using the title doctor, reverend, or professor unless you meet certain legal requirements. Other than those types of restrictions, most doing-business-as (dba) names are acceptable as long as you obtain the proper registration. Interestingly, consulting firms may take advantage of fictitious name registration; law and CPA firms may not.

Fictitious name registration is usually very easy; it should not be considered a major problem in setting up your consulting practice. First, find out the law in your state by contacting someone such as the country clerk. Typically there is a small registration fee of less than $50 and another small fee, perhaps $30 to $50, for the publication of your registration in a general circulation newspaper distributed in the area in which you intend to do business. Once publication is accomplished, you file the affidavit with your county clerk's office. In many cases, the newspapers can handle the entire matter for you. The form is simple, and filling it out takes only a few minutes. Many states allow you to obtain more than one fictitious name on the form. For some types of consulting practices, having more than one dba name can be useful; it allows you to test certain products under names other than your client's or the regular business name of your practice. Then, if the product fails in the marketplace, it will have no effect on either your image or your client's.

Fictitious name registration is in force for a predetermined fixed period, which varies by state; five years is typical. In many cases, newspapers will write you ahead of time offering to handle the renewal for you. In this way, they secure publication of the form in their newspaper.

CLIENTS' USE OF CREDIT CARDS

Credit cards, such as Visa and MasterCard, are becoming increasingly useful for the professional consulting practice. In fact, many other professionals, such as doctors and dentists, now accept credit cards from their patients or clients.

Accepting credit cards has two major benefits for you. First, it adds additional credibility. Companies or individuals that have not done business with you before will recognize the Visa or MasterCard name and will realize that those agencies investigated you before allowing you to use their services. Second, the consumer credit company will provide credit to your clients and will collect the money for you. Thus, several thousand dollars in consulting fees can be billed and paid over a period of time without your being the collection agency.

Of course, there is a disadvantage to using consumer credit companies: You pay the company a certain percentage of each billing. Usually the higher your credit card sales, the lower the percentage the consumer credit company charges. The percentage involved is generally about 4 percent of the sale.

STATIONERY AND BUSINESS CARDS

Get the highest-quality business cards and stationery that you can. These items represent you to your clientele and communicate a message about the type of firm you are. Get the most expensive you can afford. Your stationery should have at least 25 percent rag content, and the letters should be engraved. The raised print has a classic appearance. A less expensive way to achieve this raised look is with a process known as thermography. The same is true of your business cards. You can do everything using desktop publishing, but, of course, raised lettering is then not possible. This is a trade-off that you are going to have to consider: the higher-quality appearance of raised letters versus the increased expense and loss of flexibility. If you use a logo, it should be simple and representative of the type of consulting you do. "High-class professional" is what you want your stationery and business cards to say.

Many companies offer low-cost business cards on the Internet today. Most of these allow you to develop your own custom cards with your own logo. So there is no excuse for consultants not to have their own business cards, and the difference in pricing between what you can obtain over the Internet and through a local printer in many cases is greater than the cost of this book!

Here are a few business card sources:

✦ VistaPrint: www.VistaPrint.com
✦ GigglePrint.com: www.GigglePrint.com
✦ Prints Made Easy.com: www.PrintsMadeEasy.com
✦ magicprints: www.MagicPrints.com

INSURANCE AND PERSONAL LIABILITY

As a consultant, you face certain risks, some of which you can insure against and some of which you cannot. For example, you cannot insure against changes in economic and business conditions, the marketplace, or technology. Any of these can change and hurt your business. However, other types of risks can be transferred through insurance: bad debts caused when subcontractors or clients go bankrupt, disasters caused by weather or fire, theft, liabilities from negligence and other actions, and death or disability of key company executives.

You should think of insurance as a form of risk management, and do it in a four-step process.

1. **Identify** the risks to which your consulting practice will be subjected.
2. **Evaluate** the probability of occurrence of each risk. Also list the cost to you should this event occur and the cost of insurance protecting you against the risk.
3. **Choose** the best way to allow for each risk, whether to accept all or part of the risk or to transfer it through insurance.
4. **Control** the risk by implementing what you select as the best method.

The services of direct writers or agents are helpful in the risk-assessment process. A direct writer is a commissioned employee of the insurer, that is, the insurance company. An agent, on the other hand, is an independent businessperson, like you, who has negotiated with the insurer to represent it for a given territory. The agent is also compensated on a commission basis.

There are advantages in both cases. An independent agent may represent many different insurers and so is able to offer you a wider choice of coverage. Also, the independent agent, dealing with many different types of insurers, may have greater overall knowledge in the field than a direct writer whose experience is limited to the employer company. However, direct writers may cost less because their commission is lower than that of the independent agent. Also, direct writers become specialists in their line, with in-depth knowledge and experience. For a certain type of insurance of particular importance to you, this seller may know the finer details of the risk you are attempting to manage.

To locate direct writers or agents, consult your phone book or ask friends or acquaintances in business.

KEEPING OVERHEAD LOW

One of the most important pieces of advice that I can give to you for managing your consulting practice is to maintain a low overhead. Specifically, keep costs that do not directly contribute to each and every project or to marketing at the absolute minimum. Many new consultants feel, for example, that they must have a fancy office at a prestigious address. If an address is indeed necessary to your success, you can usually rent a mail drop in an upscale neighborhood. But usually the address is not really an important factor in your being hired as a consultant. The fact is that most clients do not come to your office; usually you go to theirs.

Many years ago, when I was working for a company as director of research and development, I interviewed an individual who told me the following sad tale. He and several other senior executives in a major aerospace company resigned to form their own consulting practice. Each invested enough money to last many months—they thought. Coming from a large company in which each had had an expensive office, elegant furniture, and a personal secretary, these new consultants found it impossible to control spending for what they considered minimum requirements. They leased expensive offices in a high-rent area and outfitted them with rich mahogany paneling and thick, luxurious rugs. But that rich image did not save this fledgling consulting firm from bankruptcy; in a few weeks, their money was depleted. On the other hand, I am acquainted with a wealthy search consultant who did half a million dollars in billing his first year out of his home. As his partner told me, he did hundreds of thousands of dollars in billings in his pajamas, but neither his clients nor the executives he placed ever knew.

Remember that at first you do not even need a secretary, only typing services. Even this, you can do yourself with a computer. What you definitely do not need is a secretary sitting around with nothing to do except contributing to your ego.

For most consulting practices, consider starting with a home office, especially if you are beginning part time. In my many years of consulting, I can count on one hand the number of times a client has visited the office that I maintain in my home. It happens usually if the client is in a start-up situation and thus has no office for me to go to. Occasionally the pressure of time will prevent you from traveling, and your client will come to you. One multimillion-dollar accountant calculated that since my billing rates were higher than his, it was less expensive for him to travel to my office than the other way around.

THE TELEPHONE

Today, many consultants use their cell phones for business purposes. Cell phones are convenient because you can make and receive calls wherever you are, and they are relatively inexpensive. If you are talking on your cell phone or have it turned off, callers can simply leave a voice mail message so that you get your messages quickly. Be aware, however, that you probably cannot deduct cell phone expenses for tax purposes, unless your cell phone is used only for business.

To keep overhead low and yet maintain a land-line business telephone without a secretary, you can rely on voice mail to collect your messages, or you can go with one of the two old standbys: a telephone answering service or a telephone answering machine. Again there are trade-offs, advantages, and disadvantages to both. The telephone answering machine is relatively inexpensive; a good, professional-quality machine can be purchased for several hundred dollars. The disadvantage is that some potential clients simply will not leave a message on an answering machine. However, I believe that if your answering message is carefully worded and if you promise to get back to the caller soon, you have the greatest probability of getting the message that you need to continue the business relationship.

Even though an answering service may cost more, it may not be as effective as a machine. Some answering service operators are rude and inconsiderate, and they will leave your caller on hold for long periods of time. This can be worse than a machine, where at least you control the friendliness and professionalism of the voice doing the answering. If you do use an answering service, I recommend that you check on it periodically to ensure that the operator has the highest standards of professionalism and is not losing clients through rudeness or incompetence.

Should you have a special business phone listing for a home office?

Maybe not. Business telephone listings are usually more expensive than personal telephones, and many telephone systems will charge you more to connect a business telephone than a personal telephone. However, the business listing entitles you to a special entry in the *Yellow Pages*, and if you want a special advertisement (discussed in Chapter 2), you need to be listed as a business.

You can have a personal telephone converted to the business telephone at little or no extra charge. If your practice is listed under your real name and you do not need the *Yellow Pages* listing as a consultant, it makes little sense to obtain a special business telephone—at least as defined by telephone companies. There is nothing wrong with having a telephone company install an additional personal phone that you call a business telephone. As long as you use it totally for business purposes, it should be deductible for tax purposes. If it is listed on your business card and your stationery, as far as your clients know, it is your business telephone.

FAX MACHINES

Fax machines are definitely a must. With a fax machine, you can send or receive photographs, reports, or other documents, and it is a good alternative to a computer for quick transmission. Do not get the wrong idea. You can still operate with great efficiency without owning or using a fax machine. But after you begin to see a positive cash flow, it is a handy piece of equipment to have. Fax machines are quicker than the mail. Because the information is transmitted right away over your telephone lines, you can save a lot of money on overnight couriers. Of course, to a certain degree this advantage has been superseded by e-mail, which is even faster and faxes can be hooked up to the computer and sent as e-mail attachments. However, fax machines allow you to transmit some items that would first have to be scanned if you use e-mail.

ANTICIPATING EXPENSES

One of the biggest mistakes new consultants make is failing to anticipate expenses. Recognize ahead of time that certain expenses will be necessary to set up and run your consulting practice as a business. Plan ahead for these expenses when you estimate the cost of being in business. Here are some typical consulting expenses:

+ Water, Electricity, and Gas
+ Office Supplies
+ Postage
+ Automobile Expenses
+ Telephone
+ Travel Other Than by Automobile
+ Promotional Material, Including Brochures
+ Entertainment
+ Income Taxes
+ Subscriptions to Professional Journals
+ Memberships in Professional and Other Associations

There will undoubtedly be additional expenses depending on the type of consulting you do. Make sure that you forget nothing, and anticipate them before you establish your practice.

NECESSARY RECORDS AND THEIR MAINTENANCE

Good records are necessary for several reasons. You will need them for preparing tax returns, measuring management effectiveness and efficiency, reducing material waste, and even obtaining loans. These are the essential records you should maintain:

1. A daily summary of income received (see the example in Figure 17-1)
2. An expense journal (see the example in Figure 17-2), which lists your expense payments in chronological order
3. An expense ledger summary (see Figure 17-3), in which cash and check payments are totaled by category—for example, rent, wages, and advertising
4. An inventory purchase journal (if product is in any way a part of

Figure 17-1. Daily summary of income received.

Day/Date Item Sold or Service Performed	Amount	
Total amount received today		
Total amount received through yesterday		
Total amount received to date		

your practice), which notes shipments received, accounts payable, and cash available for future purchases (as shown in Figure 17-4)

5. An employee compensation record, listing hours worked, pay rate, and deductions withheld for both part-time and full-time employees (as shown in Figure 17-5)

6. An accounts receivable ledger for outstanding invoices (as shown in Figure 17-6)

(text continues on page 238)

Figure 17-2. Expense journal.

Date	To Whom Paid	Purpose	Check Number	Amount	
			Total expenditures		

Figure 17-3. Expense journal summary.

Purpose	Total This Period		Total up to This Period		Total to Date	
Advertising						
Car and truck expense						
Commissions						
Contributions						
Delivery expense						
Dues and publications						
Employee benefit program						
Freight						
Insurance						
Interest						
Laundry and cleaning						
Legal and professional services						
Licenses						
Miscellaneous expense						
Office supplies						
Pension and profit-sharing plan						
Postage						
Rent						
Repairs						
Selling expense						
Supplies						
Tax						
Telephone						
Traveling and entertainment						
Utilities						
Wages						
Totals						

Figure 17-4. Inventory purchase journal.

Date	Inventory Ordered Carried Forward	Shipment Received/Date	Accounts Payable	Cash Available for Future Purchases
		Totals		

TAX OBLIGATIONS

As the owner of a consulting practice, you are responsible for payment of federal, state, and local taxes. Because federal taxation tends to be the most complex for new consultants, we will look at them first. There are four basic types of federal taxes that you may run into: (1) income taxes, (2) Social Security taxes, (3) excise taxes, and (4) unemployment taxes. In addition, you may be subject to state and local taxes. Let's look at each in more detail.

INCOME TAXES

The amount of federal taxes you owe depends on the earnings of your company and on your company's legal structure. If you have a sole proprietorship or partnership, your other income exemptions and non-

Figure 17-5. Employee compensation record.

Name _____   Social Security No. _____

Date	Period Worked (hours, days, weeks, or months)	Wage Rate	Total Wages	Deductions					Net Paid
				Soc. Sec.	Fed. Inc. Tax	State Inc. Tax			
			Totals						

business deductions and credits are important factors. The tax formula used is generally the same as that for the individual taxpayer. The only difference is that you file an additional form (Schedule C of Form 1040, Profit or Loss from Business or Profession) that identifies items of expense and income connected with your consulting business. If your business is a partnership, the partnership files a business return (Form

Figure 17-6. Accounts receivable ledger.

Date	Customer/Client Name	Products/Services	Amount Owed	Payments Made/Date

1065), and you report only your share of the profit or loss on your personal return.

However, there is an important difference between being a sole proprietor or a partner and being a salaried employee working for someone else. As a sole proprietor or a partner, you are required by law to pay federal income taxes and self-employment taxes *as the income is received*. You do this by completing Estimated Tax for Individuals Form 1040-ES. This is an estimate of the income and self-employment taxes you expect to owe on the basis of anticipated income and exemptions. Payment of tax is made quarterly: April 16, June 15, September 17, and January 15.

If you have a corporation, you must also pay income tax on its net profits separate from the amount taken out for salary, which is considered part of your personal income.

Every corporation whose tax is expected to be $500 or more is required to make estimated tax payments. These must be deposited with an authorized financial institution or a Federal Reserve Bank. Each deposit is made with a federal tax deposit coupon and done in accordance with the instructions on the coupon. Estimated tax is due by the fifteenth day of the fourth, sixth, ninth, and twelfth months of your corporation's tax year. If any date falls on a Saturday, Sunday, or legal holiday, the installment is due on the next regular business day.

To operate your practice, you must have the necessary funds to pay your income taxes on time. Your accountant can help you work out a budget to allow for this. You can also use the worksheet in Figure 17-7 developed by the U.S. Small Business Administration.

Withholding Income Taxes

According to the law, you must withhold federal income tax payments for your employees. These payments are passed on to the government periodically. The process begins when you hire a new employee, who must sign Form W-4, Employee's Withholding Allowance Certificate, listing any exemptions and additional withholding allowances claimed. The completed W-4 is your authorization to withhold income tax in accordance with the current withholding tables issued by the Internal

Figure 17-7. Worksheet for meeting tax obligations.

Kind of Taxes	Due Date	Amount Due	Pay to	Date for Writing the Check
Federal Taxes				
Employee income taxes and Social Security taxes	____	_____	_____	_____
	____	_____	_____	_____
	____	_____	_____	_____
Excise Taxes	____	_____	_____	_____
Owner-manager's and/or corporation's income taxes	____	_____	_____	_____
	____	_____	_____	_____
	____	_____	_____	_____
Unemployment taxes	____	_____	_____	_____
	____	_____	_____	_____
	____	_____	_____	_____
State Taxes				
Unemployment taxes	____	_____	_____	_____
	____	_____	_____	_____
	____	_____	_____	_____
Income taxes	____	_____	_____	_____
Sales taxes	____	_____	_____	_____
	____	_____	_____	_____
	____	_____	_____	_____
Franchise taxes	____	_____	_____	_____
Other	____	_____	_____	_____
	____	_____	_____	_____
Local Taxes				
Sales taxes	____	_____	_____	_____
	____	_____	_____	_____
	____	_____	_____	_____
Real estate taxes	____	_____	_____	_____
Personal property taxes	____	_____	_____	_____
Licenses (retail, vending machines, etc.)	____	_____	_____	_____
Other	____	_____	_____	_____
	____	_____	_____	_____

Revenue Service. If an employee fails to furnish a certificate, you are required to withhold taxes as if he or she were a single person with no exemptions. Before December 1 of each year, you should ask your employees to file new exemption certificates for the following year if there has been a change in their exemption status. At the end of each year, you must furnish each employee with a copy of Form W-2, Wage and Tax Statement. As you know if you have worked for someone else, the employees must file a copy of this with their income tax returns. You, as the employer, must also furnish a copy of it to the IRS on or before February 28 of each year. For complete details, contact the IRS office in your area.

And do not forget to check with your state office to find out whether you are responsible for withholding your employees' state income taxes as well.

Withholding Social Security Taxes

For Social Security taxes, you must deduct a percentage from each employee's wages, and, as an employer, you must match that sum. Check with the Internal Revenue Service for the latest rules and percentages.

The following kinds of payments are not subject to Social Security taxes:

1. Payments made more than six months after the last calendar month in which the employee worked
2. Payments made under workers' compensation law
3. Payments or portions of payments attributable to the employee's contribution to a sick pay plan
4. Most payments made to a state or local government employee (the third-party payer should contact the state or local government employer for instructions)
5. Payments made for medical care
6. Payments (generally for injury) that are not related to absence from work

Remitting Federal Taxes

Remitting federal taxes involves three steps:

1. You must report the income and Social Security taxes you have withheld from the employee's pay.
2. You must deposit the funds you withheld.
3. You must match your employees' contributions.

Use Form 941, Employer's Quarterly Federal Tax Return, to report both Social Security tax and withheld income tax. This form is filed quarterly, but the taxes themselves are paid in advance. Social Security tax and income tax withholding must be deposited regularly in a bank if they exceed a certain amount. How often these deposits must be made depends on your tax liability.

✦ If you owe less than $1,000 in tax at the end of the quarter, your deposit is made by the fifteenth of the month after the quarter ends.

✦ If you withheld less than $50,000 during the 12-month period ending last June 30, you must deposit tax monthly—by the fifteenth day of the next month—unless you meet the less-than-$1,000 exception.

Failure to deposit FICA and income tax withholding by the due date results in a 5 percent late payment penalty. You may also be charged interest on the unpaid deposit.

The due dates for Form 941 are April 30, July 31, October 31, and January 31. However, if you make timely deposits, you have 10 extra days to file the returns.

The third step, matching the contribution, is done on Form 940. Any additional details are available from your local IRS office.

EXCISE TAXES

Federal excise taxes are due on the sale or use of certain items or transactions and on certain occupations. Normally, a consultant is not involved in excise tax. However, to be absolutely certain, again check with your local IRS office.

UNEMPLOYMENT TAXES

If you pay wages of $1,500 or more in any calendar quarter, or if you have one or more employees on at least some portion of one day in each of 20 or more calendar weeks, either consecutive or nonconsecutive, your consulting practice is liable for federal unemployment (FUTA) taxes. The obligation applies even if you pay wages to different employees, and individuals on sick leave or vacation are counted as employees.

FUTA tax is reported annually on Form 940, Employer's Annual Federal Unemployment Tax Return, which is due by January 31 of the next calendar year. If you have made timely deposits, however, you have until February 10 to file.

When are deposits required? If at the end of any calendar quarter, you owe more than $100 FUTA tax for the year, you must make a deposit by the end of the next month.

FUTA tax is not withheld from your employees' wages. It is an out-of-pocket expense the employer bears.

FUTA tax is computed on the first $7,000 of wages paid to each employee during the calendar year. The tax rate varies, depending on the state in which you do business.

Obtaining an Employer Identification Number

An employer identification number is required for all employment tax returns filed with the federal government. You obtain this number by filing a Form SS-4 with your regional Internal Revenue Service Center. At the same time, you can ask for your business tax kit, IRS 454; it has additional information on taxes pertinent to each type of business or consulting practice with which you may be involved.

STATE AND LOCAL TAXES

State and local taxes vary by area. Three major types of state taxes are (1) unemployment taxes, (2) income taxes, and (3) sales taxes (as discussed under "Other Legal Necessities" earlier in this chapter). Every state has unemployment taxes; the rules vary by state and may not be the same as those of the federal government. Local taxes by counties, towns, and cities may include real estate, personal property taxes, taxes on receipt of businesses, and so forth. For more information on all these types of taxes, contact your local and state governments.

MINIMIZING TAX PAPERWORK

As you can see, many of the required taxes concern employees. If you have no employees, the amount of paperwork is significantly reduced. Instead of hiring permanent staff for your company, try to retain and pay individuals as consultants. There are restrictions on how many hours or days someone may work for you and still be considered a consultant, so be sure to check on the current regulations if you take this route.

For remitting all types of taxes, be certain to consult a good tax accountant. You will pay for the service, but this expert will save you far more in the long run than the cost of the services.

SOURCES OF ADDITIONAL INFORMATION

Here are some books that may assist you in managing your consulting practice:

Accounting and Finance Made Easy by Robert Low (Entrepreneur Press)

Adams Streetwise and Small Business Start-Up: Your Comprehensive Guide to Starting and Managing a Business by Bob Adams (Adams Media)

The McGraw-Hill Guide to Starting Your Own Business: A Step-By-Step Blueprint for the First-Time Entrepreneur by Stephen C. Harper (McGraw-Hill)

SUMMING UP

So the business is set up, you have marketed your business effectively, and you are ready to provide your service to your clients. The next chapter explains how to develop strategies for your client.

18

Developing
Strategies for
Your Client

MANY CLIENTS that do not hire you to develop a strategy are nevertheless interested in having you do this. Although it is not wise to leave your area of expertise, you should know something about strategy development.

Peter Drucker felt that the first responsibility of the leader is to establish the mission, objectives, and goals and then put it all together with a workable strategy to achieve them. Of course, numbers are important in the development of strategy, because they act as important inputs to that greatest of computers and computer programming, the human brain. Yet it is your judgment, not any assignment of numbers and percentages, that enables the development of a strategy that works. Blindly following numbers and percentages can never replace the ability of the human brain to integrate vast amounts of data, both qualitatively as well as quantitatively, and to reason its way through to a solution that works and that is optimal for a given situation. Your brain is better than any computers or computer programs, no matter how sophisticated they may be. In fact, we can introduce major error into the development of strategy when we attempt to assign numbers to elements that cannot and should not be quantified. Assigning numbers to qualitative aspects gives the appearance of truth and accuracy, when in reality we are simply cloaking judgment in a way to make it appear precise and absolute. If you have heard of the term "the tyranny of numbers," you know what the term means.

WHY MY RECOMMENDED APPROACH TO STRATEGY IS DIFFERENT

There are quantitative approaches to strategy development that use matrices going by the name of cow, star, dog, question mark, and the like. For the most part, you don't need them. The use of matrices for developing strategy really is appropriate for a portfolio of products or businesses; hence its name, portfolio management. Strategy using the product life cycle also helps you to make certain strategic decisions regarding what you should do with products or services you have introduced.

But strategy is an art. As a result, there is a concept of strategy that helps us make strategic (and tactical) decisions, whether we are managing portfolios of products or businesses or considering what to do with a product or service in a certain stage of its life cycle. This chapter will enable you to understand and use the concept with or without these other quantitative techniques.

Although we are going to use relatively nonquantitative principles as the core of our discussion, the application of these principles to strategy development can still be scientific. The scientific method is a process that is a reliable, consistent, and nonarbitrary representation of the real world. It minimizes the influence of bias and prejudice. Because numbers are so easily controlled, we frequently assume that to be scientific we must have quantifiable arguments. This is not necessarily true. Drucker, for example, rarely used numbers in his consulting. Yet his clients claimed that he made billions of dollars for him through his strategies. What is true is that we must approach the solution we seek in such a way that the output yields consistent results. In this way, we can avoid a repetition of past errors, capitalize on the greatest chances for success, and reach the predictable and repeatable conclusions we desire.

A scientific method is crucially important when employing judgment, in utilizing strategy principles, and in coordinating the many factors that must be considered in developing operational marketing strategy. The method is particularly critical when various principles conflict (and they often do) or when one principle is more important than another under different conditions (also often true).

PRINCIPLES, RESOURCES, AND SITUATIONAL VARIABLES

When we seek to apply principles of strategy in any situation, we face three aspects:

1. The Principles Themselves
2. The Resources We Have Available
3. The Relevant Variables Found in the Situation

Innumerable concepts have been put forth as the true basic principles of strategy. My own studies have resulted in ten principles that I consider universal:

1. **Commitment to a Definite Objective.** This refers to what you, as a strategist, intend to accomplish.
2. **Seizing and Maintaining the Initiative.** This means that you, not your competitor, should be in control.
3. **Economization to Mass.** No company has unlimited resources. So you need to economize where the situation allows this and concentrate your resources where it is important to be strong.
4. **Surprise.** If your competitor does not know your plans, he cannot prepare to counter your strategy initiatives.
5. **Simplicity**. The simpler your strategy, the easier for everything to come together to be implemented as you intend.

6. **Multiple Simultaneous Approaches and Objectives.** If you have alternate approaches and objectives and if you are clever, you make it difficult or even impossible for a competitor to counter your strategic moves, because if the competitor blocks one way, you can go another.

7. **The Indirect Approach.** If you approach your objective indirectly, you have a greater chance of achieving it, so instead of competing on price, you compete on delivery or service.

8. **Environment.** Select a strategy that matches your environment.

9. **Timing and Sequencing.** Doing the right thing at the wrong time is sometimes worse than not doing it or doing the wrong thing.

10. **Exploitation of Success.** Keep going until your goals are fully achieved.

The situation in question involves basically two types of variables: controllable and uncontrollable. For example, the resources you have to work with may include manpower, capital, equipment, know-how, quality of leadership, among others. They are assets that you control, and you can manipulate them to implement your strategy. You can also exert control over the familiar tactical variables. For example, in a marketing context we can control product, price, promotion, and distribution. You also face situational or environmental (uncontrollable) variables: economic conditions, business conditions, the state of technology, politics, legal and regulatory requirements, social and cultural norms, the competition, and the like.

An astute strategist looks at all aspects of the situation and selects the relevant variables in it. Each variable must be avoided, overcome, ignored, utilized, or turned to an advantage. The strategist must integrate the variables with the principles and, using the resources available, develop a plan to accomplish marketing objectives and goals.[1]

Figure 18-1 contains the three lists of the aspects of strategy necessary, side by side. Then we'll look at an example of how these aspects might be used.

Figure 18-1. Aspects of strategy development and selection.

Situational and Tactical Variables	Principles of Strategy	Available Resources
Economic and business conditions	Commitment to a definite objective	Manpower
State of technology	Seizing and maintaining the initiative	Capital
Politics	Economization to mass	Equipment
Legal and regulatory issues	Positioning	Special knowledge
Social and cultural norms	Surprise	Quality of leaders
The competition	Simplicity	Other relevant assets
Product	Multiple simultaneous alternatives	
Price	The indirect approach	
Promotion	Timing and sequencing	
Distribution	Exploitation of success	

EXAMPLE: ATTACKING A MARKET LEADER'S TOP PRODUCT

To illustrate the method, let's look at one of the most successful new product introductions ever undertaken against a market leader. In 1936, Lever Bros., number two in the soap business behind Procter & Gamble (P&G), introduced Spry vegetable shortening to compete against P&G's well-entrenched Crisco brand.[2]

The smart money said, "No way." Not only was Crisco firmly established, it had been on the market for 20 years. The Great Depression had had little effect on Crisco, so it appeared to be Depression-proof. Sales were up, and the product had no serious challengers, despite the fact that lard and butter were far less expensive. The

Crisco name had become synonymous with vegetable shortening and almost generic. When women asked for Crisco, they meant vegetable shortening. Yet within one year of introduction, Spry had captured 50 percent of Crisco's market share. Moreover, no new ingredients were used, and Spry was made from exactly the same raw materials as Crisco.

HOW LEVER BROS. DID IT

Lever Bros. was a subsidiary of Unilever of London, a giant worldwide corporation. Having been successful with a number of products in the United States, in the late 1920s, it sought another new product to launch. The company first looked at all aspects of the situation, and a vegetable shortening product seemed a good potential candidate. P&G had already proven there was a market. Although its potential competitor's product was well established, its dominance also meant there were no other major competitors or competitive products to contend with. At the time of the initial decision, both business and economic conditions were good.

Lever took a harder look into its competitor's product and found some weaknesses. Although women liked the product, they did not like other things. If refrigerated, the product turned hard and was difficult to use. If left unrefrigerated, it tended to turn rancid. The color was not consistent, and, although housewives would have preferred the product to be pure white, its color tended to be described as more of a dirty white. Moreover, the packaging was not uniform in the cans in which it was supplied, and the housewives did not like that either.

INTEGRATING THE PRINCIPLES

Looking at the principles of strategy, we can see how some were integrated with the situational variables to this point. Lever Bros. seized the initiative and committed to a definite objective. It planned to concentrate resources at the strategic position of shortening. P&G thought its product Crisco was invulnerable; thus it paid little attention and did no research with the consumer. In fact, it had even allowed quality control in manufacture and packaging to get sloppy. As a consequence, the thought that a competitor, even a major one like Lever Bros., would introduce a product to compete with Crisco was totally unexpected, even unthinkable. Lever Bros. capitalized on this belief. Coupled with good security, the company achieved complete surprise with Spry.

LOOKING AT RESOURCES

Lever Bros. decided which of the situational variables could be avoided, overcome, or taken advantage of. Moreover, it had the resources to do this and to support the general principles of strategy it was planning. Unilever had made major technological advances in Europe in the manufacture of soap, and the technology was directly transferable to the production of vegetable shortening due to hydrogenation, the major process common to both types of products. Thus, a vegetable shortening product was compatible with the Lever Bros.' experience, know-how, and technical advantage. The problems with Crisco noted by consumers were easy to overcome. Some had simply to do with stricter quality control. Financial resources and know-how were on Lever Bros.' side, but it even had one additional major advantage.

LEVER BROS.' SECRET WEAPON

Francis Conway had become president of Lever Bros. in 1913 when sales were but $1 million. By the late 1920s, sales were over $40 million, largely due to his personal leadership. Conway had met every challenge thrown at him, and he had the confidence of the parent company's leadership back in England. Unilever invested the money to build the manufacturing plants to make the product. By the early 1930s, Lever Bros. was ready to go.

ENTER THE GREAT DEPRESSION

The Depression began in October 1929 and preempted product launch. By mid-1930 it was clear this was not an economic condition that would change soon, and Lever Bros. had planned on introducing the product by then. There was tremendous pressure from within the company and the parent corporation to do so. The company had sunk a lot of money into Spry, and they wanted to get on with it. However, Conway knew his strategy and the importance of timing. He made the decision to wait. Meanwhile, he did note that the sales of Crisco did not slow, and although Spry was shelved, fine-tuning went on and research into the best promotional approach was initiated.

THE LAUNCH

In late 1935, lard and butter prices rose, creating a situation whereby the higher-priced shortening would be more price competitive. Lever Bros. did not intend to compete with P&G on price in a direct approach strategy. Instead, although it was competing with essentially an identical product, the approach was indirect in the sense that the problems with Crisco, recognized by consumers but not by the manufacturer, were all corrected in the new product, Spry.

Again, Conway economized elsewhere to concentrate and initiate a massive promotional campaign. Until this time, conventional wisdom was to introduce advertising for a new product and let it be assimilated gradually by the consumer. Conway eschewed this approach and gave it everything he had on day one. This included door-to-door salespeople distributing one-pound sample cans and free Spry cookbooks, to discount coupons and advertising even in small-town newspapers. Conway even launched a mobile cooking school that went around the country doing two-hour demonstrations. P&G was stunned, and though it improved its product and manufacturing, it never recaptured the share it had lost. Conway and Lever Bros. integrated the relevant variables with the principles and, using the resources available, developed and initiated a plan that made Spry a success despite the advantages enjoyed by P&G with Crisco.

APPLY THE PRINCIPLES SCIENTIFICALLY

Strategy is an art, but the principles are applied scientifically, not haphazardly. The strategist analyzes the situation and identifies the relevant variables. She uses numbers but does not allow them to overrule good judgment. Rather, she integrates the relevant variables with the principles. Using the resources available, she develops and then implements the marketing plan that will help attain the strategic goals and objectives.

If you want to know more about formulating strategies, especially using this methodology, I recommend my own book, *The Art of the Strategist* (AMACOM, 2004).

SUMMING UP

Once the strategy is in place, it has to be executed. Sometimes, implementation requires more than just your individual efforts, and you find yourself in charge of a consulting team. Chapter 19 explains what it takes to lead a team.

NOTES

1. This concept originated with J.F.C. Fuller, as developed in Anthony John Trythall, *"Boney" Fuller* (Piscataway, NJ: Rutgers University Press, 1977), p. 108.
2. Robert F. Harley, *Marketing Successes*, 2nd ed. (Hoboken, NJ: Wiley, 1985), pp. 68–78.

19

How to Lead Consulting Teams

ONE OF THE MOST IMPORTANT and difficult challenges you may face as a consultant is working on a team, especially if the team consists of individuals who do not normally work for you or with you but who are other independent consultants. Teamwork is never easy. You must work with different personalities, having different work schedules, different priorities, different motivations, and different ways of approaching the project or solving problems.

Occasionally the project is large and requires expertise that you may not have yourself. You will have no choice but to handle this as a team, and you will be the de facto team leader and responsible to your client for the successful completion of the project. Fortunately, there is a power of teams unequaled by that of the individual. Twenty years ago management guru Tom Peters wrote: "The power of the team is so great that it is often wise to violate apparent common sense and force a team structure on almost anything."[1]

WHY TEAMS WORK

Teams in industry have had some amazing achievements. One of General Electric's plants in Salisbury, North Carolina, increased its productivity by 250 percent using teams, compared to other General Electric plants making the same product but without teams. General Mills' plants with teams are 40 percent more productive than plants without teams. Westinghouse Furniture Systems increased productivity 74 percent in three years with teams. Using teams, Volvo's Kalimar facility reduced defects by 90 percent. In one hospital study of critical care, when patients receiving mechanical ventilation are managed by a multidisciplinary team that proactively oversees the weaning process of removing a tube used for breathing, it takes patients nearly two days less time to become acclimated as compared to the traditional process.[2] So the potential for your consultant team to do exceedingly well is real.

However, teams must share the following characteristics if they are to be effective:

+ They must demonstrate coordinated interaction and greater efficiency than when members are working alone.
+ They must enjoy the process of working together.
+ Responsibility usually rotates either formally or informally.
+ There must be mutual care, nurturing, and encouragement among team members, especially between leaders and followers.
+ There must be a high level of trust.
+ Everyone must be extremely interested in everyone else's success.

You may be interested in characteristics of high-performance teams as distinguished from those that performed less well. Keep these in mind as you manage your team.

+ Clear Goals
+ Goals Known by All
+ Goals Achieved in Small Steps
+ Standards of Excellence
+ Autonomy
+ Performance-Based Rewards
+ Competition
+ Praise and Recognition

- Feedback of Results
- Skills and Knowledge of Everyone Used
- Rules and Penalties for Performance
- Performance Measures[3]

- Team Commitment
- Plans and Tactics Used
- Adequate Resources Provided
- Continuous Improvement Expected

As you might expect, when you have a group working together toward a common goal showing these characteristics, you will see some very positive results. The group becomes not just a team, but a successful team. The team members have a degree of understanding and acceptance not found outside the group. They produce a greater numbers of ideas, and these ideas are of a higher quality than if they thought up ideas individually and met to make a list of the total. Such a team has higher motivation and performance levels, which offset individual biases and cover each other's blind spots. With fewer blind spots and performing together in such a way as to emphasize each member's strengths and make individual weaknesses irrelevant, an effective team is more likely to take risks and innovative action that leads to such levels of success as those achieved by the winning football team in a Super Bowl.

HOW SHOULD YOU LEAD A TEAM OF CONSULTANTS?

There is no way of telling you how to be a leader in 25 words or less. Volumes have been written about leadership. I should know. I wrote a couple of them myself.

I will, however, point out one critical fact: If you are team leader acting for your client, you have a major responsibility for the ultimate result. There is an old saying that it is better to have an army of lambs led by a lion than an army of lions led by a lamb. This emphasizes the extreme importance of the leader in getting the job done. The excuse that "all my team members were lambs" does not relieve you of the responsibility for success. A leader who says such a thing is really saying, "I am a lamb." So how should you lead a team of consultants? Be a lion! Then even if your team members are lambs, you will succeed.

Beyond that advice, although I cannot make you an expert leader in a few pages of suggestions, I can tell you a few things that you need to know about being a team leader.

RECOGNIZING TEAM STAGES

Psychologists and researchers of leadership have found that teams progress through four stages of development. Not only does each stage have different characteristics, but members of teams tend to ask different questions in each stage. Partly because the concerns of the team tend to be different in each stage, the leader's focus, actions, and behavior must also be different. This adjustment is important because what might be the correct action in one stage would be counterproductive in another. For example, in the second stage of development, members actually tend to be committed and even obedient. The leader's focus during this stage must be on building relationships and facilitating tasks. But look out! In the next stage, members tend to challenge each other and even their leader. You've got to focus on conflict management and examining key work processes to make them better. If you are stuck in stage 2 while your team is in stage 3, you may lose your moral authority as leader.

So, as a team leader, you must first identify what stage the team is in. Then pay attention to your focus and take actions to answer the concerns of your team while you help move them toward completing the project. With this in mind, here are the four stages of team development:

+ Stage 1:   Getting Organized
+ Stage 2:   Getting Together
+ Stage 3:   Fighting It Out
+ Stage 4:   Getting the Job Done

Let's look at each in turn.

STAGE 1: GETTING ORGANIZED

When you first get together as a team, you are going to find that many of your team members may tend to be quiet and even self-conscious because they are uncertain. They do not know what is going to happen, and they may be worried about what is expected of them. Typical questions that may occur to your fellow team members at this time are:

✦ Who are these other consultants?

✦ What are their capabilities?

✦ Are they going to be friendly or challenge me?

✦ What are they going to expect me to do?

✦ What's going to happen during this team engagement?

✦ Where exactly will we be headed and why?

✦ What are our precise goals?

✦ Where do I fit in?

✦ How much work will this involve?

✦ Is this project going to require me to give up time that I need to put in elsewhere with other clients?

As the team leader, your primary focus during stage 1 is just what the description says: organizing the team. Your actions should include making introductions; stating the mission of the team; clarifying goals, procedures, rules, and expectations; and answering questions. The idea is to establish a foundation of trust right from the start. You want an atmosphere of openness with no secrets. Although members may disagree with each other or with you, everyone gets a say and everyone's opinion is listened to and considered.

To do this, you must model these expected behaviors yourself. If you are not open, no one else will be. If you do not treat the opinions of others with respect, neither will anyone else. If you listen carefully, so will everyone else. If you argue and try to shout down others, so will those you are attempting to lead.

In stage 1, your principle focus is on getting organized. At the same time, you are laying the foundations of trust and openness for the stages that follow.

STAGE 2: GETTING TOGETHER

Congratulations! You did a great job of getting your consulting team started at the first meeting. Now you have a different challenge. At this stage, members tend to ignore disagreements and conform obediently to the group standards and expectations, as well as your directions as leader. There is heightened interpersonal attraction, and at the end everyone will be committed to a team vision. All of this is what you want.

Of course, team members still wonder and ask themselves questions, some of which may not have changed very much.

+ What are the team's expectations?
+ How much should I really give up to conform with the group's ideas?
+ What role can I perform on this team?
+ Where can I make a contribution?
+ Will I be supported in what I suggest, or will others put me down?
+ Where are we headed?
+ How much time and energy should I commit to this project?

During this stage, you have several major challenges:

+ Facilitating role differentiation
+ Showing support
+ Providing feedback
+ Articulating and motivating commitment to a vision

Facilitating Role Differentiation

To facilitate role differentiation, you need to continue to build relationships among your team members. You want your team members to contribute according to their strengths where they are most needed and to make their weaknesses irrelevant. Of course, assignments may be made strictly by specialty. However, certain assignments will not be so clear-cut. People like to be assigned the fun, glory assignments.

Problems sometimes arise when the assignment involves mainly tedious work, so these types of tasks should be distributed fairly.

You also want to assist team members in whatever tasks they are working on. You can do this by asking about their strengths and their preferences for tasks that need to be done. As they proceed, it is your responsibility to ensure that they have the resources to do the job. When there are disagreements between or among consultant team members, as leader you have to resolve the situation and keep the peace while you continually work toward your client's goals and objectives.

As a task facilitator, you yourself may function in a variety of roles. At times you may give direction or at least suggestions. You are sometimes an information seeker and at others an information giver. You must monitor, coordinate, and oversee everything that is going on. Avoid blocking others from contributing, and do not let anyone else block others' ideas or opinions either. Members try to block others in a variety of ways, including by fault finding, overanalyzing, rejecting out of hand, dominating, stalling, and some other tactics we might never anticipate. Do not let them do it!

Showing Support

You show support for others by building people up every chance you get. Build on their ideas, and be sure to give the credit to those who thought of the ideas first. And as indicated previously, let everyone be heard. Don't let someone who is more articulate, powerful, or popular put down the ideas of other team members who are less so.

Providing Effective Feedback

Providing effective feedback is not easy, but you must tell it like it is. As the leader, you will be expected to make the final decisions about what is going to work and what will not. You must do this without offending, so that individuals maintain their self-respect and continue to contribute. That's a real challenge. To best accomplish this, talk about behavior, not about personalities. Make observations, not inferences. Be as specific as possible. Share ideas and information. Do not set yourself up as a know-it-all who just gives advice. Learn the art of the possible. It is possible to give too much feedback at one time, especially if the feedback is more critical than congratulatory. In fact, critical feedback is always difficult. Look for ways of giving it that takes the sting out of it.

Criticism can take a number of relatively stingless forms. For example, when I flew in combat during the Vietnam War, we established a DSOW Award (Dumb _ _ _ _ of the Week Award) to the pilot who made the biggest screwup. That individual had to buy drinks for the rest of the squadron. President Ronald Reagan gave a small statue of a foot with a hole in it to his Secretary of the Interior when the secretary made a major public error. The statue was the Shot Yourself in the Foot Award. A lot of laughter and good humor went along with the presentation. Still, it was criticism. You might establish a pot into which people put in a dollar if they show up late to a team meeting. The money could go toward a team party or for some other team purpose. Mary Kay Ash, who built a billion-dollar cosmetic company starting with $5,000, used a sandwich technique. She first paid a compliment, then she gave the criticism, then she gave another compliment. If you are going to adopt this technique, you need to practice to get it right. Just remember that you have to give feedback for the team's sake, not for personal emotional release, not to show who's boss, and not to show how clever you are.

Articulating and Motivating Commitment

Finally, you must focus on articulating and motivating commitment to a vision. A vision is a sort of mental picture of the mission's outcome. Every consultant member has to have that vision of what things are going to look like when the project is complete. You should sell the outcome, along with the good things that will happen as a result of the team's work, in precise terms. Motivating your team means making your vision their vision also. To do this, you must get them involved with it. Ask their opinions. Modify your vision, as necessary. Ground the vision in core values that all can agree to. By all means, make it a big vision. People don't sacrifice to accomplish small, insignificant tasks. They sacrifice only for big tasks. So emphasize building a better world more than you do profitability or carrying out an assignment. What will be the benefit to the client organization and to society as a result of your work? If you can get the others involved with suggestions, ideas, and other aspects of the vision and how to achieve it, you will have attained two essential ingredients: public commitment and ownership. Get those, and you have gone a long way toward building a winning team.

STAGE 3: FIGHTING IT OUT

When you enter stage 3, the good news is that the consultant team is fully committed to a vision and fighting to get the engagement done as a major achievement. Unfortunately, because individuals have so much of themselves invested, members in this stage can become polarized, may form cliques, become overcompetitive, and may even challenge your authority as leader.

Clearly, your work is cut out for you in this stage. Your focus must be on conflict management, continuing to ensure that everyone gets to express ideas, examining key work processes to make them better, getting team members working together rather than against each other, and avoiding groupthink. All of these are pretty straightforward except for groupthink.

Groupthink is the adoption of some idea or course of action simply because the group seems to want it, not because it is a particularly good idea that has been thoroughly discussed and thought through. The most conspicuous example of groupthink has been popularized in a story called "Trip to Abilene."[4] In the story a family makes a miserable two-hour trip to Abilene and returns to a ranch in west Texas. The trip is made in a car without air conditioning on a hot, humid summer day at the suggestion of one of the family members. All members agreed on the trip, although later it turns out that they did so simply "to be agreeable." At that point, the member who suggested the idea states that he did not want to go either. He simply suggested the idea "to make conversation." You do not want this kind of thing to happen on your consultant team.

To avoid groupthink, all ideas should be critically evaluated. You should therefore encourage open discussion of all ideas on a routine basis. Some more sophisticated ideas can be evaluated better by calling in outside experts to listen or even by rotating devil's advocate assignment to bring up objections to all proposed ideas. One idea that helps many teams avoid groupthink is a policy of second-chance discussions. With this technique, all decisions taken at a meeting have their implementations deferred until one additional confirmation discussion at a later date.

During this stage, the questions on the minds of your fellow team members will include:

✦ Why can't we handle disagreements better?
✦ Why can't we learn how to communicate negative information?
✦ Can the composition of this team be changed?
✦ How can we make decisions even though there is a lot of disagreement?
✦ Do we really have the best leader?

You may wish that your fellow team members were not asking themselves these questions, especially the last one. However, it is better to be forewarned, so that you can deal with these issues, than to be surprised.

You can take a number of actions to help your team during this stage. You can think up ways to reignite and reinforce commitment to the vision. You can turn your fellow team members into teachers, helping other members with problems they may be having. In fact, you should know that using others as teachers or as leaders in subareas in the project helps to generate their public commitment. Just make certain everyone gets to be a teacher. You might think up ways to provide individual recognition, such as giving a small prize for the most accomplished during the previous week. As arguments arise, you can work on being a more effective mediator. You can look for win-win opportunities and foster win-win thinking, where both sides of an argument or an issue can benefit.

There are plenty of challenges for you as a leader in this stage. You will learn a tremendous amount about leading groups. Do it right, and your team goes into the final stage looking, acting, and performing like a real winner.

STAGE 4: GETTING THE JOB DONE

Of course, your team is getting the job done during all four stages. But if you have done things right, you are really on a roll when you get to stage 4. How soon your team gets into this stage varies greatly. Clearly, it is to your advantage to get into this stage as soon as you can and to spend the bulk of your time there finalizing the project. During this stage, on an effective team, team members show high mutual trust and unconditional commitment to the team. Moreover, team members tend to be self-sufficient and display a good deal of initiative. The team itself may give all the appearance of an entrepreneurial company. As team leader, your focus during this final stage should be on innovation, continuous improvement, and emphasizing and maximizing what your team does best: its core competencies.

Team members' questions reflect this striving for high performance.

+ How can we keep getting better?
+ How can we promote innovativeness and creativity or other qualities?
+ How can we build further on our core competencies?
+ What further improvements can be made to our processes?
+ How can we maintain a high level of contribution to the team?

As team leader, your actions are in direct alignment with these questions. Do everything you can to encourage continuous improvement. Celebrate your teams' successes. Keep providing ongoing feedback on performance. Sponsor and encourage new ideas and expanded roles for team members. Most important, help the team avoid reverting to earlier stages.

SUMMING UP

Of course, these stages of team development overlap to a certain degree. That is unimportant. Just treat the symptoms and questions of your team members as they occur, and solve each problem one at a time.

Finally, remember: Whether you enjoy leading a consulting team or not, you are the sole person responsible for everything that the team accomplishes or fails to accomplish for your client.

In the next chapter we'll look at that relatively new form of consulting open to the consultant: counseling and coaching.

NOTES

1. Tom Peters, *Thriving on Chaos: Handbook for a Management Revolution* (New York: Knopf, 1987), p. 306.
2. Jeffrey R. Dichter, "Teamwork and Hospital Medicine: A Vision for the Future," *Critical Care Nurse* (June 2003).
3. F. Petrock, "Team Dynamics: A Workshop for Effective Team Building," Presentation at the University of Michigan Management of Managers Program.
4. Jerry B. Harvey, *The Abilene Paradox and Other Meditations on Management* (Lexington, MA: Lexington Books, 1988).

20

PERSONAL CONSULTING: COUNSELING AND COACHING

OVER THE LAST 20 YEARS, a new form of consulting has grown up, and it is still growing at a phenomenal rate. One estimate on leadership development, which is classified as a subset of this field, is $50 billion[1] a year.

PersonalAlchemy, a life and executive coaching practice based in Australia, offers some pertinent facts on coaching:

+ Coaching is estimated to be $100 billion a year worldwide.
+ Coaching is the fastest growing industry in the United States, second only to information technology.
+ On Goggle alone, there are 50,000 searches per month made by individuals seeking a coach.
+ One out of every five Fortune 500 companies is reported to have hired a coach for each of their senior executives.[2]

The differences in the two estimates—$50 billion a year for leadership development alone versus $100 billion for all coaching—would seem to indicate that either the investment in individual coaching for leadership development is high or the estimate for total coaching is low. My guess is that the latter conclusion is correct.

Not everyone considers coaching a form of consulting, but I do and I am in good company. According to *U.S News & World Report*, coaching is the second largest consulting business in the country, bested only by management consulting.[3] I think this magazine has it right, and it makes it hard for any consultant to ignore this form of consulting as a potential market.

WHAT EXACTLY IS COACHING?

The International Coach Federation says that "Personal and business coaching is an ongoing professional relationship that helps people produce extraordinary results in their lives, careers, businesses or organizations."[4]

Wikipedia, the online encyclopedia, defines personal coaching as "a relationship which is designed and defined in a relationship agreement between a client and a coach. It is based on the client's expressed interests, goals, and objectives."[5]

A personal coach may use inquiry, reflection, requests, and discussion to help clients identify personal and/or business and/or relationship goals, as well as develop strategies, relationships, and action plans intended to achieve their goals. The coach works with clients to monitor their progress toward implementing their action plans. Together, they evolve and modify the plan to best suit the client's particular needs, individual situation, and environmental relationships. A personal coach provides clients with an outside and unbiased perspective on what he or she is observing about them. A personal coach may teach specific insights and skills to empower clients to move toward their goals. Finally, a personal coach encourages the client to celebrate the achievement of milestones and goals in order to recognize progress.

There are so many different types of coaching that not all of them fit this description exactly. Still, there are commonalities, and, though some practitioners may define personal coaching and other categories of coaching slightly differently, such as business or executive coaching, the basic concept is the same. Here's one example defining what coaches do:

> Coaches anchor people to their internal strengths; they inspire organizations to see vision beyond their plans. Coaching is a positive, productive partnership in which the coach helps the clients transform their life or business through:
>
> - Identifying their values, desires, dreams and goals
> - Setting forth a plan of action to move toward obtaining their goals
> - Identifying, pre-empting and if necessary, conquering obstacles to success
> - Celebrating successes—moving beyond fears and into results![6]

A personal coach is much more similar to a psychologist than to the kinds of consultants discussed in previous chapters. However, there are differences between personal coaches and psychologists or psychiatrists. According to one school for coaches, psychotherapy generally deals with emotional issues, behavioral problems, and disruptive situations and seeks to bring the client to normal function by focusing on dysfunction. On the other hand, coaching deals with functional persons who want to move toward a higher function and achieve excellence while creating an extraordinary, or at least a much better, life.[7]

Also, psychologists see their patients (also known as clients) over much longer periods. Long-term engagements are probably much less true for most consultants, attorneys, and doctors, who are usually engaged to solve a particular problem and then terminate the relationship when the current assignment with the client is completed (even if the termination is only until the next assignment in the future). For psychologists, the immediate problem is usually caused by issues that may take years to explore, analyze, and resolve. Also, some clients find the experience so beneficial that they may consider seeing a psychologist even after the original problem has long since been resolved. As a result, psychologists are trained to spot this phenomenon and actually divorce themselves from a client when it appears that the relationship no longer has value and that they are no longer needed.

Someone may continue to see a personal coach for other reasons that are different from the reasons for consulting. A client may see an executive coach because he wants a promotion for a specific job. Once he attains the promotion, he may be so satisfied that he seeks career coaching on a much longer or even a permanent basis. However, the duration of the relationship is up to the client. The relationship between coach and client is usually much shorter than for psychologists, yet longer than the typical consulting engagement. On average, the relationship between coach and client lasts about eight months to a year.

Other major differences between consulting and coaching are listed in Figure 20-1.

Figure 20-1. Differences between consulting and coaching.

Consultants	**Coaches**
Usually engaged to help businesses or other organizations	Usually engaged to help individuals or individuals within businesses or other organizations on a one-on-one basis
Hired to solve a specific problem, with the relationship generally terminated once the specific problem is solved	Hired to help solve a problem or assist in a longer-term issue requiring an ongoing relationship (although some coaches sell packages of coaching for specific time periods)
Infrequent contact with a client depending on the nature of the consulting engagement	Frequent contact with a client, usually at least once a week
May do external work for client, resulting in a product, such as a marketing plan	Helps and advises clients on doing needed work and completing projects
The expert who can get the facts the client needs	Regards the client as the expert who has the facts the coach needs
Usually work by giving answers to questions	Usually work by asking questions
Usually minimally interactive	Almost entirely interactive

There is, of course, some overlap between regular consulting and one-on-one coaching. My professor and mentor, Peter Drucker, consulted primarily by asking questions. Despite these differences, much of what has been discussed earlier is as applicable to coaching as to regular consulting.

DIFFERENT KINDS OF COACHING

As in traditional consulting, there are different types of coaches.

✦ Personal coaching may cover all types, including coaching individuals both in and outside of organizations.

✦ Life coaching is distinguished by coaching on an individual basis, is usually conducted outside an organization, and may involve almost any application of coaching skills, including dating, parenting, finding a mate, or any other subject.

✦ Business coaching typically refers to coaching the CEO or president of a small company.

✦ Executive coaching refers to coaching individuals specifically in and for the organization. The Fortune 500 companies, for example, use executive coaching when they engage coaches to work on a personal basis with their senior managers. The organizations may employ coaches to work with a group of senior managers or other employees simultaneously. This, however, is considered training, not coaching. Of course, when the training is combined with a personal one-on-one component with each of these individuals participating, it is considered coaching with a training element.

HOW COACHING GOT STARTED

There is some controversy about how coaching got started. One theory is that it began with the personal development programs that caught on in the early 1980s. Companies took participants on wilderness treks and gave them other short- and long-term challenges to build self-confidence and to develop personal skills that spilled over into performance in their personal lives. Because these programs employed personal hands-on coaches and were successful, the companies decided to expand this type of coaching to businesses. If champion athletes, actors, singers, and other performers had coaches, why not business executives? Once again the success from individual coaching in corporations was at least as phenomenal as that seen in personal self-development for other purposes. Fortune 500 companies and the leading business magazines such as *Harvard Business Review, Industry Week,* and *Fortune* all agreed. Documented before-and-after results confirmed the benefits. Coaching then spread to other activities that included coaching in spiritual things, dating, marriage, and any other area in which individuals sought a higher level of performance.

HOW IS COACHING DONE?

Coaching is usually accomplished by interacting with a client once or more a week. The encounter can be in person, by telephone, or over the Internet. The period is usually about an hour long, although some coaches use free introductory sessions of a half-hour or so to get started so that clients can decide whether they wish to continue. Because the objective is to help clients to achieve what they want to achieve, the clients choose the topics for discussion at every meeting. Although coaches provide advice, they generally start by asking questions and getting their clients to think through their own issues.

A good example is the encounter between Peter Drucker and the then new General Electric (GE) CEO Jack Welch, described earlier in this book. Welch had apparently brought up the subject of GE-owned businesses and the fact that they were a mixed bag, with too many of them to concentrate GE's resources effectively. Peter Drucker then asked Welch the famous two questions that led to billons of dollars in profits for GE: (1) "If GE weren't already in a business, would you enter it today?" (2) "If the answer is no, what are you going to do about it?" Note that Drucker did not supply any information or strategy at all. He merely asked questions.

LEARNING TO BE A COACH

The skills you already possess as a consultant, in addition to the information contained in the preceding chapters of this book, will all be very helpful to you should you decide to get into this relatively new aspect of consulting. The overwhelming criterion is that you offer real value to your client—that you have the training and experience and that you are competent in your chosen area. Many coaches maintain a referral list of coaches in other areas, and like consultants, if they do not feel that they can help a client because the need is outside their area of expertise, they can refer the prospect to someone else who has the required expertise.

If you have this book, you probably have a special expertise and therefore the basic knowledge to be successful. Many have started and become successful coaches with far less. Refer again to Chapter 1 and especially the section entitled "What Makes an Outstanding Consultant?" The same qualities make good coaches. However, like any professional, you want to learn all you can about your profession. There are many seminars on coaching, and some so-called coaching colleges offer entire programs on effective coaching. Here are a few that offer seminars or even certification on coaching:

- American Management Association: http://www.amanet.org/seminars/seminar.cfm?basesemno=2506
- Behavioral Coaching Institute: http://www .behavioral-coaching-institute.com/Registration.html
- College of Executive Coaching: http://www .executivecoachcollege.com
- International Coach Federation: http://www.coachfederation .org/ICF/
- Teachers College, Columbia University: http: //continuingeducation.tc.columbia.edu/default.aspx?pageid=631

COACHING FEES

Like consulting, the amount you charge for coaching varies greatly. According to one survey, fees range from $40 to over $300 per hour, with the average being $132 an hour.[8] The same advice on setting price given in Chapter 7 applies here. Because there is so much variance and coaches tend to be more open about their fees on their web sites, I recommend that you visit some of these sites. Use a search engine to do a search for personal, executive, and other types of coaching.

MARKETING COACHING SERVICES

Reread the advice offered in Chapters 2 through 4. Again, you can conduct an Internet search for coaches who are currently advertising coaching on their web sites to see how coaching services can be packaged and how the web site is used to help bring in clients. However, as with consulting, although a web site is very useful, it should not be your primary method of marketing. With so many competitors out there on the World Wide Web, you will be very difficult to locate. However, most of the methods used for obtaining consulting clients work for coaching clients as well.

SUMMING UP

Coaching represents a significant opportunity for any trained or experienced consultant and an additional method of helping others to success.

NOTES

1. Jeffrey E. Auerbach, "Executive Coaching: How Psychology Helps Leaders Develop," *The California Psychologist* (September/October 2007), V. 40, N. 5, p. 15.
2. Rajiv Vij, "The Coaching Process," *PersonalAlchemy*, accessed at http://www.personalalchemy.org/coachingindustry.html, May 2, 2008.
3. Reported in Holly Burns, "Life Coaching Industry Growing but Still Unregulated," *Charleston Regional Business Journal* (October 20, 2003), accessed at http://www.charlestonbusiness.com/news /2882-life-coaching-industry-growing-but-still-unregulated December 3, 2008.
4. International Coach Federation, accessed at http://www.coachfederation .org/ICF/, May 2, 2008.

5. "Coaching," *Wikipedia Encyclopedia*, accessed at http://en.wikipedia .org/wiki/Personal_coaching#Personal_coaching, May 1, 2008.

6. *Pathways Associates*, accessed at http://pathways-associates .com/what/000001.html, May 1, 2008.

7. "What Is Coaching?" *The Institute for Life Coach Training*, accessed at http://www.lifecoachtraining.com/about/whats_coaching.shtml, May 2, 2008.

8. Stephen Fairley and Chris E. Stout, *Getting Started in Personal and Executive Coaching: How to Create a Thriving Coaching Practice* (Hoboken, NJ: Wiley, 2003), p. 20.

Epilogue

THERE IS NO QUESTION that you can become a successful consultant (either full or part time) and make a valuable contribution to your clients and to society. Everything you need to know to market and to put your own expertise in any particular field into practice has already been given to you in the pages of this book. The questions that remain unanswered are those that will arise as you begin actual work as a consultant.

This is as it should be, for certain aspects of your consulting work are unique not only to your category of consulting, type of industry, or geographic area but also, more important, to your personality, style, and way of doing business. All totaled, the answers to these questions constitute your differential advantage over all the others doing identical work, and a sustained differential advantage over your competition will be the primary factor in your success.

A great adventure awaits you, with many challenges, some disappointments, and the thrill of victory along the way. Further, your journey will involve not only monetary rewards but also the satisfaction of doing what you want and doing it well.

But no book, regardless of how complete or thorough it may be, can begin this journey for you. This you must do for yourself. Without your beginning, your taking action, your taking the steps toward starting your consultancy, there can be nothing. So the rest is up to you.

I wish you the great success that only you yourself can achieve.

APPENDIX

A

REFERENCES USEFUL TO CONSULTANTS

GENERAL CONSULTING

The Basic Principles of Effective Consulting by Linda K. Stroh and Homer H. Johnson (Mahwah, NJ: Lawrence Erlbaum Associates, 2005)

Become a Top Consultant by Ron Tepper (Hoboken, NJ: Wiley, 1987)

The Complete Guide to Consulting Success, 3rd ed. by Howard Shenson, Ted Nicholas, and Paul Franklin (Chicago: Dearborn Trade, 1997)

The Consultant's Handbook: How to Start and Develop Your Own Practice by Stephan Schiffman (Cincinnati, OH: Adams Media, 2000)

The Consultant's Manual by Thomas L. Greenbaum (Hoboken, NJ: Wiley, 1994)

Consulting for Dummies, 2nd ed. by Bob Nelson and Peter Economy (Foster City, CA: IDG Books Worldwide, 2008)

Flawless Consulting: A Guide to Getting Your Expertise Used, 2nd ed. by Peter Block (Sudbury, MA: Jossey-Bass, 1999)

Getting Started in Consulting, 2nd ed. by Alan Weiss (Hoboken, NJ: Wiley, 2003)

How to Become a Successful Consultant in Your Own Field, 3rd ed. by Hubert Bermont (Roseville, CA: Prima Publishing, 1997)

How to Succeed as an Independent Consultant, 4th ed. by Herman Holtz (Hoboken, NJ: Wiley, 2004)

Million Dollar Consulting: The Professional's Guide to Growing a Practice, 4th ed. by Alan Weiss (New York: McGraw-Hill, 2002)

The Overnight Consultant by Marsha D. Lewin (Hoboken, NJ: Wiley, 1995)

The 10 Hottest Consulting Practices: What They Are, How to Get into Them by Ron Tepper (Hoboken, NJ: Wiley, 1995)

CONSULTING FOR THE GOVERNMENT

The Entrepreneur's Guide to Doing Business with the Federal Government by Charles Bevers, Linda Christie, and Lynn Price (Upper Saddle River, NJ: Prentice-Hall, 1989)

How to Sell to the Government by William A. Cohen (Hoboken, NJ: Wiley, 1981)

MARKETING FOR SMALL BUSINESSES AND CONSULTANTS

Big Ideas for Small Service Businesses: How to Successfully Advertise, Publicize and Maximize Your Business or Professional Practice by Marilyn and Tom Ross (Buena Vista, CO: Communication Creativity, 1994)

Building a Mail Order Business, 4th ed. by William A. Cohen (Hoboken, NJ: Wiley, 1996)

The Consultant's Guide to Getting Business on the Internet by Herman Holtz (Hoboken, NJ: Wiley, 1997)

Expanding Your Consulting and Professional Services by Herman Holtz (Hoboken, NJ: Wiley, 1986)

Get Clients Now! A 28-Day Marketing Program for Professionals and Consultants by C. J. Hayden and Joe Vitale (New York: AMACOM, 1999)

Marketing Your Consulting and Professional Services by Dick Connor and Jeff Davidson (Hoboken, NJ: Wiley, 1997)

138 Quick Ideas to Get More Clients by Howard L. Shenson and Jerry Wilson (Hoboken, NJ: Wiley, 1993)

Selling Services: Marketing for the Consulting Professional by Paul O'Neil (Hudson, MA: Psi Successful Business Library, 1998)

PROBLEM SOLVING FOR CONSULTANTS

Awaken Your Birdbrain: Using Creativity to Get What You Want by Bill Costello (Bowie, MD: Thinkorporated, 1999)

The Confident Decision Maker: How to Make the Right Business and Personal Decisions Every Time by Roger Dawson (New York: Quill, 1995)

Consultations, 2nd ed. by Robert R. Blake and Jane S. Mouton (Reading, MA: Addison-Wesley, 1976)

Creative Problem Solving by Donald J. Noone (New York: Barrons Educational Series, 1998)

Creative Solution Finding: The Triumph of Breakthrough Thinking over Conventional Problem Solving by Shozo Hibino, Gerald Nadler, and John Farrell (Roseville, CA: Prima Publishing, 1999)

Decision Traps: Ten Barriers to Brilliant Decision-Making and How to Overcome Them by J. Edward Russo and Paul J.H. Schoemaker (New York: Fireside, 1990)

The Entrepreneur and Small Business Problem Solver, 2nd ed. by William A. Cohen (Hoboken, NJ: Wiley, 1990)

Handbook of Business Problem Solving by Kenneth J. Albert, ed. (New York: McGraw-Hill, 1980)

The Marketing Problem Solver by Donald Weinrauch (Hoboken, NJ: Wiley, 1987)

101 Creative Problem Solving Techniques: The Handbook of New Ideas for Business by James M. Higgins (Winter Park, FL: New Management, 1994)

EXECUTIVE SEARCH

Executive Recruiters Almanac by Steven Graber, ed. (Cincinnati, OH: Adams Media, 1998)

Secrets of a Corporate Headhunter by John Wareham (New York: Jove Publications, 1984)

Secrets of the Executive Search Experts by Christian Schoyen and Nils Rasmussen (New York: AMACOM, 1999)

NEWSLETTERS AND JOURNALS

Consultant's Craft Newsletter
Summit Consulting Group
P.O. Box 1009
East Greenwich, RI 02818-0964
800-766-7935 or 401-884-2778
Fax: 401-884-5068
info@summitconsulting.com

Consultants News
1 Phoenix Mill Lane, 3rd floor
Peterborough, NH 03458
888-259-1500 or 603-924-6390
Fax: 603-924-4460
subscribe@kennedyinfo.com

Consulting Magazine
1 Washington Park, Suite 1300
Newark, NJ 07102
212-563-6054
consultingmag@kennedyinfo.com
http://www.consultingmag.com

Management Consultant International
1 Phoenix Mill Lane, 3rd floor
Peterborough, NH 03458
888-259-1500 or 603-924-6390
Fax: 603-924-4460

http://www.consultingcentral.com/newsletters/management-consultant-international?C=qwZOletMth3McZZW&G=6FQbhe1VnU3PkUm9

Marketing Energizer Zine For Consultants
Hanson Marketing Group, Inc.
8011 Navajo Street
Philadelphia, PA 19118
215-753-2620
Fax: 215-753-9223
bhanson@hansonmarketing.com
http://www.hansonmarketing.com/freezine.html

USEFUL MATERIAL FOR CONSULTANTS ON THE INTERNET

American Demographics
Demographics of special interest to marketers
http://adage.com/americandemographics/

American Express Small Business Exchange
Information on creating a business plan, managing a business, and expert advice on small business problems
https://home.americanexpress.com/home/open.shtml

Commercial Services of the U.S. Department of Commerce
Numerous programs having to do with export, including trade statistics abroad
http://www.ita.doc.gov/uscs/

Hoovers Online
Company information and profiles on more than 2,700 companies, both public and private
http://www.hoovers.com

infoUSA, Inc.
Order in-depth profile on any business, get the address and phone number of any business
http://www.infousa.com

Kennedy Information Research Group
General information on consulting, trends, fees, etc.
http://www.kennedyinfo.com

Linkexchange
Banner exchange, starting, promoting, and managing a web site;
selling online, and more
http://www.linkexchanged.com

MCNI
Forums, free consultant listing, search service, book store, and more
http://www.mcni.com

Small Business Advisor
Advice and short reports for small businesses
http://www.isquare.com

Statistical Abstract of the United States
Demographics of all types; numerous sites the following URL is for the
home page
http://www.census.gov/compendia/statab/

Trade Show Central
Search directory for 33,000 trade shows worldwide
http://www.tscentral.com:80/html/ven_fac.html

U.S. Small Business Administration
Information on starting a business, expanding one, local Small Business
Administration resources, shareware, and more
http://www.sbaonline.sba.gov

SAMPLE CONSULTANT'S BROCHURE

I PUT THE SAMPLE BROCHURE in this appendix together myself, and if you have a computer and a color printer, you can do the same. The beauty of this brochure is in its flexibility and cost. Because you are printing it yourself with a computer printer, you don't need to pay anything until you have a prospective client and need one. And even then you pay for only what you need. Yet, the brochure is extensive and has everything in it. This particular brochure emphasizes my seminars on leadership. However, I can not only tailor its subject matter, but I can also include the latest information for a specific client.

Here's what you do. Buy a package of letter-sized folders. I like white, but any color will do. Also buy a package of white, full-sized labels ($8\frac{1}{2}$ x 11 inch); Avery size 5165 works just fine.

Using your word processing program, write and lay out the design for the front and back of your folder. Because the labels are self-adhering, all you need to do is print them out and affix them to the front and back, respectively, of your folder.

Inside the folder you will find a pocket on either side, plus a place to insert your business card. You can print out special business cards using your computer and printer as well. In the left-hand pocket, I put articles that I have written or that have been written about me. In the right side, I put letters from satisfied clients, a partial client list, a short biographical background, and descriptions of my consulting (or in this case of my seminars). I also include a black-and-white photograph. As you can see, you can vary the contents of the pockets according to your client and the situation.

SAMPLE BROCHURE COVER

Here's an example of the front cover of my brochure.

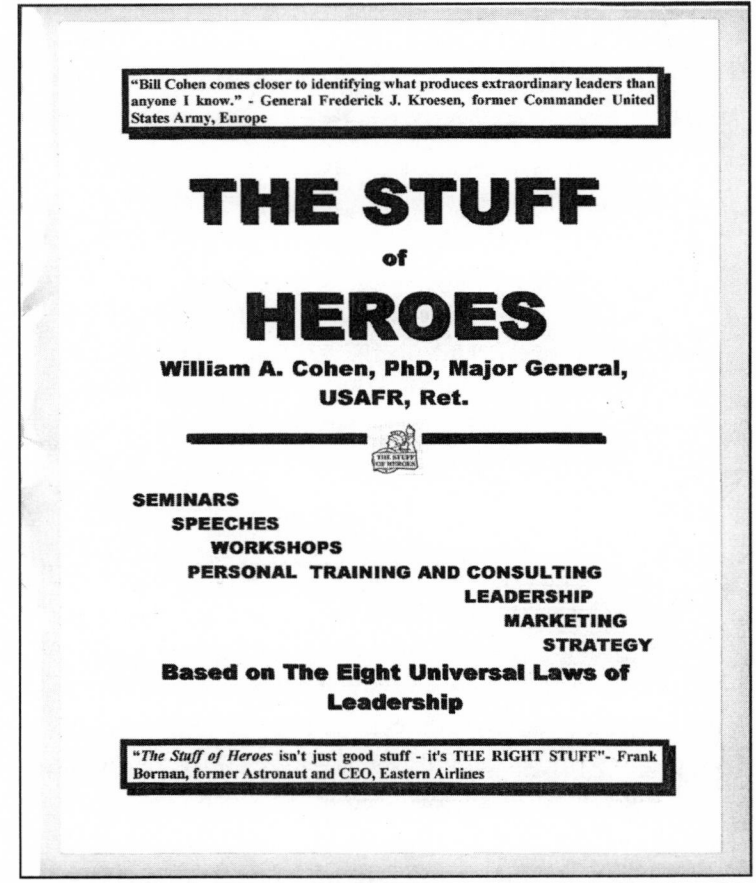

SAMPLE BROCHURE INTERIOR

This and the next page show what the interior of my brochure looks like.

Effective change processes usually include a change navigator, who may be an internal or external consultant. The navigator make possible the results desired by the change leader by coaching people with different agendas and perspectives who may support or oppose the change. The change navigator brings these people into alignment around the change.

Change leadership involves a partnership between the change navigator and the leaders and employees to develop change processes and capabilities.

• Change navigators help develop new skills, and offer a broad experience of overcoming change-related challenges.

• Change leaders get the ear of their people, develop commitment, and create plans that fit the culture.

The navigator works through relationships to design learning processes and systems that enable people to design, implement and sustain changes that produce desired results, solve unexpected problems, and develop the capability for initiating future changes.

Because different people have different understandings, interests, roles and information about a change, the navigator has to re-sell and re-define what is being done. This demands partnership, and an ability to change course, refine the direction, envision the outcome, say difficult and unpopular things to the leaders, and bring unpleasant realities to light. If the navigator is defensive, closed, unavailable or arrogant, people may reject his or her help.

Change navigators are also learners who listen to feedback and learn to question assumptions. They explore

WILLIAM A. COHEN

Laws of Leadership

If you don't maintain your integrity, you will never be fully trusted by those you lead.

I HAVE TRIED TO IDENTIFY principles of leadership that are universal in all situations. The basis of my research was a survey sent to more than 200 former combat leaders and conversations with hundreds more. I sought those who had become successful in other organizations after leaving the armed forces. I asked them to list what they considered to be the three most important principles.

Their responses confirm there are universal principles that successful leaders follow to boost productivity and achieve extraordinary success.

The strength of the results of my investigation motivated me to name these principles the *eight universal laws of leadership:*

1. Maintain absolute integrity. Without basic trust between leader and followers, the leader is forever suspect. Integrity means doing the right thing. Lack of integrity can have terrible consequences. Even if a leader loses a fight, by main-

Get out in front where you can see and be seen.

happen? Accept that, and press on. If you aren't committed, no one else will be.

5. Expect positive results. The higher your goals, the higher goals you will achieve. There is a direct relationship between the goals you expect and what you get. Successful leaders expect positive results and maintain a positive attitude regardless of external realities. If you expect to succeed or expect to fail, you're right. So, although it makes sense to be ready for the worst, expect the best.

6. Take care of your people. If you take care of your people, they will take care of you. Loyalty is a two-way street. You cannot expect others to support your interests if you ignore theirs. J.W. Marriott once said: "We take care of our people, and they take care of our guests."

7. Put duty before self. If you are a leader, your duty encompasses accomplishing your mission and taking care of your people. Usually, the mission must come first. Sometimes, you must take care of your people first, or you may never accomplish your mission. All leaders must put the interests of the mission and their followers before their own. If your mission and your people don't come before you, you are not the leader.

8. Get out in front. The only way to

Profile of a Peak Performance Expert

Dr. Bill Cohen is Professor of Marketing and Leadership, former department chairman and Institute Director at California State University Los Angeles and is a retired major general from the U.S. Air Force Reserve. He has also taught at the University of California Los Angeles, University of Southern California and Claremont Graduate University.

Among his 35 books translated into 11 languages and over 100 articles resulting from his research, are the best selling books *The Stuff of Heroes* (Longstreet Press, 1998) and *The Art of Leader* (Prentice Hall, 1990). The latter was named a Best Business Book of the Year by Library Journal. The former was

nominated   998 by
Manageme   f world
class lead   ls and
admirals, p   ne 500
companies.   es and
universities

Amor   alifornia
State Unive   Forge
George Wa   (1985),
and the C   Award
(1996). He   999, he
was named   s from
around the   awards
include the   juished
Flying Cros   ak leaf
clusters.

Dr. C   d trade

APPENDIX
C

THE CONSULTANT'S QUESTIONNAIRE AND AUDIT

PART I: ORGANIZATION

Company: _____

Division: _____

Address: _____

City, State, and Zip Code: _____

Web Site: _____

Other Division Locations: _____

_____

_____

_____

Company Officers and Other Key Executives: _____

_____

_____

_____

Primary Contact for This Engagement: _____

Title: _____

Address: _____

City, State, and Zip Code: _____

Phone Number: _____

Fax Number: _____

E-mail: _____

Backup Contact for this Engagement: _____

Title: _____

Address: _____

City, State, and Zip Code: _____

Phone Number: _____

Fax Number: _____

E-mail: _____

Note: Obtain relevant company organization charts.

PART II: PRODUCTION (FOR MANUFACTURERS)

What percentage of production is:

_____ %   Job-order (custom) manufacture?

_____ %   Repetitive (standard) manufacture?

100%   Total

What percentage of production is:

_____ %   Private label for someone else?

_____ %   Sold under your own name?

100%   Total

Do you subcontract? _____

_____ %   If yes, what percentage of your total work?

Who are your major subcontractors? _____

_____

_____

_____

Are you satisfied with their work? _____

_____

_____

_____

_____ %   What percentage of your production do you export?

What countries do you export to? What is the percentage of export to each country?

_____   _____ %

_____   _____ %

_____   _____ %

_____ %   At what current percentage of production capacity are you now operating?

_____ %   What additional percentage could you add to total capacity (100%) in order to accommodate additional sales?

How many months would it take to reach this figure? _____ months

_____ %   What is the minimum percentage of capacity at which you must operate in order to break even?

How seasonal is your production?

____ Not at all ____ Slightly   ____ Fairly   ____ Highly   ____ Totally

At which season(s) is production at its peak?

_____

At which season(s) is production at its minimum?

_____

To what extent are your production operations regulated by governmental controls?

____ % Federal ____ % State   ____ % Local

Who are your major suppliers? Are you satisfied with them?

_____ _____ %
_____ _____ %
_____ _____ %
_____ _____ %

PART III: MARKETS SERVED

The basic questions from Peter Drucker:

Who are your customers?

What do they (not you) value?

If possible, give estimates for the following:

	Last Year	Three Years Ago
Total industry sales	$ _____	$ _____
Your sales	$ _____	$ _____
Your market share	$ _____	$ _____
FRED—Major competitor's share	$ _____	$ _____
Second-ranking competitor's share $ _____	$ _____	$ _____
Third-ranking competitor's share $ _____	$ _____	$ _____

_____ % Consumer market   _____ % Industrial market

Describe each consumer market or industrial market by SIC code.* List your products or services, the channels used to distribute them, and your approximate percentage share of each market.

Market	Products	Channel(s)	Market Share

*This is a code developed by the federal government to describe products and services and the companies that offer them.

List your major competitors.

Name and Address	Strongest Markets	Why Strong in These Markets?	Strongest Products	Why Strong with These Products?

What new competitors have entered the marketplace in the past three years?

_____

_____

_____

Have any done unusually well? If so, in what markets, with what products, and why? _____

_____

_____

_____

_____

PART IV: PRODUCTS

Approximately how many different individual products do you manufacture?

_____

$_____ What is the dollar amount of your average sale (to your end customer)?

How many times is your average product purchased by the same customer in a single year? _____

_____% Approximately what percentage of your customers are repeat customers?

What is the average purchase life of your customers?_____

Why do they stop buying from you?_____

_____

_____

Which of your products have the highest margins?_____

_____

_____

Do you sell any "loss leaders"? _____

_____

_____

_____

_____

_____

Has their effectiveness ever been tested against that of other items? If so, which items, and how?

_____

_____

_____

_____

_____

_____

_____

_____

List your products below by sales and profits:

Product	Annual Sales	Annual Profits
_____	$ _____	$ _____
_____	$ _____	$ _____
_____	$ _____	$ _____
_____	$ _____	$ _____

_____ $ _____ $ _____
_____ $ _____ $ _____
_____ $ _____ $ _____

Have you considered dropping those products that account for low profits? If low-sales/low-profit products are being retained, indicate why:

_____
_____
_____
_____
_____
_____
_____
_____

Do you have an ongoing new-product research and development program?

_____

When was your last new product introduced? _____

_____

When was your last major product modification introduced? _____

_____

How do you do new-product research and development? _____ In-house

_____ Subcontract

Why do you do new-product research and development?

___ Meet the competition
___ Counter product obsolescence
___ Reduce production costs
___ Reduce material costs
___ Enter new markets
___ Increase sales
___ Other _____

How do you screen potential products for development? _____

_____

_____

PART V: MARKETING RESEARCH

Do you have an ongoing market research program?

Do you have correct information on:
___ Who's buying your products?
___ Why they're buying?
___ Where your products are being bought?
___ Who's making the purchase decision?
___ How to best reach your customers through advertising?
___ The effectiveness of advertising programs?
___ Your competitors' products?
___ Your competitors' strategies?
___ Potential markets?
___ Relative effectiveness of different channels of distribution?
___ New applications of your products?
___ Export potential?
___ Related products demanded by your customers?
___ Relative effectiveness and efficiency of salespeople?
___ Packaging effectiveness?
___ Pricing sensitivity?
___ Image and positioning of your product relative to others?
___ Publicity possibilities?
___ Operating ratios in your industry?

What trade associations do you belong to? _____

_____

_____

What trade magazines or journals do you subscribe to? _____

_____

_____

Do you use the market research available from associations and magazines?

_____

Do you use the market research available from the Internet?_____

If you make use of internally generated market research, which organizations within your company provide this research, and what research do they provide?

_____

_____

_____

_____

_____

_____

What outside organizations have assisted you in doing research?

_____

_____

_____

_____

_____

_____

PART VI: MARKET SEGMENTS

Consumer Market

What segments of the market do your present customers represent?

_____

_____

_____

_____

_____

_____

Are your products more:
___ Habitual purchase?
___ Impulse purchase?
___ Planned purchase?

In your market, which are the most important factors for buying?

___ Price   ___ Features   ___ Appearance

___ Quality   ___ Performance   ___ Other: _____

_____

_____

Who influences the decision to buy your products?

___ Men	___ Lawyers
___ Women	___ Religious leaders
___ Children	___ Mechanics
___ Doctors	___ Contractors
___ Dentists	___ Tradespeople
___ Educators	___ Fraternal or social groups
___ Beauticians	___ High-income or influential people
___ Barbers	___ Others: _____

_____

_____

Industrial Market

Who makes the purchase decision for your product? If more than one individual, indicate all. _____

_____

_____

Outline the sequence of events as to how this decision is made. Include other factors or individuals influencing this decision._____

_____

_____

PART VII: PRICING

How do you decide on the price for your products?_____

_____

_____

What's your warranty policy? _____

_____

_____

_____

What's your service policy? _____

_____

_____

_____

Any other special policies of importance?_____

_____

_____

_____

PRICING CHECKLIST

Examining Costs, Sales Volume, and Profits. The questions in this part should be helpful when you look at prices from the viewpoint of costs, sales volume, and profits.*

Pricing and Costs. The company that sets the price for an item by applying a standard markup may be overlooking certain cost factors that are connected with that item. The following questions are designed to help you gather information that should be helpful when you are determining prices on specific types of items.

	Yes	No
1. Do you know which of your operating costs remains the same regardless of sales volume?	____	____
2. Do you know which of your operating costs decrease percentagewise as your sales volume increases?	____	____
3. Have you ever figured out the breakeven point for your items selling at varying price levels?	____	____

*This section (which continues until the beginning of Part VIII) is adapted from Joseph D. O'Brien, "A Pricing Checklist for Managers" published by the U.S. Small Business Administration.

Yes   No

4. Do you look behind high gross margin percentages?
   (For example, a product with a high gross margin
   may also be a slow turnover item with high handling
   costs. Thus it may be less profitable than lower-margin
   items that turn over fast.)   ____ ____

5. When you select items for price reductions, do you
   project the effects on profits? (For example, if a food
   marketer considers whether to run canned ham or rump
   steak on sale, an important cost factor is labor. Practically
   none is involved in featuring canned ham; however, a rump
   steak sale requires the skill of a meat cutter, and this labor
   cost might mean little or no profits.)   ____ ____

Pricing and Sales Volume. An effective pricing program should also
consider sales volume. For example, high prices may limit your sales
volume, while low prices may result in a large but unprofitable volume.
The following questions should be helpful in determining what is right
for your situation.

Yes   No

6. Have you considered setting a sales volume goal and then
   studying it to see if your prices will help you reach it?   ____ ____

7. Have you set a target of a certain number of new customers
   for next year?   ____ ____

   If so, how can pricing help to get them?   _____

   _____

8. Should you limit the quantities of low-margin items that any
   one customer can buy when such items are on sale?   ____ ____

   If so, will you advertise this policy?   ____ ____

9. What is your policy when a sale item is sold out before the end
   of the advertised period? Do you allow disappointed customers
   to buy the item later at the sale price?   ____ ____

Pricing and Profits. Prices should help bring in sales that are profitable over
the long pull. The following questions are designed to help you think about
pricing policies and their effect on your annual profits.

Yes   No

10. Do you have all the facts on costs, sales, and competitive
    behavior?   ____ ____

11. Do you set prices with the hope of accomplishing definite
    objectives, such as a 1 percent profit increase over last year? ____ ____

12. Have you set a given level of profits in dollars and in percentage
    of sales?   ____ ____

13. Do you keep records to give you the needed facts on profits,
    losses, and prices?   ____ ____

14. Do you review your pricing practices periodically to make sure
    that they are helping to achieve your profit goals?   ____ ____

Judging the Buyer, Timing, and Competitors. The questions in this part
are designed to help you check your practices for judging the buyer (your
customer), your timing, and your competitors.

The Buyer and Pricing. After you have your facts on costs, the next point
must be the customer—whether you are changing a price, putting in a
new item, or checking out your present price practices. Knowledge of
your customers helps you determine how to vary prices in order to get the
average gross margin you need for making a profit. (For example, to get
an average gross margin of 35 percent, some retailers put a low markup at
10 percent, for instance—on items that they promote as traffic builders
and use high markup, sometimes as much as 60 percent, on slow-moving
items.) The following questions should be helpful in checking your
knowledge about your customers.

Yes   No

15. Do you know whether your customers shop around and for
    what items?   ____ ____

16. Do you know how your customers make their comparisons?   ____ ____
    _____ By reading newspaper ads?
    _____ Store shopping?
    _____ Hearsay?

17. Are you trying to appeal to customers who:
    _____ Buy on price alone?
    _____ Buy on quality alone?
    _____ Combine the two?

Yes   No

18. Do any of your customers tell you whether your prices are in line with those of your competitors?   ____ ____
    ____ Higher?
    ____ Lower?
    ____ Competitive?

19. Do you know which items (or types of items) your customers call for even though you raise the price?   ____ ____

20. Do you know which items (or types of items) your customers leave on your shelves when you raise the price?   ____ ____

21. Do certain items seem to appeal to customers more than others when you run weekend, clearance, or special-day sales?   ____ ____

22. Have you used your individual sales records to classify your present customers according to the volume of their purchases?   ____ ____

23. Will your customers buy more if you use multiple pricing (for example, three for thirty-nine cents for products with rapid turnover)?   ____ ____

24. Do your customers respond to odd prices more readily than to even prices, for example, ninety-nine cents rather than one dollar?   ____ ____

25. Have you decided on a pricing strategy to create a favorable price image with your customers? (For example, a retailer with eight thousand different items might decide to make a full margin on all medium or slow movers while featuring at low price levels the remaining fast movers.)   ____ ____

26. If you are trying to build a quality price image, do your individual customer records, such as charge account statements, show that you are selling a larger number of higher-priced items than you were twelve months ago?   ____ ____

27. Do your records of individual customer accounts and your observations of customer behavior in the store show price as the important factor in their:
    ____ Buying?
    ____ Service?
    ____ Assortments?
    ____ Some other consideration?

Time and Pricing. Effective merchandising means that you have the right product at the right place, at the right price, and at the right time. All are important, but timing is the critical element for the smaller retailer. The following questions should be helpful in determining what is the right time for you to adjust prices.

Yes No

28. Are you a "leader" (rather than a "follower") in announcing your price reductions? (Followers, even though they match their competitors, create a negative impression on their customers.) ____ ____

29. Have you studied your competitors to see whether they follow any sort of pattern when making price changes? (For example, do some of them run clearance sales earlier than others?) ____ ____

30. Is there a pattern to the kinds of items that competitors promote at lower prices at certain times of the month or year? ____ ____

31. Have you decided whether it is better to take early markdowns on seasonal or style goods or to run a clearance sale at the end of the season? ____ ____

32. Have you made regular annual sales—such as anniversary sales, fall clearance, or holiday cleanup so popular that many customers wait for them rather than buying in season? ____ ____

33. When you change a price, do you make sure that all customers know about it through price tags and so on? ____ ____

34. Do you try to time reductions so they can be promoted in your advertising? ____ ____

Competition and Pricing. When you set prices, you have to consider how your competitors might react to your prices. The starting place is learning as much as you can about their price structures. The following questions are designed to help you check out this phase of pricing.

Yes No

35. Do you use all the available channels of information to keep you up-to-date on your competitors' price policies? (Some useful sources of information are: things your customers tell you; competitors' price lists and catalogs, if used; competitors' advertising; reports from your suppliers; trade paper studies; and shoppers employed by you.) ____ ____

Yes No

36. Should your policy be always to:
   _____ Try to sell above or below competition?
   _____ Or only to meet the competition?

37. Is there a pattern to the way your competitors respond to your price cuts?   ____ ____

38. Is the leader pricing of your competitors affecting your sales volume to such an extent that you must alter your pricing policy on individual items (or types of items) or merchandise?   ____ ____

39. Do you realize that no two competitors have identical cost curves (This difference in costs means that certain price levels may be profitable for you but unprofitable for your competitor or vice versa.)   ____ ____

Practices That Can Help Offset Price. Some companies take advantage of the fact that price is not always the determining factor in making a sale. They supply customer services and offer other inducements to offset the effect of competitors' lower prices. Delivery service is an example. Providing a comfortable shoppers' meeting place is another. The following questions are designed to help you take a look at some of these practices.

Yes No

40. Do the items or services you sell have advantages for which customers are willing to pay a little more?   ____ ____

41. From personal observation of customer behavior in your store, can you estimate about how much more customers will pay for such advantages?   ____ ____

42. Should you change your services so as to create an advantage for which your customers will be willing to pay?   ____ ____

43. Does your advertising emphasize customer benefits rather than price?   ____ ____

44. Are you using the most common nonprice competitive tools? (For example, have you tried to alter your product or service to the existing market? Have you tried stamps, bonus purchase gifts, or other plans for building repeat business?)   ____ ____

45. Should policies on returned goods be changed so as to better impress your customers?   ____ ____

Yes   No

46. If you sell repair services, have you checked out your guarantee policy?   ____ ____

47. Should you alter assortments of merchandise to increase sales?   ____ ____

PART VIII: DISTRIBUTION

How much of your product line is:

_____ % Manufactured by you?

_____ % Manufactured for you by someone else?

100 % Total

Is your distribution:

_____ Regional? In what areas? _____

_____

_____

_____ National? What are your strongest areas? _____

_____

_____

_____ International? What are your strongest foreign countries?_____

_____

_____

_____

What systems of distribution do you use?_____

_____

_____

_____

How do you subdivide your product lines in your sales organization?

_____ Geographic territories   _____ Type of product

_____ Type of customer   _____ Other: _____

_____

How do you decide on methods of distribution and which distributors to use?

_____
_____
_____
_____
_____

PART IX: SELLING

Do your salespeople, agents, or distributors have exclusive territories?

_____
_____
_____

How many people do you have selling your product, and what are their responsibilities?_____

_____
_____

How do you compensate your salespeople? _____

_____
_____
_____

Do you offer any special sales incentives?_____

_____
_____

Who prepares your product catalogs? _____

_____
_____

What aids to selling do you, your distributor, or your agent provide to people selling your product? _____

_____
_____

Do you provide any type of formal sales training? Explain type, subjects, length of programs, etc. _____

_____

_____

How frequently do you hold sales meetings or conferences? What subjects are covered? _____

_____

_____

What branch offices do you maintain? _____

_____

_____

How do you select or recruit your agents and salespeople? _____

_____

_____

How do you set sales quotas? _____

_____

_____

What trade discounts do you offer? _____

_____

_____

What terms of sale do you use? _____

_____

_____

Do you grant any special concessions or offers to stimulate sales?_____

_____

_____

_____ % What is your percentage of returned goods?
_____ % What is your percentage of goods returned due to damage?
_____ % What is your percentage of bad debts?

What is the average time for collection of amounts owed to you?_____

How frequently do your salespeople send in reports?_____

How do you maintain your sales records?_____

_____

_____

What is your ratio of sales made to number of calls made?_____

Are your "cold calls" supplemented by any other type of communication such as direct mail?_____

_____

_____

_____

How do you control your salespeople's activities?_____

_____

_____

_____

What percentage of your salespeople's time is spent on:

_____ % Planning?

_____ % Preparation?

_____ % Travel?

_____ % Calls on prospects?

_____ % Calls on established customers?

_____ % Other?

100   % Total

What are the following yearly gross sales figures of your salespeople?

$_____ Average gross

$_____ Lowest gross

$_____ Highest gross

$_____ What is the average amount spent on promotion activities that back up sales per salesperson per year (total spent yearly on sales promotion, advertising, and publicity divided by number of salespeople)?

$_____ What is the average amount spent on sales activities per salesperson per year (total spent on recruiting, training, expense accounts, and compensation divided by number of salespeople)?

PART X: ADVERTISING

What media do you use to promote to your customers? _____

_____
_____
_____
_____
_____
_____

What advertising (including direct mail and telephone) have you done, and what were the costs over the last year? What were the results? _____

_____
_____
_____
_____
_____

How were results measured for these ads? _____

_____
_____
_____
_____
_____

Have you used the Internet for advertising? What were the results?_____

_____

_____

_____

_____

_____

_____

_____

Do you have an advertising agency? _____

Name: _____

Contact: _____

Address: _____

Phone number: _____

Fax number: _____

E-mail:_____

PART XI: PROMOTION

What types of sales promotion have you done (discounts, coupons, contests, etc.), and what were the costs? What were the results?_____

_____

_____

_____

_____

_____

PART XII: PUBLICITY AND PUBLIC RELATIONS

What type of public relations program did you engage in over the previous year, and what were the costs? What were the results?_____

_____

_____

_____

_____

_____

PART XIII: MANAGEMENT OPERATIONS

What type of planning does the organization do? _____

_____

_____

_____

_____

_____

_____

How is budgetary control of operations planned and maintained? _____

_____

_____

_____

_____

PART XIV: FINANCIAL CHECKLIST
ARE YOU MAKING A PROFIT?

Analysis of Revenues and Expenses. Since profit is revenues less expenses, you must first identify all revenues and expenses for the period under study to determine what your profit is.*

    Yes   *No*

1. Have you chosen an appropriate period for profit determination?   ____ ____

   For accounting purposes, businesses generally use a twelve-month period, such as January 1 to December 31 or July 1 to June 30. The accounting year you select doesn't have to be a calendar year (January to December); a seasonal business, for example, might close its year after the end of

---

*This section (which continues until the beginning of Part XV) is adapted from Narendra C. Bhandari and Charles S. McCubbin, Jr., "Checklist for Profit Watching" published by the U.S. Small Business Administration.

the season. The selection depends upon the nature of your business, your personal preference, or possible tax considerations.

                                                                          Yes   No

2. Have you determined your total revenues for the accounting period?   ____ ____

   In order to answer this question, consider the answer to the following questions.

   $____ What is the amount of gross revenue from sales of your goods or service (*gross sales*)?

   $____ What is the amount of goods returned by your customers and credited (*returns and rejects*)?

   $____ What is the amount of discounts given to your customers and employees (*discounts*)?

   $____ What is the amount of net sales from goods and services (net sales = gross sales *[returns and rejects + discounts]*)?

   $____ What is the amount of income from other sources, such as interest on bank deposits, dividends from securities, and rent on property leased to others (*nonoperating income*)?

   $____ What is the amount of total revenue (*total revenue = net sales + nonoperating income*)?

3. Do you know what your total expenses are?   ____ ____

   Expenses are the cost of goods sold and services used in the process of selling goods or services. Some common expenses for all businesses are:

   $____ Cost of goods sold (cost of goods sold = beginning inventory + purchases – ending inventory)

   $____ Wages and salaries (don't forget to include your own—at the actual rate you'd have to pay someone else to do your job)

   $____ Rent

   $____ Utilities (electricity, gas, telephone, water, etc.)

$____ Supplies (office, cleaning, and the like)

$____ Delivery expenses

$____ Insurance

$____ Advertising and promotion costs

$____ Maintenance and upkeep

$____ Depreciation (here you need to make sure your depreciation policies are realistic and that all depreciable items are included)

$____ Taxes and licenses

$____ Interest

$____ Bad debts

$____ Professional assistance (accountant, attorney, etc.)

There are, of course, many other types of expenses, but the point is that every expense must be recorded and deducted from your revenues before you know what your profit is. Understanding your expenses is the first step toward *controlling them and increasing your profits.*

FINANCIAL RATIOS

A *financial ratio* is an expression of the relationship between two items selected from the income statement or the balance sheet. Ratio analysis helps you evaluate the weak and strong points in your financial and managerial performance.

Yes   No

4. Do you know your current ratio?   ____ ____
   The *current ratio* (current assets divided by current debts) is a measure of the cash or near cash position (liquidity) of the company. It tells you if you have enough cash to pay your company's current creditors. The higher the ratio, the more liquid the company's position, and hence the higher the credibility of the company. Cash, receivables, marketable securities, and inventory are current assets.

   Naturally you need to be realistic in valuing receivables and inventory for a true picture of your liquidity, since some debts may be uncollectible and some stock obsolete. Current liabilities are those that must be paid in one year.

5. Do you know your *quick ratio*?   ____ ____

Quick assets are current assets minus inventory. The *quick ratio* (or acid-test ratio) is found by dividing quick assets by current liabilities. The purpose, again, is to test the company's ability to meet its current obligations. Because it doesn't include inventory, quick ratio is a stiffer test of the company's liquidity. It tells you if the business could meet its current obligations with quickly convertible assets should sales revenues suddenly cease.

6. Do you know your total debt to net worth ratio?   ____ ____

This ratio (the result of total debt divided by net worth, then multiplied by 100) is a measure of how the company can meet its total obligations from equity. The lower the ratio, the higher the proportion of equity relative to debt, and the better the company's credit rating will be.

7. Do you know your average collection period?   ____ ____

You find this ratio by dividing accounts receivable by daily credit sales. (Daily credit sales = annual credit sales divided by 360.) This ratio tells you the length of time it takes the company to get its cash after making a sale on credit. The shorter this period, the quicker the cash inflow is. A longer than normal period may mean overdue and uncollectible bills. If you extend credit for a specific period (say, thirty days), this ratio should be very close to the same number of days. If it's much longer than the established period, you may need to alter your credit policies. It's wise to develop an aging schedule to gauge the trend of collections and identify slow payers. Slow collections (without adequate financing charges) hurt your profit, since you could be doing something much more useful with your money, such as taking advantage of discounts on your own payables.

8. Do you know your ratio of net sales to total assets?   ____ ____

This ratio (net sales divided by total assets) measures the efficiency with which you are using your assets. A higher than normal ratio indicates that the company is able to generate sales from its assets faster (and better) than the average concern.

	Yes	No

9. Do you know your operating profit to net sales ratio? ____ ____

This ratio (the result of dividing operating profit by net sales and multiplying by 100) is most often used to determine the profit position relative to sales. A higher than normal ratio indicates that your sales are good, that your expenses are low, or both. Interest income and interest expense should not be included in calculating this ratio.

10. Do you know your net profit to total assets ratio? ____ ____

This ratio (the result of dividing net profit by total assets and multiplying by 100) is often called return on investment, or ROI. It focuses on the profitability of the overall operation of the company. Thus it allows management to measure the effects of its policies on the company's profitability. The ROI is the single most important measure of a company's financial position. You might say it's the bottom line for the bottom line.

11. Do you know your net profit to net worth ratio? ____ ____

This ratio is found by dividing net profit by net worth and multiplying the result by 100. It provides information on the productivity of the resources the owners have committed to the company's operations. All ratios measuring profitability can be computed either before or after taxes, depending on the purpose of the computations. Ratios have limitations. Since the information used to derive ratios is itself based on accounting rules and personal judgments as well as facts, the ratios cannot be considered absolute indicators of a company's financial position. Ratios are only one means of assessing the performance of the company and must be considered in perspective with many other measures. They should be used as a point of departure for further analysis and not as an end in themselves.

SUFFICIENCY OF PROFIT

The following questions are designed to help you measure the adequacy of the profit your company is making. Making a profit is only the first step; making enough profit to survive and *grow* is really what business is all about.

Yes No

12. Have you compared your profit with your profit goals?   ____ ____

13. Is it possible your goals are too high or too low?   ____ ____

14. Have you compared your present profits (absolute and ratios) with the profits made in the last one to three years?   ____ ____

15. Have you compared your profits (absolute and ratios) with profits made by similar companies in your line?   ____ ____

A number of organizations publish financial ratios for various businesses, among them Dun & Bradstreet, Robert Morris Associates, the Accounting Corporation of America, NCR Corporation, and Bank of America. Your own trade association may also publish such studies. Remember, these published ratios are only averages. You probably want to be better than average.

TREND OF PROFIT

Yes No

16. Have you analyzed the direction your profits have been taking?   ____ ____

The preceding analyses, with all their merits, report on a company only at a single time in the past. It is not possible to use these isolated moments to indicate the trend of your company's performance. To do a trend analysis, you should compute performance indicators (absolute amounts or ratios) for several time periods (yearly for several years, for example) and lay out the results in columns side by side for easy comparison. You can then evaluate your performance, see the direction it's taking, and make initial forecasts of where it will go.

MIX OF PROFIT

Yes No

17. Does your company sell more than one major product line or provide several distinct services?   ____ ____

If it does, a separate profit and ratio analysis of each should be made: to show the relative contribution of each product line or service; to show the relative burden of expenses of each product or service; to show which items are most profitable, which are less so, and which are losing money; and to show which are slow and fast moving. The profit and ratio analyses of each major item help you uncover the strong and weak areas of your operations. They can help you to make profit-increasing decisions to drop a product line or service or to place particular emphasis behind one or another.

RECORDS

Good records are essential. Without them a company doesn't know where it's been, where it is, or where it's heading. Keeping records that are accurate, up-to-date, and easy to use is one of the most important functions of the owner-manager, his or her staff, and his or her outside counselors (lawyer, accountant, banker).

Basic Records

Yes   No

18. Do you have a general journal and/or special journals, such as one for cash receipts and disbursements?   ____ ____

    A general journal is the basic record of the company. Every monetary event in the life of the company is entered in the general journal or in one of the special journals.

19. Do you prepare a sales report or analysis?   ____ ____

    a. Do you have sales goals by product, department, and accounting period (month, quarter, year)?   ____ ____

    b. Are your goals reasonable?   ____ ____

    c. Are you meeting your goals?   ____ ____

    If you aren't meeting your goals, try to list the likely reasons on a sheet of paper. Such a study might include areas such as general business climate, competition, pricing, advertising, sales promotion, credit policies, and the like. Once you've identified the apparent causes, you can take steps to increase sales (and profits).

BUYING AND INVENTORY SYSTEMS

Yes   No

20. Do you have buying and inventory systems?   ____ ____

    The buying and inventory systems are two critical areas of a company's operation that can affect profitability.

21. Do you keep records on the quality, service, price, and promptness of delivery of your sources of supply?   ____ ____

22. Have you analyzed the advantages and disadvantages of:

    a. Buying from suppliers?   ____ ____

    b. Buying from a minimum number of suppliers?   ____ ____

23. Have you analyzed the advantages and disadvantages of buying through cooperatives or other such systems?   ____ ____

24. Do you know:

    a. How long it usually takes to receive each order?   ____ ____

    b. How much inventory cushion (usually called safety stock) to have so you can maintain normal sales while you wait for the order to arrive?   ____ ____

25. Have you ever suffered because you were out of stock?   ____ ____

26. Do you know the optimum order quantity for each item you need?   ____ ____

27. Do you (or can you) take advantage of quantity discounts for large-size single purchases?   ____ ____

28. Do you know your costs of ordering inventory and carrying inventory?   ____ ____

    The more frequently you buy (smaller quantities per order), the higher your average ordering costs are (clerical costs, postage, telephone costs, etc.), and the lower the average carrying costs are (storage, loss through pilferage, obsolescence, etc.). On the other hand, the larger the quantity per order, the lower the average ordering costs, and the higher the carrying costs. A balance should be struck so that the minimum cost overall for ordering and carrying inventory can be achieved.

29. Do you keep records of inventory for each item?   ____ ____

These records should be kept current by making entries whenever items are added to or removed from inventory. Simple records on 3 x 5-inch or 5 x 7-inch cards can be used, with each item being listed on a separate card. Proper records will show, for each item, quantity in stock, quantity on order, date of order, slow or fast seller, and valuations (which are important for taxes and your own analyses).

Other Financial Records

	Yes	No

30. Do you have an accounts payable ledger?

This ledger shows what, whom, and why you owe. Such records should help you make your payments on schedule; any expense not paid on time could adversely affect your credit. But even more importantly, such records should help you take advantage of discounts that can help boost your profits.

31. Do you have an accounts receivable ledger?

This ledger shows who owes money to your company. It shows how much is owed, how long it has been outstanding, and why the money is owed. Overdue accounts could indicate that your credit-granting policy needs to be reviewed and that you may not be getting the cash into the company quickly enough to pay your own bills at the optimum time.

32. Do you have a cash receipts journal?

This journal records the cash received by source, day, and amount.

33. Do you have a cash payments journal?

This journal is similar to the cash receipts journal but shows cash paid out instead of cash received. The two cash journals can be combined if convenient.

34. Do you prepare an income (profit and loss, or P&L) statement and a balance sheet?

These are statements about the condition of your company at a specific time; they show the income, expenses, assets, and liabilities of the company. They are absolutely essential.

35. Do you prepare a budget?   ____ ____

You could think of a budget as a "record in advance," projecting future inflows and outflows for your business. A budget is usually prepared for a single year, generally to correspond with the accounting year. It is then, however, broken down into quarterly and monthly projections.

There are different kinds of budgets: cash, production, sales, and the like. A cash budget, for example, shows the estimate of sales and expenses for a particular period of time. The cash budget forces the company to think ahead by estimating its income and expenses. Once reasonable projections are made for every important product line or department, the owner-manager has set targets for employees to meet for sales and expenses. You must plan to ensure a profit. And you must prepare a budget to plan.

PART XV: MATERIALS TO ASK FOR

- Sales brochures
- Price lists
- Public relations materials
- Product description and photographs
- Special forms
- Annual report
- Financial statements
- Sample advertisements and promotional materials
- Information given out at recent trade shows
- Organizational charts

ASSOCIATIONS OF MANAGEMENT CONSULTANTS

Association of Executive Search Consultants
12 East 41st Street, 17th Floor
New York, NY 10017
212-398-9556
Fax: 212-398-9560
aesc@aesc.org
http://www.aesc.org

Association of Management Consulting Firms
380 Lexington Avenue
New York, NY 10168
212-551-7887
Fax: 212-551-7934
info@amcf.org
http://www.amcf.org

Association of Professional Consultants
P.O. Box 51193
Irvine, CA 92619-1193
1-800-745-5050
Fax: 714-527-4210
apc@consultapc.org
http://www.consultapc.org

Canadian Association of Management Consultants
4 King Street West, Suite 815
Toronto, Ontario, Canada M5H 1B6
416-860-1515 or 1-800-268-1148
Fax: 416-860-1535 or 1-800-662-2972
consulting@cmc-canada.ca
http://www.camc.com

Institute of Management Consultants
2025 M Street NW, Suite 800
Washington, DC 20036
202-857-5334
Fax: 202-367-2134
office@imcusa.org
http://www.imcusa.org

Professional and Technical Consultants Association
P.O. Box 2261
Santa Clara, CA 95055
1-800-747-2822
Fax: 866-746-1053
info@patca.org
http://www.patca.org

INDEX